TOUCHING AT A DISTANCE

EDINBURGH CRITICAL STUDIES IN SHAKESPEARE AND PHILOSOPHY
Series Editor: Kevin Curran

Edinburgh Critical Studies in Shakespeare and Philosophy takes seriously the speculative and world-making properties of Shakespeare's art. Maintaining a broad view of 'philosophy' that accommodates first-order questions of metaphysics, ethics, politics and aesthetics, the series also expands our understanding of philosophy to include the unique kinds of theoretical work carried out by performance and poetry itself. These scholarly monographs will reinvigorate Shakespeare studies by opening new interdisciplinary conversations among scholars, artists and students.

Editorial Board Members
Ewan Fernie, Shakespeare Institute, University of Birmingham
James Kearney, University of California, Santa Barbara
Julia Reinhard Lupton, University of California, Irvine
Madhavi Menon, Ashoka University
Simon Palfrey, Oxford University
Tiffany Stern, Shakespeare Institute, University of Birmingham
Henry Turner, Rutgers University
Michael Witmore, The Folger Shakespeare Library
Paul Yachnin, McGill University

Published Titles
Rethinking Shakespeare's Political Philosophy: From Lear to Leviathan
Alex Schulman
Shakespeare in Hindsight: Counterfactual Thinking and Shakespearean Tragedy
Amir Khan
Second Death: Theatricalities of the Soul in Shakespeare's Drama
Donovan Sherman
Shakespeare's Fugitive Politics
Thomas P. Anderson
Is Shylock Jewish?: Citing Scripture and the Moral Agency of Shakespeare's Jews
Sara Coodin
Chaste Value: Economic Crisis, Female Chastity and the Production of Social Difference on Shakespeare's Stage
Katherine Gillen
Shakespearean Melancholy: Philosophy, Form and the Transformation of Comedy
J. F. Bernard
Shakespeare's Moral Compass
Neema Parvini
Shakespeare and the Fall of the Roman Republic: Selfhood, Stoicism and Civil War
Patrick Gray
Revenge Tragedy and Classical Philosophy on the Early Modern Stage
Christopher Crosbie
Shakespeare and the Truth-Teller: Confronting the Cynic Ideal
David Hershinow
Derrida Reads Shakespeare
Chiara Alfano
Conceiving Desire in Lyly and Shakespeare: Metaphor, Cognition and Eros
Gillian Knoll
Immateriality and Early Modern English Literature: Shakespeare, Donne, Herbert
James A. Knapp
Hazarding All: Shakespeare and the Drama of Consciousness
Sanford Budick
Touching at a Distance: Shakespeare's Theatre
Johannes Ungelenk

Forthcoming Titles
Making Publics in Shakespeare's Playhouse
Paul Yachnin
The Play and the Thing: A Phenomenology of Shakespearean Theatre
Matthew Wagner
Shakespeare's Staging of the Self: The Reformation and Protestant Hermenuetics
Roberta Kwan
Hospitality in Shakespeare's Drama
Sophie Battell
Shakespeare, Levinas and Adaptation
Lisa Starks

For further information please visit our website at: edinburghuniversitypress.com/series/ecsst

TOUCHING AT A DISTANCE

Shakespeare's Theatre

◆ ◆ ◆

JOHANNES UNGELENK

EDINBURGH
University Press

Edinburgh University Press is one of the leading university presses in the UK. We publish academic books and journals in our selected subject areas across the humanities and social sciences, combining cutting-edge scholarship with high editorial and production values to produce academic works of lasting importance. For more information visit our website: edinburghuniversitypress.com

© Johannes Ungelenk, 2023, 2024 under a Creative Commons Attribution-NonCommercial licence

This publication was supported by funds from the Publication Fund for Open Access Monographs of the Federal State of Brandenburg, Germany.

Edinburgh University Press Ltd
13 Infirmary Street
Edinburgh EH1 1LT

First published in hardback by Edinburgh University Press 2023

Typeset in 12/15 Adobe Sabon by
IDSUK (DataConnection) Ltd

A CIP record for this book is available from the British Library

ISBN 978 1 4744 9782 4 (hardback)
ISBN 978 1 4744 9783 1 (paperback)
ISBN 978 1 4744 9784 8 (webready PDF)
ISBN 978 1 4744 9785 5 (epub)

The right of Johannes Ungelenk to be identified as the author of this work has been asserted in accordance with the Copyright, Designs and Patents Act 1988, and the Copyright and Related Rights Regulations 2003 (SI No. 2498).

CONTENTS

Acknowledgements vi
Abbreviations viii
Series Editor's Preface ix

Introduction: Theatrical Contagions 1

1. Theatre's Offence: *Hamlet* and *The Tempest* 38

2. Touching the Depth of the Surface: *Richard III* 80

3. Caressing with Words: *Much Ado About Nothing* 148

4. Touching Fractions: *Troilus and Cressida* 186

Coda: A Philology of Touch 243

Bibliography 251
Index 268

ACKNOWLEDGEMENTS

I would like to thank Tobias Döring for his generosity and inspiring guidance. I am grateful to Sandra Fluhrer, Hanna Sohns and Alexander Waszynski for hours of enjoyable and intellectually stimulating discussions, as well as the rigour of their feedback. I am indebted to the DFG-network 'Berühren: literarische, mediale und politische Figurationen', under whose direction the project began, providing me with many opportunities to discuss parts of the study with colleagues.

Work on this book coincided with me taking up a post at the University of Potsdam, and I would like to thank my wonderful colleagues for giving me such a warm welcome and the perfect conditions with which to pursue this study. I am grateful to Anna Hordych for her feedback on the introduction and to Jassin Braun, Alma Knispel, Isabel Grahn and Valerie Pflaumer for assisting with literature research and the manuscript. I would also like to thank the invaluable Munich Shakespeare Library and Asal Shahrimoghaddam for her help in lifting its treasures. I am indebted to Joe Green, who has skilfully and prudently polished my English prose.

I am grateful to Ewan Fernie for encouraging me to go to Edinburgh University Press, and to Michelle Houston and Susannah Butler for their assistance and support during the publication process. The study has profited immensely from the helpful feedback of Kevin Curran, Eric S. Mallin and an anonymous reviewer.

An earlier version of an excerpt from Chapter 1 was published in German in *Tangieren – Szenen des Berührens*, edited by Sandra Fluhrer and Alexander Waszynski. An abridged version of Chapter 5 appeared in *Arcadia*. I am grateful to the editors and reviewers for their comments on these sections of the book.

Above all, I would like to thank my wife, Daniela, and my little son, Moritz. You are the joy of my life – this book is dedicated to you.

ABBREVIATIONS

adj.	adjective
Ado	*Much Ado About Nothing*
adv.	adjective
emph.	emphasis
etym.	etymology
gr.	ancient Greek
Ham.	*Hamlet*
3H6	*King Henry VI, Part 3*
lat.	Latin
l./ll.	line(s)
Lr.	*King Lear*
Mac.	*Macbeth*
MND	*A Midsummer Night's Dream*
MV	*The Merchant of Venice*
n.	noun
OED	*Oxford English Dictionary*
Oth.	*Othello*
prep.	preposition
R3	*Richard III*
SD	stage direction
TC	*Troilus and Cressida*
TGV	*The Two Gentlemen of Verona*
Tmp.	*The Tempest*
transl.	translation
v.	verb

SERIES EDITOR'S PREFACE

Picture Macbeth alone on stage, staring intently into empty space. 'Is this a dagger which I see before me?' he asks, grasping decisively at the air. On one hand, this is a quintessentially theatrical question. At once an object and a vector, the dagger describes the possibility of knowledge ('Is this a dagger') in specifically visual and spatial terms ('which I see before me'). At the same time, Macbeth is posing a quintessentially philosophical question, one that assumes knowledge to be both conditional and experiential, and that probes the relationship between certainty and perception as well as intention and action. It is from this shared ground of art and inquiry, of theatre and theory, that this series advances its basic premise: Shakespeare is philosophical.

It seems like a simple enough claim. But what does it mean exactly, beyond the parameters of this specific moment in *Macbeth*? Does it mean that Shakespeare had something we could think of as his own philosophy? Does it mean that he was influenced by particular philosophical schools, texts and thinkers? Does it mean, conversely, that modern philosophers have been influenced by him, that Shakespeare's plays and poems have been, and continue to be, resources for philosophical thought and speculation?

The answer is yes all around. These are all useful ways of conceiving a philosophical Shakespeare and all point to lines of inquiry that this series welcomes. But Shakespeare is philosophical in a much more fundamental way as well. Shakespeare is philosophical because the plays and poems actively create new worlds of knowledge and new scenes of ethical encounter. They ask big questions, make bold arguments and develop new vocabularies in order to think what might otherwise be unthinkable. Through both their scenarios and their imagery, the plays and poems engage the qualities of consciousness, the consequences of human action, the phenomenology of motive and attention, the conditions of personhood and the relationship among different orders of reality and experience. This is writing and dramaturgy, moreover, that consistently experiments with a broad range of conceptual crossings, between love and subjectivity, nature and politics, and temporality and form.

Edinburgh Critical Studies in Shakespeare and Philosophy takes seriously these speculative and world-making dimensions of Shakespeare's work. The series proceeds from a core conviction that art's capacity to think – to formulate, not just reflect, ideas – is what makes it urgent and valuable. Art matters because unlike other human activities it establishes its own frame of reference, reminding us that all acts of creation – biological, political, intellectual and amorous – are grounded in imagination. This is a far cry from business-as-usual in Shakespeare Studies. Because historicism remains the methodological gold standard of the field, far more energy has been invested in exploring what Shakespeare once meant than in thinking rigorously about what Shakespeare continues to make possible. In response, Edinburgh Critical Studies in Shakespeare and Philosophy pushes back against the critical orthodoxies of historicism and cultural studies to clear a space for scholarship that confronts aspects of literature that can neither be reduced to nor adequately explained by particular historical contexts.

Series Editor's Preface

Shakespeare's creations are not just inheritances of a past culture, frozen artefacts whose original settings must be expertly reconstructed in order to be understood. The plays and poems are also living art, vital thought-worlds that struggle, across time, with foundational questions of metaphysics, ethics, politics and aesthetics. With this orientation in mind, Edinburgh Critical Studies in Shakespeare and Philosophy offers a series of scholarly monographs that will reinvigorate Shakespeare Studies by opening new interdisciplinary conversations among scholars, artists and students.

Kevin Curran

Trust not my reading nor my observations,
Which with experimental seal doth warrant
The tenor of my book; (*Ado* 4.1.165–7)

INTRODUCTION: THEATRICAL CONTAGIONS

At the end of Shakespeare's *Troilus and Cressida*, Pandarus, the character who has tragically set Troilus up with Cressida, is left alone on the stage. He gives an epilogue that terminates with a threat – or is it a promise?

> Till then I'll sweat and seek about for eases,
> And at that time bequeath you my diseases. (*TC* 5.11.55–6)[1]

Pandarus is a logical choice for the epilogue's speaker. He has been a matchmaker, a go-between in the play world, and it is his task now, at the end of the performance, to eliminate one final manifestation of distance. By dissolving the theatrical situation, he collapses the insurmountable boundary that has kept apart the fictive world of the play and the real world of the audience. He reintroduces the actors to reality and brings them back into regular contact with the members of the audience, something which was, on occasion, ritually celebrated through a dance that involved both the cast and some, mostly prominent, spectators. The threat of spreading (venereal) disease might be understood as a darkly humorous allusion not only to some more intimate form of contact taking place behind the scenes, but also to rumours of actors being likely carriers of syphilis – speculations about a venereal reason for Shakespeare's baldness are still alive today. There is, however, a different and more interestingly comic twist to Pandar's statement. Although the audience has been kept at a distance during the performance, they are very likely to develop the symptoms that Pandarus describes as characteristic for his 'diseases': the audience probably share his 'aching bones' (5.1.50) and the 'rheum in mine eyes' (5.3.104). These symptoms do not, however, go back to Pandarus collapsing the theatrical situation at the end of the play but are, on the contrary, produced by the situation that Pandarus dissolves, by the two or three hours of standing in the pits or sitting on wooden benches while being exposed to a theatrical performance. The 'rheum in the eyes' – that is, tears – is a conventional indicator of a suffering inflicted by theatre. Pandar's epilogue thus subtly implies that his – or the play's – goal has been reached. The audience has been contaminated with theatrical emotions: 'a fearful contagion between world and stage' (Hobgood 'Feeling Fear in *Macbeth*' 38) has taken place, and the disease has been spread among the spectators. The manner of infection testifies to a capacity of theatre that is at the centre of this study: theatre's capacity for 'touching at a distance'.

'Touching at a distance' is a paradoxical notion: Touch, as a sense of nearness (a *Nahsinn*, according to Edmund Husserl), does not know of distance. It is, in its own sensory realm, constitutively 'blind' to distance. Nevertheless, as we have seen with Shakespeare's *Troilus and Cressida*, theatre may point to a conceptual and political potential for touch that surmounts the neat distinction of the senses; a potential which comes from touch that may even be formative for the functioning of the sensual domains of seeing and hearing, senses which are primarily activated when watching a Shakespeare play.

The art of play-acting looks back on a long and rich history, over which it has constantly been reinvented and renewed, and during which its cultural status, its conventions and its very material have undergone significant alterations. However, most of its variants – and this is perhaps the only fragile licence for talking about 'theatre' in the singular – share the structure that the formula 'touching at a distance' attempts to capture. Theatre is constituted by 'distance'. It is structured around an unbridgeable divide between stage and audience.[2] Although only separated by an invisible boundary, this distance at the heart of theatre is absolute: the onstage fiction and the audience's reality meet, but, for structural reasons, they cannot merge. Nevertheless, since Aristotle, theatre has been characterised by what happens 'across' this boundary, by the theatrical emotions that are produced between stage and audience. It is a particularity of theatre that these emotions are experienced in real time, simultaneous to their theatrical generation. The co-presence of actors and audience (cf. Fischer-Lichte) provides the foundation of theatre's capacity to produce emotions. As a result, the theatrical situation is constituted by a paradoxical tension: the tension between the structural distance of fiction and the nearness of (bodily) co-presence. It is to this tension, or, to use Stephen Greenblatt's terminology, this 'friction between boundaries' ('Fiction and Friction' 85), that my study is dedicated.

Any reconstruction of theatre's emotional effectiveness is located somewhere in a spectrum opened up by the two poles of fictional distance and bodily co-presence: being 'moved' or emotionally 'touched' by a play can be understood more or less literally. Whereas the ancient theory of humours encourages a rather literal, physiological interpretation of theatre's emotions that emphasises the impact of bodily co-presence, the history of Western theatre registers a growing control or economy of effects, especially in the later seventeenth and eighteenth centuries. '[T]he use of "emotion" as a rough synonym for [passion and affection] involves forgetting the very motion it contains,' writes Shankar Raman (120).

The distance of fiction begins to require a more extensive process of mediation or translation that accompanies and steers theatre's effects, so that being 'moved' becomes morally and didactically embedded, thereby acquiring a rather 'metaphorical' tinge. The world, its episteme and its social organisation has changed – especially with human rationality taking over its ordering centre. However, despite mediation and translation, theatre's tension of distance and presence subsists. The manifold attempts at channelling the emotions instead betray the fact that theatre's co-presence of bodies keeps challenging the supremacy of rational control and its economy of mediation.

'Touching at a distance' is not only paradoxical – it is also tautological. As theoreticians like Jacques Derrida and Jean-Luc Nancy have shown (cf. Derrida *On Touching*; Nancy 'Rühren'), touch, though characterised as a sense of nearness, also implies separation. No matter whether violent or soft, touch requires distance to come about. Even at the moment of contact the bodies involved remain separate, hold a certain unbridgeable distance. It is only for as long as they do not merge, do not lump together, that touch continues to produce an effect. Although perhaps the most intuitive access to the world surrounding us, touch turns out to be very complex at heart. Its characteristics break with much that we hold 'natural': like the fruit fly under the microscope, touch, when scrutinised more closely, presents us with a surprisingly 'new', a surprisingly 'different' world that had existed right next to us in the most banal of guises.

Although touch appears to assure us of the materiality of anything that we encounter in the world – confer the 'touchstone' to check the authenticity of coins – it challenges, on a more philosophical level, the very notion of substantiality. Touch never comes to touch at the 'thing', its defining core, itself; touch only ever encounters limits (cf. Derrida *On Touching* 6). It shifts the ontological paradigm from the question of essence (*ti esti?* – 'what is/exists?') to a question of surfaces and their modulations. It thereby also introduces an ineluctable, constitutive temporality. In contrast to the concept of substance that is built on timelessness, touch is inseparable from time. It is a movement towards contact and away from it; a movement that is defined by having a beginning and an end – a process of approaching and distancing. Instead of a thing, touch is rather a rhythm. It is a fragile gesture which is not individuated by its lastingness, its indifference to the corrosive troubles of the world but, on the contrary, by the difference it makes.

The impact of touch is characterised by its radical mutuality. As the notion of con-tact suggests, it takes at least two to touch, and, what is more, these two get involved in a sphere of togetherness. They touch 'together', which means that the pattern of active and passive, with which we are used to make sense of our world, is suspended (cf. Nancy *Being Singular Plural* viii). At the moment of touching, even the most violent of encounters does not know an active subject and a passive, suffering object. Together they are affected: the hammer smashing the watermelon loses kinetic energy at the moment of touch, suffers a certain recoil, will leave the encounter marked by the melon's juice and flesh. Its stickiness will remind us of what has taken place if nobody decides to erase the traces that touching the melon has left.[3] The particularity of touch's radical mutuality will shine out when we compare it to exemplary scenes of knowledge and truth production. I look out of the window and see 'a tree'. I can name the object, I can describe the greenness of its leaves. My observations about the tree can only claim the attribute of truth if they do not make a difference, if they do not interfere with what they 'register'.[4] I take without giving; a fundamental asymmetry defines the scene of knowledge; the tree does not do anything, it does not look back,[5] it just lets itself be taken as what 'it is'. Despite the distance that the perceiving subject keeps to the object, it appropriates this very object, makes it part of the world in which it reigns. Appropriation means nothing less than the opposite of touch: destroying any separating distance, including something into an absolute nearness without being affected, that is, changed by it.

Touch, on the contrary, entails exposing oneself to the other. Touching and being touched are one and the same. Nevertheless, despite the nearness that touch implies, a distance is maintained. Touch always touches at a distance: since touching does not know of appropriation, since it does not drag the other into an abstract realm controlled by the subject's understanding, the other remains other. There is therefore no guarantee that the touching encounter will be successful – that is, joyful, interesting or profitable. Quite the opposite, exposing oneself to the other in order to make a touching encounter possible implies taking a risk: the risk of cutting or burning oneself, of being affected in a harmful manner. Contact entails the threat of con-tagion.

It is therefore hardly surprising that Western society and epistemology have found ways to hedge the dangerous gesture of touch in frameworks that reduce the risks of uncontrolled contagion. Immanuel Kant's *Critique of Pure Reason* and its programme of converting 'groping about' into 'the secure course of a science' (106)[6] is a case in point: paradoxically, the risk of touch is banned not by introducing distance (the distance of seeing), but by abandoning the characteristic distance of touch. It is not the other that we encounter when making sense of the world, but something of ourselves, our own transcendental apparatus. Instead of touching at a distance, knowledge and truth is produced by way of self-affection. The familiarity introduced by the Kantian transcendentalism is based on the positing of a constitutive hierarchy: the transcendental subject reigns over the realm of the phenomena, because everything that it encounters in this realm is pre-shaped to be appropriated. Transcendentalism is an apparatus that generates a sphere of universal nearness. At the same time, it seals itself off hermetically from any unfamiliar, 'strange' otherness that could disturb the quiet familiarity 'inside'.

The theatrical situation, structurally, constitutes an apparatus of the opposing kind: instead of abandoning, it guarantees distance. It creates a contact surface that, making reality encounter fiction, forecloses appropriation. Exposing oneself to its touches, that is, becoming involved in the nearness of its characteristic co-presence, means affirming the risks of being affected. Theatre provides its visitors with an opportunity to enjoy contact to the uncontrolled 'other', to forces that overpower the agency of the individual self. 'Early modern spectators were not victimized by infectious affect,' writes Allison P. Hobgood. Their passions 'might have been something not to master, but to indulge in, alongside other equally vulnerable spectators' (Hobgood 'Feeling Fear in *Macbeth*' 45).

It is certainly true that it constructs a 'safe' framework for experiencing intense emotions: the audience can be sure that no severe bodily harm will be done to them during the performance. However, it is the ambivalence of risk that fuels theatre's production of emotions. Theatrical enjoyment is based on suffering – in other words, on the loss of control. According to Aristotle, tragedy famously produces 'pleasure which comes from pity and fear' (75). How exactly this transformation of emotions is brought about remains all but clear. Theatre has never stopped being a space for experimentation, a space where 'touching at a distance' and its production of emotions has to be tried out – and is never guaranteed to be successful. The vehemence of anti-theatrical opposition to play-acting[7] testifies to the fact that the theatrical 'touch' can hardly claim the 'cleanliness' of only rousing the emotions intended: its contact is always held under suspicion of contagion.

With its affinity to touch, *Troilus and Cressida* is not a solitary case in Shakespeare's dramatic oeuvre. On the contrary, 'touching at a distance', I would like to argue, is one of the trademarks of his theatrical art. He is probably unrivalled in the intensity and the persistence with which his plays are concerned with the paradoxical tension unfolding in between the stage and the audience that defines the theatrical situation.

Shakespeare's theatre masterfully exploits this tension in order to generate the strongest of emotions. In contrast to, for example, the plays of Jean Racine, those by Shakespeare have proven capable of 'touching at a distance' in a historical sense, too: despite the fact that more than 400 years have passed since their first performances, they still touch us today. The distance between Shakespeare and us is not just a number. We are living in a world that is different in many aspects: the structure of society, the way in which we make sense of the world and ourselves, the way we stage and consume theatre plays. And yet, Shakespeare's dramatic art still works, is still effective. One reason for this astonishing and fascinating longevity and freshness may be that Shakespeare's theatre has always 'touched at a distance': as 'the very gatekeeper of futurity' (Wilson 21) it is addressed to a 'future' audience, to an audience (yet) to come.[8] This does not mean that Shakespeare was 'ahead of his time' or that we would have made a step towards realising Shakespeare's 'ideal viewer' – we have not 'become early modern' (cf. Charnes 'We Were Never Early Modern').'Shakespeare's drama might be drawn as much towards a future beyond our apprehension as back to its place of origin in the past', writes Kiernan Ryan (65). His art does not anticipate a certain attitude from the spectator or a particular state of the world. It does not sketch a (didactical) frame of (moral) consent that would unite spectacle and audience. On the contrary, it is the deviation of any actual audience from the plays' 'audience to come' that is responsible for the capacity to generate emotions. The plays do not aim for consent; they aim to make a difference. Once the distance separating play and audience was overcome, once the spectacle found its genuine, proper spectator, a spectator that was completely 'up for it', Shakespeare's theatre would immediately lose its affective power. Without irritation, without contact with the unknown and the uncontrolled, fiction is robbed of its friction: touching without distance is not only impossible; it is, above all, devoid of the power to 'move' (towards becoming something unforeseen).

The untimeliness which characterises Shakespeare's theatrical touch may account for its enormous affective energy; however, it also renders it fragile. Keeping contact with the audience (in spite of the constitutive distance) is therefore a main concern of his poetics, all the more since the early modern theatre not only aimed for artistic but also (and probably mainly) economic success. This is achieved, in parts, by means that we, who do not share the early modern horizon, can only reconstruct: Shakespeare's use of stories that his contemporaries were familiar with from other plays, poetry or prose of their time; allusions to historical or political events, to gossip or to his colleagues' work; the integration of the (folk) tradition, mythology or the shared cultural heritage. All this has become the subject of annotations in scholarly editions but has lost its effect on modern theatre audiences. We are today left with a second strategy that Shakespeare extensively employs for keeping contact with the audience: he exposes the theatrical contact. This can be done in a variety of ways: 1) by transgressing the logics of fiction and metaleptically merging the internal and external communicative system (addressing the audience, using shifters like *now* and *this* which refer both to the fictional and the audience's reality), moments that Terence Hawkes calls 'supra-textual contact, where 'the play's own continuity appears to break down and it seems suddenly to leap out at us, [. . .] to touch us directly and often wordlessly' (Hawkes 'Conclusion' 138); 2) by putting this contact on stage in the form of plays-within-plays or scenes analogous to them, for example with scenes of eavesdropping, where an onstage audience represents the real audience and displays the effect of their listening to the characters' (dramatic) speech or of their being exposed to some sort of spectacle; 3) by making characters speak about the phenomena of 'touching at a distance' and thereby (also) commenting on the theatrical situation. The strategy of keeping contact by exposing it clearly works with metatheatrical means. However, Shakespeare's metatheatricality does not so much attempt to explain or reflect upon the theatrical situation – it is not to be misunderstood as a modern gesture of showing control by displaying theatre's invisible conditions of possibility – but rather tries to increase the spectators' involvement. In contrast to the modern stage and its theatrical machinery, on Shakespeare's early modern stage there were hardly any invisible theatrical illusions which could be interrupted. The metatheatrical gesture of exposing theatre's contact zone rather drags/invites 'the world' onto the stage, or exposes its entanglement with problems or characteristics of theatricality. Jennifer Waldron speaks of the creation of a 'metatheatrical awareness as an embodied and collective process', which depends upon live theatre as 'a specifically communal, intersubjective phenomenon during which many people sense or feel a similar event at the same time' (408).

That is why many of the famous metatheatrical passages in Shakespeare can be read as the playwright's 'deepest' philosophical statements (cf. Prospero's 'Our revels now are ended' speech (*Tmp.* 4.1.148–63)). His concern with theatre's paradoxical tension between distance and co-presence does not consist in balancing it out according to external (moral, didactical) standards, but in enhancing and exploiting it; his theatrical art, including its metatheatricality, does not avoid but facilitates contagion.[9]

The fact that Shakespeare's dramatic art explores theatre's capacity for 'touching at a distance' so intensely can be explained with epistemological, cultural and material reasoning. For Elizabeth D. Harvey, 'the early modern period is especially significant as a historical moment for [an] investigation of touch, because we can witness then the nascent stages of a consolidation of beliefs about the body's relation to knowledge, sexuality and reproduction, artistic creativity, and "contact" with other worlds, both divine and newly discovered geographical realms' ('Introduction' 2). Katherine A. Craik and Tanya Pollard likewise emphasise the role of the body in early modern reality and thinking, pointing to 'assumptions about the intrinsically material and physiological nature of emotion, an especially rich site for exploring the nature of affect'(3). Farah Karim-Cooper explicates the role that these insights assign to touch in the early modern period: 'To feel things deeply or to be moved emotionally is to be *touched* in Shakespeare' ('Touch and Taste' 217).

There may also be quite material reasons for the affinity to touch observed in Shakespearean drama. It is above all the particularities of the early modern platform stage that must be taken into account.[10] The public playhouses – among them Shakespeare's iconic Globe – encouraged 'touch' in a variety of ways. From an architectonic view, they were rather small wooden structures that could house an astonishingly large crowd of spectators – up to 1,500 people in a space 90–100 feet in diameter for The Globe (cf. G. Egan). Theatre literally brought its customers into contact, not only as a result of its crowdedness, but also as a place where all kinds of 'trading' took place during the performance. As Farah Karim-Cooper notes, 'tactile crowding' also raised 'anti-theatrical concerns' ('Touch and Taste' 220), which portrayed theatres as 'dangerous places of touch' (*The Hand* 159): 'Theatres were places where, in addition to the pricks and stings of drama, actual groping, prickling, stealing hands threatened not just the soul and the body, but the purse as well' (*The Hand* 158). Carla Mazzio suggests that the word 'assembly', historically used to refer to the theatre audience, gave a better understanding of the early modern theatre than speaking of spectators, 'because it implied not only a coming together of persons, but a physical touching of bodies in space' ('Acting with Tact' 162).

Associating these touches with contagion, as Pandarus does in the Epilogue to *Troilus and Cressida*, is not far-fetched: the main public theatres of Shakespeare's time were located in the 'Liberty of the Clink', an entertainment district in Southwark which was also famous for its dense concentration of brothels. The theatrical 'touch' not only profited from the same liberties as the trade of prostitution, but to a certain extent even appears to have been dependent on them. Crossing the River Thames and heading to the Liberty of Clink is not to be separated from a calling of the senses, no matter whether the journey ended in a bear-baiting performance, a whorehouse or watching *Julius Caesar* at The Globe. While today's theatregoing has mostly become a practice of social distinction, the early modern public playhouse displayed quite the opposite characteristic: as is still the case in the industry of prostitution, it suspends social hierarchies and brings people from very different backgrounds into contact, people that are most unlikely to meet in 'real life'. Antitheatrical pamphlets took offence at the fact that 'theater blurred distinctions between sexes and classes' (Sanders 401):

> in Stage Playes for a boy to put one the attyre, the gesture, the passions of a woman; for a meane person to take upon him the title of a Prince with counterfeit porte, and traine, is by outward signes to shew the selves otherwise then they are, and so with in the compasse of a lye [...]. (Gosson E5r)

However, the blurring of social distinctions exceeded the theatrical representation on stage. In The Globe, these 'dangerous', potentially contagious contacts would not only take place between the socially dubious caste of actors on stage and the lords and ladies in the galleries, but also within the audience itself, which ranged from the common men to the noblemen. The contact surface facilitating all of these improbable encounters was the body. Exposing one's body to all kinds of uncontrollable touches formed a central part of the early modern theatrical experience.

The architecture of the playhouse, with its hierarchy of pit and galleries that followed a simple financial principle, hardly compensated for the 'democratic' experience of rubbing shoulders on the way to one's more or less distinguished place. It facilitated touch in a more abstract, structural sense, however: it provided the material conditions for a theatrical practice that is shaped by *mutuality*. In contrast to most modern theatre buildings, the construction of the early modern public playhouse was not governed by a principle of vision and illusion, but of proximity: it is not structured around an ideal, abstract axis of sight, resulting in a stretched rectangular layout, but in a circle that minimises the distance between actors and audience and guarantees a certain proximity, even for those on the back benches. Astonishingly enough, the best seats in The Globe, in the 'Lord's Rooms' which were at the back of the stage, above the tiring rooms, were probably the ones with the worst view – but located closest to the actors. Apart from the physical proximity generated by the public playhouses' architecture, it is their lighting that contributed most to the characteristic mutuality of the early modern theatrical experience: the natural shared light on which the public playhouses, as roofless outdoor theatres, were dependent illuminated stage and audience alike. As a result, the interaction between actors and spectators was very different from the way that we are used to experiencing it in modern theatre buildings, with a proscenium stage and artificial lighting.[11]

The contrast of the brightly illuminated stage and the darkness of the auditorium tells a lot about the conventions of modern theatre that are shaped by a central asymmetry: the audience watches the spectacle on stage, but they cannot be seen. While the actors expose their bodies to the bright spotlight, those of the audience are sheltered in darkness. The generation and consumption of illusion governs the 'interaction' taking place between stage and audience. Artificial lighting and the asymmetry that it produces significantly weaken the experience of theatre's characteristic bodily co-presence, so much so that any direct interaction between actor and spectator – in speeches addressed to the audience, for example – has to be faked if the lighting situation is kept the way it probably has been for the rest of the play. The actor, blinded by the spotlight, simply cannot discern the spectators in the dark auditorium – and, more importantly, the spectators do not even notice the asymmetry which makes their being addressed part of the theatrical illusion.

By contrast, the shared light in the early modern playhouse supported the experience of co-presence. The shared daylight made it part of the visual perception and enabled genuine, symmetrical interaction between stage and audience. This mutual contact of seeing and being seen, of being exposed to each other, did not so much imply a break of illusion but subsisted as a constant, an ever-present component of the early modern theatre performance. '[C]ontact among the audience', writes Farah Karim-Cooper, 'was a condition of performance in Shakespeare's theatres, which raises the question as to how tactility might affect the reception of the plays [. . .]' ('Touch and Taste' 214). Shakespeare's frequent metatheatrical allusions to his audience's reality thus answer and connect to this component of the theatrical experience: his art is persistently concerned with maintaining contact with the audience, which is facilitated and intensified both by the spatial proximity of the stage and the lighting allowing for genuine interaction. However, for the very same reasons, this contact is also fragile: in the early modern theatre, there was a lot more to see and to interact with than the actors on stage – for example, the illustrious visitors to the 'Lord's Rooms' right above it. Unlike the modern proscenium, with its use of perspective modelled on an ideal individuum consuming the play, watching a performance in The Globe was an inherently social, collective act: getting in touch with the stage inevitably entailed getting in touch with the fellow playgoers. Theatre was not only watched collectively, but watching others watch theatre formed part of this social event. Shakespeare's metatheatricality mirrors these second-order observations, thereby also attempting to channel the complex social dynamics of the crowd and using it for the theatrical generation of emotions.

The bareness of the platform stage called for another form of mutuality at the heart of early modern theatre: the spectators could not simply passively consume and enjoy the play that was prepared for them. The cooperation of their fantasy was required to transform the few optical and the many verbal cues into 'vivid scenes'. It is only as a result of their mutual contact that stage and audience, together, produced the theatrical illusion which had the power to move the spectators. Moreover, as Bruce R. Smith suggests, the interaction between actors and spectators was not a silent process, but one that formed part of the experience of the play: 'Globe audiences were not so passive,' he writes, '[t]hey were actively encouraged to return sound to the actors in form of applause' ('Within' 193).

Claiming that Shakespeare's plays are particularly capable of 'touching at a distance' thus does not merely admire the huge amount of energy that his art proves able to generate on stage, energy that would be powerful enough to travel distances and still affect the recipients. The question of intensity should not be answered without first paying attention to the particular quality of the contact that Shakespeare's theatre establishes between stage and audience. The idea of my book is to understand this theatrical contact in a literal way:

as a 'touch' performed by actor and spectator together (lat. *cum-tangere*), as a mutual touching, taking place between the two. Or, in Bruce R. Smith's words: 'What is touching about "Shakespeare"? The in-between' (*Phenomenal Shakespeare* xviii).

Touching at a Distance is not without precedent. The paradigm of touch has become part of Shakespeare Studies through the inspiring work of Elizabeth D. Harvey, Carla Mazzio, Bruce R. Smith, Lowell Gallagher and Shankar Raman, Farah Karim-Cooper and Tiffany Stern, and many others.[12] Interest in touch grew out of an attention shift towards the sensory/sensual, the bodily and affective side of the early modern theatre performance. Bruce R. Smith coined the term 'historical phenomenology' ('Premodern Sexualities' 320) for a methodological framework which formulates the basic conditions and intellectual goals of this turn towards the senses. Smith emphasises that it is not 'a desire to speak', as for New Historicism, but 'a desire to *feel* with the dead' ('Phenomophobia' 481) that drives historical phenomenology. Interestingly, the search for 'an affective bond with the past' (Curran and Kearney 355) implies questioning the traditional hierarchy of the senses. Whereas, according to Smith, 'current methodologies' 'are predominantly visual', '[h]istorical phenomenology is interested in all the senses' ('Premodern Sexualities' 326). Drawing on insights from 'sensory history, the cultural history of emotion, and the affective turn within the social sciences', write Kevin Curran and James Kearney, 'historical phenomenology [...] offered scholars of Shakespeare and his world new ways to explore visual, tactile, aural, olfactory, and emotional dimensions of early modern culture, which might otherwise resist critical engagement' (354). Whether explicitly endorsing the label 'historical phenomenology' or not, all criticism concerned with touch and early modern theatre likely builds on the aforementioned 'intersection of three disciplines' (354). Nevertheless, research developed from a common interest in touch can take quite different directions: 1) It is almost a precondition for further research to follow the historicist impulse to better understand the role, working and (different) hierarchies of the senses in early modernity, especially as, according to Constance Classen, '[t]he omission of tactile experience is noticeable not only in the field of history, but across the humanities and social sciences' (xi). 2) As Gallagher and Raman have shown, rewriting the history of the senses brings up complex epistemological issues. Taking into account the plurality of interacting senses, new answers to the old questions of truth and knowing are required. 3) Knowledge about the early modern working of the senses promises a better understanding of the *early modern* 'effects of plays [. . .] on minds, bodies, and souls' (Craik and Pollard 1), with the pragmatic dimension of performance coming into focus.

With his influential study *The Acoustic World of Early Modern England: Attending to the O-Factor*, Bruce R. Smith established a model that many scholars have followed. Directing our attention to senses other than the hegemonic sense of vision – in Smith's case, first to the realm of the acoustic, later to that of touch[13] – proved to be a promising path towards a new understanding of the (historical) theatrical experience. Farah Karim-Cooper spells out this strategy for a foregrounding of touch. She suggests that Shakespeare's plays themselves challenge the established hierarchy of the senses, creating a constellation that can then be used to reconstruct the experience of early modern playgoing:

> Shakespeare's assertion of tactility as a primary medium of human connection and mutual affection challenges the medieval and early modern hierarchy of the senses, which traditionally placed touch at the lowest end of the spectrum with sight or hearing at the highest. (Karim-Cooper *The Hand* 9)

From her diagnosis, she derives the project she has been working on in various texts: 'examining touch not just as a sense at work in the theatres, but as a physical and conceptual effect of performance' (Karim-Cooper 'Touch and Taste' 216). Karim-Cooper makes it clear that she inherited the question – a virulent question – that her research addresses: 'Patricia Cahill had asked: [W]hat would happen if we were to think of the interactions between early modern players and playgoers as a tactile encounter?', 'what might it mean to be touched by a play?' (216).[14]

This very question is at the heart of my study. However, taking up Karim-Cooper's words, it is the 'conceptual effects' rather than the reconstruction of the historical 'physical' experience that I am looking for. I share Michael Witmore's perspective, who regards theatre 'as lived inquiry or parcel of vernacular intellectual culture' (420). Shakespeare's theatre has not only the 'the ability to physically touch its spectators' (Karim-Cooper *The Hand* 157), but, excels in the capacity of 'conceptualizing [a thrilling] philosophy [of touch] on stage' (Witmore 420). It is the combination of the two that accounts for the particular knowledge that Shakespeare's plays foster: they perform 'communication as contamination' (Cavell 12).

In my study, interest in the conceptual potential of Shakespeare's theatre, in its embodied philosophy of touch, upstages the historical reconstruction of the early modern theatrical experience.[15] However, *Touching at a Distance* cannot bracket knowledge about the early modern humoral body or the 'materiality of the playhouses' (Karim-Cooper and Stern 'Introduction' 2). On the contrary, it is these epistemological and material conditions that inform the conceptual experiments of Shakespearean theatre and account for their innovative impulses for our thinking today. Reconstructing the conceptual potential of early modern theatrical touch is thus only possible on the firm ground of historical knowledge. The difference in focus between my work and that of my colleagues is that what can usually be found in introductions or overview sections – the conceptual characteristics of touch – are instead at the centre of my readings. Inversely, the historical knowledge about touch and the senses, as well as the material conditions of the cultural site theatre that my colleagues have studied in detail, is rather briefly summed up in my introduction and will only emerge in the main part to assist the close reading and the conceptual work undertaken there.

Although the strategy might be different, the basic insights are the same. As has been sketched out by scholars working in the field of Shakespeare Studies and the senses, touch is a complex but fascinating 'phenomenon'. 'Touch evokes at once agency and receptivity, authority and reciprocity, pleasure and pain, sensual indulgence and epistemological certainty' ('Introduction' 2), writes Elizabeth D. Harvey in the introduction to her pioneering *Sensible Flesh*. The paradoxical combination of characteristics indicates a trait of touch that Carla Mazzio has called its 'resistance [. . .] to conceptual models' ('Acting with Tact' 160), 'to specificity, conceptual stasis' ('Acting with Tact' 162). Theatre, as a processual art of events, might provide a better framework for exploring 'the reciprocal, fleeting, and "nonteleological" aspect of touch' ('Acting with Tact' 161), its 'economy in which taking leads not to contraction but to abundance, an intersubjective, chiastic dynamic' (Tribble '"O, she's warm"' 73), than philosophy's static texts. Patient, extensive close readings of the following chapters will substantiate this claim. We will see that Shakespeare's drama resonates with Carla Mazzio's suggestion that touch instantiates a 'social and erotic interaction [. . .] quite different from other manually inflected forms of engagement such as "manipulation," "grasping," and "clutching"' ('Acting with Tact' 161). This distance, differentiating touch from grasping or clutching, is at the centre of my book. Criticism of Shakespearean tactility has rarely and fleetingly touched this distance, for example when Margaret Healy suggests that 'you could be "touched" in this period without being touched – without the mediation of the senses' (23), or when Carla Mazzio observes that 'touch can seem all the more alluring and powerful when objects are held at a distance' ('Acting with Tact' 165). Following these cues means moving away from the immediateness of sensory experience and towards a more abstract level. In this understanding, touch does not feature as a supplementary sensory channel, but rather provides the conceptual framework for theatre's overall desired impact – a framework to which hearing and seeing as senses of distance contribute substantially.[16]

Shakespeare's plays, especially in their most explicitly metatheatrical passages, show clear traces of the conceptual particularities of touch. Apart from touch's characteristic mutuality, inherent in the material conditions of the performance in the early modern playhouse, a short glance at some catchphrases from Prospero's 'Our revels now are ended' speech suffices to encounter the other main traits of touch that I have detailed previously. As its famous first line (*Tmp.* 4.1.148) already indicates, Shakespeare's metatheatricality is concerned with temporality: a theatre performance makes the audience experience a beginning and an end. As there is no curtain and no special lighting that would 'externally' demarcate the plays' limits, both were rather fragile situations. As the conventional prologues and epilogues expose, these liminal moments demanded the spectators' cooperation. Together with the actors, the audience would bring about a little world whose constitutive ephemerality resonated with the fundamental condition of each and everyone's existence in the crowd. The experience to which the dissolution of this theatrical world gives rise is highly unsettling, because it questions substantiality, the very foundation of our ontological intuition: it is an 'insubstantial pageant' (*Tmp.* 4.1.155) that has touched us and that, in its temporality, resembles our own existence – 'We are such stuff / As dreams are made on, and our little life / Is rounded with a sleep' (*Tmp.* 4.1.156–7), as Prospero tells the audience. He also characterises the alternative ontology that the spectators encounter when watching a play: 'the baseless fabric of this vision' (*Tmp.* 4.1.151) is the interesting formulation that he uses for describing theatre's 'material'. With these words, Prospero ties theatre's etymological starting point, 'vision' (gr. θεάομαι, *theáomai*, 'to look upon'), to the question of surface and touch. The noun 'fabric' carries the traces of fabrication, that is, fictionality, and continues the textile metaphor that traditionally associates verbal artefacts with the art of weaving. It is the adjective 'baseless' that exposes the alternative ontological status, the non-substantial nature of the theatrical material. At the same time, it indicates that it is not this material's core, the essence behind its fabricated surface, but the surface itself, the fabric's texture, that accounts for theatre's powerful effects: fiction's frictions (cf. Greenblatt 'Fiction and Friction'), rather than the smooth transmission of a 'deeper' message, are responsible for the theatrical contagion of Shakespeare's plays.

With his 'baseless fabric of this vision', Prospero sets the scene for the investigations I would like to pursue in the following chapters of this book. In Chapter 1, I analyse how Shakespeare's *Hamlet* insistently resorts to the notion of touch, in scenes that deal with what is constitutively non-palpable: the famous ghost scenes stage a vision whose 'baseless fabric' severely touches all that dare to expose themselves to it. I will read *Hamlet* as a story of contagion that tells, at the same time, the story of theatre's power to generate emotions. Reconstructing all the 'touching at a distance' that takes place onstage will allow us to explore the theatrical situation and the structuring role that touch plays in it. Some side glances to *The Tempest*, whose metatheatrical scenes are not only deeply related to *Hamlet* but even occasionally seem to comment on the earlier tragedy, will help with working out the conceptual implications that the theatrical paradigm of touch brings with it.

Chapter 2 is dedicated to *Richard III* and its explorations of histrionic surfaces. The dark history play invites its spectators to sound the deepness of theatre's 'baseless fabric'. In contrast to my reading of *Hamlet* and *The Tempest*, the analysis of *Richard III* does not keep to a description of the theatrical situation but focuses on the existential questions that the theatrical world of touch raises. The 'deep dissembler' Richard, who once even mimes the 'deep tragedian' (*R3* 3.5.5) on stage, carries his metatheatricality to the spectators. He makes them accomplices of his crimes. They become involved not only because he lets them in on his plans from the beginning, but also and mainly because the superficial world of dissembling that he presents to them uncannily resonates with their historical reality: accelerated by the turbulences of changing official religion thrice within a generation, the confidence in the foundation on which the world was built decreased rapidly (cf. Döring).

The obsession of *Richard III* with the power of surfaces and surface modulations has its finger on the pulse of early modernity. Shakespeare's play employs a promising candidate for taming the growing complexity of the world: modern subjectivity. Richard's characteristic loneliness, his being individualised by being different, by being separated from the collective, exaggerates the basic conditions of modern existence so as to expose them to the audience. As we will see, Richard is, however, less of an outsider than he appears to be. The formula that he embodies, being = dissembling = play-acting = being, guides the behaviour of most of the characters. This is not to say that they are as morally corrupted as he is; they rather share a reality of life that has become 'baseless'. It is here that theatricality and the early modern historical experience of the world resonate: the fragility of touch – the challenge of temporality and doubtful substantiality, the suspension of absolute hierarchies and new social relations based on mutuality that bring a loss of control – not only characterises the medium of theatre but also shapes the societal status quo in which Shakespeare's audiences are involved. This resonance makes theatre a privileged place where strategies of coping with the fragility of touch can be developed and put to the test.

Shakespeare's *Richard III* raises fundamental issues connected to the problem of touch that the following chapters will continue to elaborate on: the problem of speaking and acting truthfully, the nature of social bonds, the rituals (of touch) that are involved in establishing them and the question of gender/sex that appears to be structurally linked to the problem of touch as such, and that surfaces in all of its dimensions. The constitutive mutuality that the notion of touch introduces is not quite compatible with the hierarchies of the patriarchal regime: as I will attempt to show, the power of touch is a power of temptation that is associated with femininity, even in the case of a male protagonist like Richard.

Chapter 3, on *Much Ado About Nothing*, is dedicated to the verbal, the linguistic dimension of this power of temptation. It examines contrasting language uses, exposed to be effective differently: speech acts of contract that work within a patriarchal framework, and anarchic, subversive speech acts of contact that defy categorisation. It is again the outsider figures, Beatrice and Benedick, who establish a social connection that is exposed to be 'baseless': their relationship is not only 'founded' on deceptions but is also, paradoxically, established by the partners' shared resistance to any verbal – that is, contractual – acknowledgement of their love. While Beatrice and Benedick celebrate and enjoy the fragility of contact, the corresponding couple of the main plot, Hero and Claudio, tragically experience the crisis of contract: contract, founded on divine and patriarchal authority, has obviously lost the power to regulate love and relationships.[17] The fragility of touch has irrevocably contaminated the traditional foundations of social life. As in *Richard III*, the outsiders' 'deviant' behaviour appears to answer to a world that has changed. Their speech acts, contractually, do nothing: they do not even communicate. They 'only' caress the dialogue partner. Shakespeare clearly experiments with the social conditions of his time. He does so by affirming the power of theatrical speech that works surprisingly similarly to Benedick's and Beatrice's verbal caresses.

In the fourth and final chapter, I will analyse the problem of social bonds that is negotiated in *Troilus and Cressida*. The structural setting resembles that of *Much Ado*: Troilus and Ulysses embody an old, traditional order of the world that is out of joint, whereas Cressida's behaviour and her way of interacting indicate a different and new regime of social regulation that is about to take over. With its complex superposition of (touches of) love and war, *Troilus and Cressida* brings together many of the aspects discussed in the preceding chapters: rituals of touch, anarchic speech acts and a gendered perspective on the world that associates touch and temporality with 'frail' femininity and temptation. With unrivalled intensity, the play puts before the spectators' eyes that the basic condition of touch, that is, exposing oneself to another, entails an incalculable risk. Hector tragically falls for the vulnerability inherent in touch and the audience suffers with him, because they share this existential precondition on which modern society is 'founded'. The gloomy, inescapable atmosphere of societal crisis that *Troilus and Cressida* creates emphasises that the fragility of touch is not to be overcome. The fractions – no matter whether Greek, Trojan or those of loving couples – cannot simply be reunited to form a new, authentic entity. Generating at least some form of social cohesion therefore remains a challenge: a challenge of touching at a distance.

In *Troilus and Cressida*, Shakespeare gives this challenge a body and a voice: the character Pandarus not only sets

Troilus up with Cressida; he also goes between stage and audience when addressing the spectators and speaking the epilogue. In his person, the touches performed on stage are connected to theatre's reaching beyond its fictional world and touching the viewers in the audience. Pandarus embodies the main argument of my book: touching at a distance as a historico-social problem negotiated on stage that is intrinsically linked to theatricality and its generation of emotions.

It is by extensive, close readings that the following chapters attempt to work out the significance of 'touching at a distance' in Shakespeare's plays. My study considers texts from all the major genres that characterise Shakespeare's dramatic oeuvre: comedy (*Much Ado*), history (*Richard III*), tragedy (*Hamlet*), the problem play (*Troilus and Cressida*) and romance (*The Tempest*). I have decided not to privilege gestures of 'actual' physical touch performed on stage over touches that are talked about or only linguistically implied by the characters' words. '[T]here was no binary between the materiality of theatre and the emotional, metaphorical and poetic registers of the plays themselves,' write Farah Karim-Cooper and Tiffany Stern ('Introduction' 3). According to Katherine A. Craik and Tanya Pollard, '[u]nderstanding the period's psychophysiology requires recognizing that the boundaries between metaphorical and literal language were radically unstable' (7). Instead of categorising different functions of *one* predefined notion of touch (for example, 'physical touch on stage', serving different purposes in different plays), my study aims to gather all the manifold instances of touch in the plays (whether 'metaphorical' or 'literal', minute semantic details or significant acts on stage) in order to look for their contribution to a larger socio-cultural regime of touch. It is very often not the stage action (such as kissing, caressing or beating) but the small 'metaphoric', linguistic details (such as the use of the word 'contagion' or Shakespeare's playing with the rich semantic spectrum of 'touching' in apparently insignificant formulations) through which this paradigm of touch can be traced and which then provide the background for a better understanding of the explicit, onstage 'haptics'.

Many of the keywords that the study claims for Shakespeare's paradigm of touch – such as contagion, proximity, contact, encounter, exposure or vulnerability – chime with the conceptual apparatus of the proliferating field of Affect Studies.[18] In fact, all the characteristics ascribed above to the specificity of the 'theatrical touch' – mutuality, temporality, critique of substantiality – and the intrinsic link to emotions have been used by scholars in their attempts to define 'affect'. Scanning through prominent formulations in Affect Studies, at times it appears hard to distinguish between affect and what I would conceptualise as 'touch': 'Bodies take the shape of the very contact they have with objects and others', writes Sarah Ahmed (1), resorting to the mutuality implied by the haptic notion of 'contact' in order to sketch out what she will later call 'affect'. The criterium of 'being moved by the proximity of others' (11), also established by Ahmed, holds true not only for affect, but also for touch, as I argue. The same could be said of the definition given by Röttger-Rössler and Slaby in the introduction to their edited volume *Affect in Relation*:

> Affect is what unfolds 'in-between' – in between interacting agents, in between actors and elements in communal everyday practices, within processes of transmission, be they medial, symbolic or aural, and in the involvement, absorption or immersion when the boundaries of the self become porous (or when they have not even been properly drawn to begin with). (Röttger-Rössler and Slaby 2)

Is Shakespeare's theatre not a prime example of the (theatrical) experience of 'the involvement, absorption or immersion' at a very early time of nascent modern subjectivity, 'when the boundaries of the self [. . .] have not even been properly drawn'? The resonances between affect and my interest in touch are strongest in Brian Massumi's pioneering work, which may be said to be closest to the Deleuzian pedigree of Affect Studies. Affect, according to Massumi, 'is not ownable' (28), and it has to be understood as 'an excluded middle, prior to the distinction between activity and passivity' (32) – two traits that I have, under slightly different names (impossibility of appropriation and mutuality), also ascribed to the concept of touch. Even the central paradox of touch – its bringing together immediacy and distance – can be found at a prominent place in *Parables for the Virtual*: first, when Massumi characterises the 'self-relation' (responsible for difference's most basic identity effect) as being 'immediate [. . .] even though it requires distance to occur' (14), and also later when he describes the affective field, where affective potential is 'in contact [. . .] as by action at a distance' (43).

Massumi's actualisation of Nietzsche's 'actio in distans' (cf. *Nachlaß 1869–1874* 572) is the closest his theory comes to a current of Continental philosophy against which Affect Studies has effectively established itself: deconstruction, represented mainly by Jacques Derrida and thinkers influenced by him, such as Luce Irigaray and Jean-Luc Nancy. This approximation is, however, balanced by a fundamental critique that fuels his whole project: 'Our entire vocabulary has derived from theories of signification' (27), Massumi writes, a credo that holds together not only the field of Affect Studies but the whole current of new materialisms. Deconstruction, which is, especially in its Anglo-American reception, associated with 'the discursive', with signification, with (ontological) effects of language, therefore has to be overcome. 'Touch' as a non-discursive gesture appears to be a promising starting point for a new conceptual vocabulary, one that is not rooted in theories of signification. However, although some derivates of touch, like contagion, have been adapted by Deleuze and scholars in his tradition, it is not Affect Studies that can claim to have worked out the conceptual potential of touch most explicitly and productively – but thinkers associated with 'deconstruction': Jacques Derrida (cf. *On Touching*), Jean-Luc Nancy (cf. *Corpus*; 'Rühren') and Luce Irigaray (cf. 'This Sex Which is Not One'). 'Touch' thus forms an interesting contact point or zone of proximity between two currents of thinking that are usually held to be rivals. Unfortunately, touch as a zone of proximity between Deleuzian and Derridean thinking has not led to fruitful encounters. Instead, the proximity appears to have triggered reflexes of distancing, such as Derrida's book on touch accusing Deleuze's philosophy of what could be called 'presentism' – of the lack of distance and absence in his thinking of encounter and becoming (cf. *On Touching* 123–6).

My argument of (re)establishing contact between the two rests on the fact that it is productive distance – Nietzsche's 'actio in distans' – or, in other words, a thinking of difference, that drives the philosophies of both Derrida and Deleuze. The tension which results from reading the two together seems a good mutual corrective: Derrida might remind Deleuzians (Affect Studies?) of the need for distance, for absence and non-presence as the basis for becomings and open futures, of a necessary ingredient that prevents Deleuze's philosophy from shifting into a colourful idyll of presence, of involvedness and the anything goes of encounters, all present, all already there (a liberalist perspective identifiable in some parts of the reception of Deleuze's writings);[19] the resonance between Deleuze and Derrida (cf. Kirby) might bring attention to the fact that Derrida's 'différance' or 'deconstruction' is not limited to linguistic phenomena – as his late work, especially on touch, shows.

Touching at a Distance, read from front to back, might be conceived of as Deleuzian, with a deconstructivist corrective;

read backwards, deconstructivist with Deleuzian sympathies. The book shares a proximity with deconstruction and Deleuzian Affect Studies, but chooses to maintain a certain distance from both. The reason for this 'perspective apart' lies in its subject matter: Shakespeare's theatre combines the presence of performance and the distance of fictional words. Reconstructing Shakespeare's theatrical touches cannot dispense with 'the discursive', as it is (mainly) words that touch. Methodically, the study therefore leans towards the deconstructive: texts are read with attention to detail and a readiness to follow the unheard voices of the peripheral. Thematically, the interest in touch brings the manifold nondiscursive forces – (also and mainly) of discourse into focus. Theatre may be the best place to experience these forces and may raise awareness of the fact that touch (and perhaps also affect) cannot and should not be as easily and categorically separated from 'the discursive' as the strategic demarcations introduced by recent philosophical currents make us think.

Touch, in other words, turns out to be a surprisingly productive way of rethinking theatricality. Recent studies in theatre's performativity (such as James Loxley and Mark Robson's *Shakespeare, Jonson, and the Claims of the Performative*) detail the paradoxical tension at work in the theatrical situation that resonates strongly with what I have identified as the central paradox of touch: 'theater puts us in both its world and ours, in a manner which puts its characters both within and out of reach', a tension that they characterise as a 'combination of nearness and inaccessibility' (115). Unlike in older studies of metatheatricality, Loxley and Robson aim for the unforeseeable productivity of this paradoxical proximity. When claiming that 'the empirical [the performance or its interruption] and the transcendental [the audience's conditions of experience] can touch', that 'possibilities – are touched by impossibilities' (Loxley and Robson 115), they affirm the contagion that takes place through the contact of heterogeneous, incompatible spheres. The distinction of 'play/world' has become 'porous' (Loxley and Robson 125) – a state (usually produced by theatrically conscious moments) for which Bridget Escolme has found the very helpful term of a 'mutual vulnerability' (154) of 'performer/figure' and audience.

Analysing Shakespeare's theatricality with recourse to the notion of touch cannot claim to be a 'new' approach; as shown by the few quotations, touch is already latently present in recent studies of performativity. However, its conceptual potential has not yet been fully developed. Compared to prevalent guiding concepts like 'performance' and 'performativity', touch, as an abstract, 'neutral' notion with regard to theatricality, may bring certain advantages to the examination of theatre's specific forces. Touch implies both sides of the productive paradox that Loxley and Robinson ascribe to the theatrical situation: it combines 'nearness and inaccessibility', presence and distance. In contrast, performance and performativity have a strong tendency to strengthen the aspect of presence and directness, and weaken the distance introduced by text and fictionality. The goal must be to combine attention for the complex forces of dramatic performance (worked out, among others, by William B. Worthen) with a sense of the intricacies of fictionality. It is the distance introduced by fictionality against which the forces of approximation, the forces aiming at transgressing the fourth wall, build up. The fascination and the force of theatricality lie in the complicated in-between that is actualised as a tension between proximity and distance.

As a consequence, the 'older' tradition of reading Shakespeare metatheatrically has become all but obsolete under the new paradigm of performativity. The textual work undertaken by critics such as James Calderwood, Robert Egan, Harry Berger, Robert Weimann and Douglas Bruster exercises a formative influence on my study. It brings attention to the precious moments where Shakespeare's theatre turns to its own theatricality, which is not, as I would argue, a gesture of closure, not the gesture of losing contact to the world which it is often read as. When metatheatrically reflecting on itself, Shakespeare's theatre exposes distance – perhaps the distance that Massumi sees as the condition of every self-relation? This is less surprising than it sounds: it is this very distance, the distance between stage and audience, between fiction and world, that is at the heart of theatre. As can be wonderfully worked out through close readings, theatre does not merely thematise and celebrate itself in these metatheatrical moments: it is its paradoxical and productive in-betweenness – its complicated touch – that comes to the fore.

The following chapters have to deal with another instance of the tension between nearness and distance: we are not only confronted with the presence of performance and the distance of fictional words, but with the presence of performance and the distance of fictional words fabricated four hundred years ago. The question of historical distance versus the proximity of presence is, of course, much debated in Shakespeare Studies. The most prominent and rival positions in the academic struggle to deal with 'the distance between critic and historical subject' (Rzepka 156) are New Historicism and Critical Presentism: whereas New Historicism emphasises the epistemic and cultural distance separating modern readers from early modern culture and society, Critical Presentism, introduced by Terence Hawkes, Ewan Fernie, Hugh Grady, Cary DiPietro and others, affirms 'Shakespeare's presence in the present' (Wilson 13), as Richard Wilson puts it. In other words, Critical Presentism is interested in the resonances of Shakespeare's plays with present political constellations and challenges. As Ken Jackson has observed, Smith's Historical Phenomenology maintains the position of an '"in-between"' (473): 'Smith produces exhilarating readings of Shakespeare that are neither "presentist" nor ahistorical' (470). As the title of my book might indicate, this in-between position is also appealing for my purposes. However, the in-between I have decided for affirms the tension between proximity and distance in the 'making and remaking of this plain, zone of contact between us and all the things we mean or sense in speaking of the early modern' (Gallagher and Raman 'Introduction' 18) in a more radical fashion than Smith – perhaps 'neither presentist nor historical'. On the one hand, *Touching at a Distance* brings early modern texts and twentieth-century theory into contact; it embraces Presentism's 'critical and productive use of anachronism' (DiPietro and Grady 'Presentism, Anachronism' 47). On the other hand, it refrains from 'collapsing the distance between [present and past]' ('Presentism, Anachronism' 47); it refrains from reading the plays 'through the lens of contemporary politics' exactly because, in contrast to DiPietro and Grady, it does not aim to 'make the play[s] our own' (DiPietro and Grady 'Presentism, Anachronism' 59). My study shares the goal of engaging 'with the very motive forces that produce difference' (Hawkes *Shakespeare in the Present* 2–3) that Terence Hawkes formulates in *Shakespeare in the Present* – with 'difference' mainly signifying the hope for political or societal impulses. However, it prefers not to anchor the anachronistic encounters in a present 'familiar' to us, or to make them happen in 'our' present. The wished-for defamiliarisation appears to me all too limited and a 'mutual vulnerability' not quite in practice when we bring Shakespeare in harmony with our present challenges and hope for unforeseen answers to questions which are still ours.

Contact does not presuppose a shared space or time; it does not presuppose '(unified) presence'.[20] The way of getting in touch with Shakespeare's theatre and its forces practised in my study attempts to hold the tension of the in-between: neither anchoring my work in a past (that is, fabricating histories of early modern culture) nor in 'our' present (making use of Shakespeare's theatre for our contemporary problems and challenges) but holding oneself in-between the two, risking 'mutual vulnerability'. In other words: touching at a distance is all that I can do. I expose myself to Shakespeare's texts in an attempt to establish the largest of contact surfaces possible. This means unfolding Shakespeare's text to the minutest semantic detail and making use of all that can be reconstructed about the material conditions of early modern performance. Exposing myself to Shakespearean drama also means bringing my own intellectual horizon to the text, presenting some typically 'modern' philosophemes to Shakespeare's words, in order to facilitate resonance. Stanley Cavell's 'unsettling the matter of priority (as between philosophy and literature, say)' (1) in order to avoid illustration or application has been methodically formative for my study. In my case, 'the company of philosophy' (Cavell 2) in reading Shakespeare consists, among others, of the following thinkers: Hans Blumenberg and Jean-Luc Nancy contribute to the first chapter; Maurice Blanchot, Friedrich Nietzsche and Jacques Derrida to the second; the latter features again in the third, this time entering into dialogue with Roland Barthes and John Austin; while the fourth chapter draws on concepts by Carl Schmitt, Niklas Luhmann and Luce Irigaray.

There can be no doubt that the endeavour of my book is fragile. The anachronism of its material indicates that its fabric has to be called 'baseless': as for the audience of a theatre performance, there is no authentic common ground between 'Shakespeare' and a twenty-first century scholar that would guarantee the success of a touching encounter. This certainly does not release me from the duties of academic integrity and honesty. The risk of anachronism is taken for strategic reasons. My study aims not merely to 'truthfully' report the history of touches that happened inside and outside the theatre long ago: its goal is to spread the contagion that Shakespeare's theatre has brought into the world. It is up to you, the readers, to determine whether this fails or not: to feel the tickling, the aches – or whatever symptoms may testify to having been touched – at a distance.

> Till then I'll sweat and seek about for eases,
> And at that time bequeath you my diseases. (*TC* 5.11.55–6)

Notes

1. Quotations from Shakespeare's plays both here and in the following refer to the Arden3 editions.
2. The term 'immersive theatres', expanded upon by Josephine Machon and others, covers a wide spectrum of contemporary exceptions to the rather 'classical' theatrical setting that I focus on. However, although immersive theatres define themselves mainly by abandoning 'the "usual" set of rules and conventions' (Machon 26) responsible for the 'delineation of space (auditorium/stage) and role (static-passive observer/active-moving performer)' (Machon 27), that is, the fundamental distance between audience and (stage) performance, what they seek is, in parts, not too different from the things that I claim to find in Shakespeare's theatre: mutuality, symmetry, 'experiencing more fully' (Machon 26), 'bodily engagement' (Machon 26) and '[i]ntimacy, involvement and communitas' (Machon 37). Touch plays a major role in immersive theatre, where it is understood as the expression and realisation of 'a desire for genuine physical connection'. Unlike immersive theatre's celebration of the directness and presence of the effects of performance (which takes its allure from the apparent indirectness and conventionality of classical theatre), it is my goal to emphasise the role of distance that drives the affective power of touch. The strategic distinction of immersive versus 'classical' theatre instead covers up the specific theatrical potential, for which distance is an essential structural ingredient, a potential that is at work both in 'immersive' and 'conventional' forms of performances.

3. In *Beschreibung des Menschen* ('Description of Man') the philosopher Hans Blumenberg argues that what he calls the human touchability (*Betreffbarkeit*) is the condition of possibility for responsibility: 'It is the body [*der Leib*] that demarcates the spatiotemporal line that emanates from the deed. The person responsible can be touched [*betroffen*] along this line and can be held accountable' (783; my transl.).
4. It is this 'security' at the heart of the epistemological primal scene that the popular interpretation of Schrödinger's cat shatters.
5. When the tree begins to look back in Heidegger's *What is Called Thinking?* most 'serious' philosophers think it a scandal: 'We stand outside of science. Instead, we stand before a tree in bloom, for example – and the tree stands before us. The tree faces us. The tree and we meet one another, as the tree stands there and we stand face to face with it' (41).
6. In German, Kant aims at turning 'bloßes Herumtappen' into 'den sicheren Gang einer Wissenschaft' (Kant *Kritik der reinen Vernunft* B VII), German *tappen* being etymologically related to *tasten* ('to touch'), cf. the Grimms' *Deutsches Wörterbuch*, 'tappen, v.'.
7. Cf. Barish, *The Antitheatrical Prejudice*, which is a classical, exemplary text representing a huge field of research. Antitheatrical polemics feature regularly in discussions of touch in Shakespeare. See, for example, Farah Karim-Cooper, 'Touch and Taste in Shakespeare's Theatres' or Carla Mazzio, 'Acting with Tact'.
8. The notion of an 'audience to come' is inspired by Gilles Deleuze's concept of 'a people to come' (cf. Deleuze *Cinema 2* 221–4; G. Deleuze and F. Guattari *What is Philosophy?* 219).
9. I use the notion of contagion with regard to Gilles Deleuze and Félix Guattari's 'definition': 'We oppose epidemic to filiation, contagion to heredity [. . .]. The difference is that contagion, epidemic, involves terms that are entirely heterogeneous: for example, a human being, an animal, and a bacterium, a virus, a molecule, a microorganism' (Deleuze and Guattari *A Thousand Plateaus* 241–2). It is the capacity of contagion

to be effective across boundaries that renders this notion interesting for analysing theatre. For exemplary employments of 'contagion' in the field of theatre studies, see the volume *Ansteckung. Zur Körperlichkeit eines ästhetischen Prinzips* ('Contagion. On the Corporality of an Aesthetic Principle'), edited by Mirjam Schaub, Nicola Suthor and Erika Fischer-Lichte, esp. Erika Fischer-Lichte's article 'Zuschauen als Ansteckung' ('Watching as Contagion'). Contagion has recently been adapted to the field of Early Modern Studies, as the volumes *Contagion and the Shakespearean Stage*, edited by Darryl Chalk and Mary Floyd-Wilson, and *Theatres of Contagion: Transmitting Early Modern to Contemporary Performance*, edited by Fintan Walsh indicate. Closest to my interest in Shakespeare's theatrical contagions is Allison P. Hobgood's wonderful article 'Feeling Fear in *Macbeth*', from which I have quoted repeatedly in this introduction.

10. William B. Worthen develops a very similar argument to the one sketched out over the following paragraphs in the first pages of his *Shakespeare and the Force of Modern Performance*.

11. 'Sight is [. . .] historically and materially situated,' writes Evelyn Tribble in her article 'Sight and Spectacle', emphasising the 'ubiquity of artificial lighting' in 'contemporary assumptions about sight and light' ('Sight and Spectacle' 237).

12. Other notable studies are Marjorie O'Rourke-Boyle's *Senses of Touch: Human Dignity and Deformity from Michelangelo to Calvin*, Katherine Row's *Dead Hands: Fictions of Agency* and Daniel Heller-Roazen's *The Inner Touch*, which serves as an important point of reference for many Shakespeare scholars.

13. 'In several senses, the book you are holding in your hands is a handbook,' begins *Phenomenal Shakespeare*. 'It provides a manual for how to do historical phenomenology. But it is also a book about hands' (*Phenomenal Shakespeare* xvii).

14. Michael Witmore repeats the latter part of Cahill's question almost verbatim in his essay 'Phenomenology and Sensation: Shakespeare, Sensation, and Renaissance Existentialism' (424).

15. Adam Rzepka diagnoses a centre of 'turns' in the concept of experience: 'Now, in the new turn away from the long turn against that sense of proximity, "experience" is quietly marking the stations of a return' (156), he writes, emphasising the complexity of the term and arguing for a 'turbulent, hybrid poetics unfolding at the peripheries of knowledge production' (171).
16. The concept of synaesthesia has been used to make this point (cf. Waldron). Farah Karim-Cooper speaks of the 'synaesthetic concept of tactile vision' (*The Hand* 163).
17. As Niklas Luhmann argues in *Love as Passion: The Codification of Intimacy*, it is literature that slowly paves the way for the development of 'love' as a 'generalised symbolic medium of communication' that regulates the nexus of romantic love and (marital) relationships in modern society.
18. Brian Massumi's *Parables of the Virtual*, Eve Kosofsky Sedgwick's *Touching Feeling: Affect, Pedagogy, Performativity*, Teresa Brennan's *The Transmission of Affect* and *The Affective Turn: Theorizing the Social*, edited by Patricia Ticineto Clough, should be mentioned as landmarks of Affect Studies.
19. 'What motivates the affective turn is a desire for a univocal ontology that eliminates even modest flirtations with alterity or otherness because such flirtations hint at transcendence and idealist philosophy,' notes Ken Jackson (470). The philosophical projects of Derrida and Nancy may serve as prime examples of thinking alterity not necessarily leading to idealist philosophy. On the contrary, as they show, it is alterity and a thinking of the event as the immanence of transcendence that prevents any materialism from developing into an idealist philosophy in disguise.
20. One legacy of Michel Foucault's thinking might be the complication of the notion of historicity, which no longer presupposes 'history' as '(unified) presence'. This is not only a question for New Historicism – we all face this complication, or rather, this challenge.

CHAPTER 1

THEATRE'S OFFENCE: *HAMLET* AND *THE TEMPEST*

'Who's there?' – The Tangible Problems of Unfolding the Theatrical Situation

'Who's there?' – this famous question opens William Shakespeare's *Hamlet*.[1] It is not yet the encounter with 'the ghost' that evokes this question, although it certainly prepares the ground for its impending appearance on stage. It concerns another 'spectral apparition' that is 'natural' only inside the fictional world of the play: there it is two minor characters, two sentinels, one taking over the shift of watch from the other, who have to identify each other in the dark of the night.[2] For the theatre audience, however, as part of the external communication system, the first words of Shakespeare's *Hamlet* pronounce and expose a fundamental and delicate process of theatrical art: 'Who's there?', this question automatically raises in the viewers, whenever an actor makes his first entrance on the stage. The convention of theatre wants that the play answers this question by conjuring up a somehow spectral, because hybrid body; a body which is and is not just the actor's body. A stage character is to be established who is present but not quite, who is in need of embodiment by an actor who resides in/comes from another world, one that does not exist for the characters in the fictional world.

Hamlet opens with a metatheatrical gesture. It exposes on stage the uneasy and dramaturgically difficult situation of acquainting the theatre audience with the fictional world of the play they are beginning to watch. The spectators are waiting for some dramaturgical help from the fictional world to name and characterise the figure who has just entered the stage. However, the second person on the platform refuses the audience this conventional favour by shifting the question in an interesting way: 'Nay, answer me,' it says, 'Stand and unfold yourself' (*Ham.* 1.1.2). Staying with the metatheatrical reading, this imperative concerns the audience itself – it questions the supposedly asymmetrical theatrical setting. It troubles the distinction between the passive, anonymous watchers, who merely consume the play, and the active actors on stage, who present their craft to the audience.

In the fictional world, the darkness of the nightly scene – probably indicated by a lantern carried by one of the actors – prevents that the imperative 'unfold yourself' can be understood in a visual way, demanding a gesture of showing, disclosing or displaying, that is, 'laying open to the view'. Instead, the request 'to unfold yourself' asks the encountering other to 'disclose or reveal' itself 'by statement or exposition' – the *OED* lists the quotation from *Hamlet* as an example of this 'linguistic' meaning of the verb *unfold* ('unfold, *v.1*'; 2.).

It might be indicative for Shakespeare's theatre that this particular use of *unfold* transposes the visual denotations of the verb ('To disclose or lay open to the view; to display. Also *fig.*' (*OED*, 'unfold, *v.1*'; 3.)) into the realm of words. Although theatre is characterised by its very name as an institution of sight (gr. θεάομαι, *theáomai*, 'to behold, view, contemplate'), the dominant medial channel of Shakespeare's art of theatre is certainly established by the power of words.

However, paraphrasing the imperative 'unfold yourself' with 'explain who you are' cuts off important connotations that are crucial for a fuller understanding of the opening scene. It covers the central fact that whosoever decides or is forced to 'unfold himself' makes himself the vulnerable object of another's 'handling' – be it the gaze or some other way of 'being dealt with'. 'Unfolding' is a gesture of exposing oneself, of presenting the other a maximum of attack surface. It implies abandoning the protection of hiding oneself in the darkness or behind shields. In contrast to the active, autonomous position as the subject of a speech act, 'unfolding' merely prepares the ground for something to come, for something that the encountering other will do with what has just opened up, what has been unfolded. As a gesture, it therefore undermines the classical active/passive distinction: although acting intentionally, the 'subject' (dis)places itself into a passive, a waiting position. By expanding the (social, bodily) contact zone it facilitates encounters that might happen to it 'from without' and that are initiated by others.

The imperative at the beginning of *Hamlet* carries the traces of this paradoxical suspension of active and passive. It not only qualifies the autonomy of the subject that is called upon to 'act'; the request to 'unfold' is also accompanied by another imperative that highlights the passivity, the waiting position which the other is to take: 'Stand and unfold yourself' (*Ham.* 1.1.2). It is here that we return to the metatheatrical reading of this little dialogue. The imperatives are an answer to the question 'Who's there?' that I have suggested to be also the characteristic question of the audience at the beginning of a play. The spectators' question: 'who is this fictional character that the actor who has just entered the stage represents' ('Who's there?') is answered with: 'stand, stay still and expose yourself, open yourself up to what the play will do with you during the next two hours' ('Stand and unfold yourself'). The groundlings in the pit certainly feel addressed by the request to stand – and might do even more so if the actor voicing the imperative speaks the words in the rough direction of the audience, indicating his inability to locate the person who is approaching.

The spectators in the theatrical setting obviously do not primarily expose themselves to be seen or heard – as spectators it is they who see and hear. However, by seeing and hearing they expose themselves to something that the play does to them, to what Farah Karim-Cooper has called 'the tactile assault' that the sight and sounds of performance can 'impose upon the bodies, minds and souls of early modern audience members' (*The Hand* 157). These 'tactile' effects that theatre produces can be tragic or comical, cathartic or entertaining. Although seeing and hearing obviously play a crucial role in the theatrical constellation, they are both only means involved in the generation of theatre's effects. As the first two lines of *Hamlet* indicate, theatre cannot be reduced to observing and listening. On the one hand, the paradigm of the visual, which describes best the distant and superior position of the audience watching a play performed for them is not particularly suited to approach the question of how theatre achieves its effects. The visual and its metaphoric field are deeply and inextricably entangled with notions of knowledge and truth – literally with 'in-sight'. As a consequence, analysing theatre under the paradigm of the visual or of communication ('What is it that we see?', 'What is the message communicated to us?') is always in danger of reconstructing theatre as an institution of cognition. It forgets that the complex theatrical experience is a much more bodily affair than the paradigm of seeing and understanding can account for. Howard Marchitello observes the interplay between perception and bodily vulnerability which is negotiated in the play itself: 'In *Hamlet* the organs of perception – eyes, ears, nose, mouth, and skin – are simultaneously the means through which one apprehends the material world and the loci of a profound material vulnerability' (142). This vulnerability entails 'a process of change that perturbs the ostensible stability of the eye's domain' (Raman 135).

On the other hand, we can only develop a sense of theatre's particular capacity of 'moving' the spectators by linking this capacity with the prominence of theatre's dominant visual and aural medial channels. Theatre does not merely 'touch' its spectators as a result of the characteristic co-presence of actors and audience (cf. Fischer-Lichte); the two senses of distance, seeing and hearing, emphasise the spatial (and fictional) division of stage and audience which theatre has the power to traverse. Theatre moves, theatre touches – but it touches from a distance.

In the following I would like to tackle the question of theatre's affective effects with this paradigm of 'touching from a distance' in mind – and with Shakespeare as my guide. I think that the two lines discussed above give only a first glimpse of what *Hamlet* as a whole is (among other themes, obviously) concerned with: theatre's process of 'concerning', of 'offending' – of touching – that takes place in-between stage and audience.

Enter the Ghost – 'Touching this dreaded sight'

Barnardo's frightened encounter with what turns out to be Francisco, the fellow sentinel from whom he takes over the nightly guard, foreshadows the first highlight of Shakespeare's *Hamlet*: the entrance of the king's ghost. In fact, the ghost has actually been concerned in Barnardo's initial anxiety. As he tells Horatio, he has encountered a strange apparition the nights before. In his question 'Who's there?', it is therefore also the fright of the past nights that speaks. The ontological reality of the apparition is obviously still in doubt, so that Barnardo and his comrade Marcellus have asked Horatio, a socially superior authority and a learned man, to be present at their watch in order to become witness of the unnatural events. The latter is sceptical about the 'factual background' of the two sentinels' ghost story:

MARCELLUS
Horatio says 'tis but our fantasy
And will not let belief take hold of him
Touching this dreaded sight twice seen of us. (*Ham.* 1.1.22–4)

The Arden3 editors paraphrase the uncommon 'Touching' with 'concerning' and thus work out the overall message of Marcellus's speech act: Horatio simply does not believe in what Barnardo and Marcello claim to have seen. However, as the metaphor 'taking hold of' indicates, the complex wording of Marcellus's statement is grouped around the semantic field of 'touching'. It thereby generates meaning that exceeds its superficial message. 'Touching this dreaded sight' voices an interesting paradox, an impossible passage from one sense, the visual, to another, to the haptic.[3] Shakespeare's *Hamlet*, like the later *The Winter's Tale*, 're-examines the relationship of vision and touch' (Tribble '"O, she's warm"' 74). The sight, this sight, is given; the task seems to consist in translating the visual into touch. 'Touching' is the challenge.

Theatre, I would like to claim, is deeply familiar with this transfer, this passage. As its name indicates, it starts from sight but only to aim for touch, for moving the spectators. Theatre does, however, not overcome, or harmonise the paradox that Shakespeare's 'Touching this dreaded sight' exposes. It rather operates with this paradox as its basic condition. Theatre touches from a distance, it touches in a constellation that resembles the visual one, but operates differently and follows its own, non-visual but much more bodily goal.

The metatheatrical reading which I have tried to develop from the fragment of Marcellus's statement can be accused of one decisive lack of consistency regarding the direction of touch: whereas the theatre analogy seems to demand that it is the (theatrical) spectacle, 'the sight', that touches the spectator, the grammatical construction of Marcellus's statement – if we take the liberty of reading 'Touching' as a somewhat 'forgotten', 'impersonalised' present participle – rather suggests that Horatio (metaphorically) touches the apparition. However, the context in which the phrase is embedded suspends the unambiguity of the haptic direction: Horatio is said not to 'let belief take hold of him / Touching this dreaded sight' (*Ham.* 1.1.23–4). Marcellus's statement thus tells us of a double movement of touch that brings together both directions. In between the two lines it even performs the contact between a touch which is suffered ('letting take hold of') and one that is actively initiated ('touching' in its grammatical function as present participle). In other words, we here encounter again the structure of the imperative 'unfold yourself' which opened this first scene of *Hamlet*. Horatio's con-tact to the 'real' nature of the ghost is barred, because he has not been willing to expose himself enough to it, 'will not let belief take hold of him'. Although he has obviously been somehow 'concerned' with the apparition in discussions about its nature that he has had with the sentinels, although they have 'touched' upon the 'dreaded sight' with words, Horatio has not yet been contaminated with the emotional trouble that the ghost spreads. His position towards the 'sight' is yet the one as which he is famously introduced: he is 'a scholar' (*Ham.* 1.1.41).[4] He judges over what others think to have observed repeatedly – he makes theory (again from gr. θεάομαι, *theáomai*, 'to behold, view, contemplate') in its literal sense. Horatio does not 'let belief take hold of him' while he, in a theoretical manner, 'touches' on this 'dreaded sight', while he refers to it, while he makes it his subject matter, without being involved himself. He touches on it merely theoretically, that is, without being touched by it himself. This is the attitude of the scholar. It translates touch into theory, into the paradigm of the visual, which is defined by the fundamental asymmetry of 'touching without being touched'. The scholars of the Arden3 edition mimic the scholar Horatio by glossing 'touching' ('Touching this dreaded sight') with 'concerning': the Latin *cernō* can be understood as a synonym of *videō* and is thus closely connected to the sphere of the visual. What gets lost in the editors' and Horatio's scholarly dealing with the question of the ghost is the emotions produced by the sentinels' encounter with the apparition. It is these strong affects that characterise this encounter and make Marcellus speak of 'this dreaded sight'.⁵

From Horatio's scholarly perspective, the apparition is 'but [their] fantasy', nothing but 'a making visible' (gr. φαντασία, phantasía). It is no coincidence that this 'making visible' strikingly describes what theatre in fact appears to do: enacting 'fancies', as Prospero describes his 'art' of producing a court masque in *The Tempest* (cf. *Tmp.* 4.1.120-122). The lines preceding the entrance of the ghost in *Hamlet* thus call up a critical attitude towards the theatrical art that is topical since Plato's prominent critique in *The Republic* (cf. *The Republic. Books 6-10* 595a-608a). It considers theatre inferior on ontological grounds: as merely representation or even projection, without 'real' substance, and therefore at best irrelevant if not corruptively misguiding. In this ontological hierarchy, the ghost holds a position similar to that of theatre; as ghost he lacks ontological density, so to speak – he is too far away from the originality of the ideas in order to be a trustworthy messenger of truth (cf. Derrida *Specters of Marx* 5).⁶

However, Shakespeare's *Hamlet* premises these theoretical metatheatrical reflections only to negate them as an outside view on theatre that necessarily misses its core. In fact, Horatio has not come as a scholar. He has abandoned his books. His joining the sentinels during their nightly watch has to be understood as a gesture of 'unfolding'. He has left behind the intellectual sphere in which he holds a position of control to expose himself to elements over which he has no authority. By (dis)placing himself into the uneasy, because vulnerable, position of waiting, he contributes his share for enabling a touching encounter. Touch cannot be conveyed discursively – it has to be performed and suffered, at the same time. And this is exactly what happens.

The ghost appears, as if conjured up by Barnardo, who has just begun telling the story of the past encounters, and the touching experience takes place. The symptoms which Horatio shows indicate unmistakeably that he has been contaminated with the very emotional trouble from which Francisco and Barnardo have already been suffering since their first encounters with the ghost

BARNARDO
How now, Horatio, you tremble and look pale.
Is not this something more than fantasy?
What think you on't?
HORATIO
Before my God, I might not this believe
Without the sensible and true avouch
Of mine own eyes. (*Ham.* 1.1.52–7)

Belief has 'taken hold of him' in quite a literal sense: 'the truth of [his] experience is registered somatically' (Marchitello 139), abstract vision has to be supplemented by a 'sensible', 'bodily', non-intellectual impression. '[U]ltimately bodily experience alone convinces him,' writes Sarah Outterson-Murphy (259). Exposing himself to '[t]ouching the ghost' serves as the 'true avouch'.

In her article dedicated to *Hamlet*'s reflections on the 'interactive physical experience of playgoing' (253), Outterson-Murphy works out that the medical vocabulary like 'contagion', 'infection' and 'symptoms' associated with what she calls 'ghostly performance' (254) is not mere imagery. Shakespeare's theatre is embedded in 'a culture in which humors and spirits had emotional effects and theater could mold the spectator's physical body' (253–4). A passage from Robert Burton's *Anatomy of Melancholy* serves Outterson-Murphy to argue that, in the early modern age, 'contagious emotion' (260) was a medical reality:

> [A] corrupt and false Imagination [. . .] works not in sicke and melancholy men only, but even most forcibly sometimes in such as are found, it makes them suddainely sicke, and alters their temperature in an instant. And sometimes a strong apprehension, as *Valesius* proves, will take away Diseases: in both kindes it will produce reall effects. Men if they see but another man tremble, giddy, or sicke of some fearful disease, their apprehension and feare is so strong in this kinde, that they will have the same disease. (Burton 125)

When the 'Ghost unleashes its spectators' emotions', he shapes them 'through its own infectious bodily power', Outterson-Murphy writes (257). This physical, material process – which touches from a distance – has the capacity of spreading to the audience: 'the complex response to the Ghost' in *Hamlet* 'models the vulnerability [. . .] of theatrical spectatorship itself' (254). The audience exposes themselves deliberately to the 'reall effects' of an overactive imagination.

Certain keywords which are dropped in the first ghost scene indicate that it negotiates and reflects on theatre and its emotional effects. When Horatio says that the ghost 'harrows [him] with fear and wonder' (*Ham.* 1.1.43), he calls up two important Aristotelian concepts of theatre: φόβος, *phóbos*, 'fear', and τὸ θαυμαστὸν, *tò thaumastòn*, 'tragic wonder' (cf. 1452a).

A glance at Shakespeare's *Tempest* might underline that Shakespeare habitually draws on these concepts to exhibit the metatheatrical quality of a scene.[7] The island on which Prospero restores his daughter's rights by confronting his rivals with a series of spectacles is clearly identifiable as a dramatic reflection on theatre and its effects. When, in the fifth act, the characters attempt to put their experiences on the island in words, the notions we discovered in *Hamlet* pervade the description:

> GONZALO
> All torment, trouble, wonder and amazement
> Inhabits here. Some heavenly power guide us
> Out of this fearful country. (*Tmp.* 5.1.104–6)

These metatheatrical reflections in *The Tempest* also elaborate on another notion that plays a major role in the first scene of *Hamlet*: belief. Horatio was first accused of not letting 'belief take hold of him'. After encountering the ghost he refers back to his initial disbelief, concluding that he 'might not this believe' without the 'true avouch' of his 'own eyes'. This oscillation between belief and disbelief also shapes the experience of the characters in *The Tempest*: 'Whether this be / Or be not, I'll not swear' (*Tmp.* 5.1.122–3), Gonzalo says, for example, while Sebastian and Antonio decide that, after one of the overpowering spectacles, they will 'believe / That there are unicorns' '[a]nd what does else want credit' (*Tmp.* 3.3.21–5). It is again late in the fifth act that Prospero declares this question of believe to be a characteristic of the (theatre) island:

PROSPERO
                          You do yet taste
Some subtleties o'th' isle that will not let you
Believe things certain. (*Tmp.* 5.1.123–5)

These 'subtleties o'th' isle' not merely suspend the stability of a certain epistemological framework; they involve severe bodily/medical 'infringements': 'an unsettled fancy', for example, that is caused by 'brains / [. . .] boiled within th[e] skull' (*Tmp.* 5.1.59–60), as Prospero explains.[8] It is similar dangers that Horatio fears when Hamlet wants to follow the ghost all on his own. He fears that it 'might deprive [his] sovereignty of reason, / And draw [him] into madness' (*Ham.* 1.4.73–4). In Horatio's reasoning, it is the 'very place', outside, somewhere on the battlements of Elsinore, that 'puts toys of desperation / Without more motive into every brain' (*Ham.* 1.4.73–8). This place, at this hour, is apparently in itself 'touching':

HAMLET
The air bites shrewdly; it is very cold.

HORATIO
> It is nipping, and an eager air. (*Ham.* 1.4.1–2)

The personifications of air in *Hamlet* foreshadow, I would suggest, the important metatheatrical role which air will play in *The Tempest*. Ariel, the character that embodies the theatrical medium, the central play-actor of Prospero's spectacles, already carries the element in his name. He, who is 'but air' (*Tmp.* 5.1.21), acts out Prospero's fancies. The resulting performance is itself repeatedly associated with the life-enabling element, for example when Prospero speaks himself of the 'airy charm' (*Tmp.* 5.1.54) that his 'potent art' (*Tmp.* 5.1.50) has brought forward. It is therefore no coincidence that the play as a whole is called *The Tempest* – a rather unusual Shakespearean title. *The Tempest* is, as a play, literally three hours of 'air made thick', as Thomas Heywood has the Presenter in his *Four Prentices of London* tell the audience when they are to imagine 'stormy tempests, that disturbe the Maine' (Heywood 175), 'air made thick' which becomes 'thin' again, only when the performance is over:

PROSPERO
> Our revels now are ended. These our actors,
> As I foretold you, were all spirits and
> Are melted into air, into thin air; (*Tmp.* 4.1.148–50)

The 'eager air' on the battlements of Elsinore thus provides the predestined setting for a theatrical encounter. The nightly air bites even more shrewdly, intensifies its 'nipping' to yet another degree, when old Hamlet's ghost – itself 'as the air, invulnerable' (*Ham.* 1.1.144) – emerges from it. Its disquieting effect is exposed when Hamlet returns to Horatio and Marcellus after having conversed with the ghost in confidence. Hamlet is obviously changed, his reason appears to be disrupted:

> HORATIO
> These are but wild and whirling words, my lord.
> HAMLET
> I am sorry they offend you – heartily,
> Yes, faith heartily.
> HORATIO
>   There's no offence, my lord.
> HAMLET
> Yes, by Saint Patrick, but there is, Horatio,
> And much offence too. Touching this vision here
> It is an honest ghost – that let me tell you. (*Ham.* 1.5.132–7)

Like the 'victims' of Prospero's spectacles, Hamlet seems to leave the encounter with the ghost and the 'eager air' showing traces of madness. The question whether this madness is feigned, a spectacle staged by Hamlet himself, or 'real', might turn out to miss the point. Instead, Horatio's words deserve close attention. The metaphor he chooses to express Hamlet's disturbed state of mind, 'wild and whirling', alludes to a field that has been dominant since the beginning of the scene: the field of weather, of 'active air', so to speak. Hamlet's words are themselves 'eager air', air that 'bites' and is 'nipping'. As he himself notices, 'they offend': they 'strike against', they 'transgress' a certain order of social graces. They do not keep the distance that is due.[9]

'It is offended' – The Contagion of 'touching this vision here'

The notion of offence is the key concept Shakespeare employs to characterise the way in which the ghost interacts with other characters. The notion is introduced in the first encounter with the ghost which Shakespeare's *Hamlet* stages: 'It is offended' (*Ham.* 1.1.49), Marcellus comments, when the ghost retreats, falsely attributing its leaving the stage to having attempted to talk to it. It is four scenes later that the audience gets to know that there was more truth in Marcellus's words than he was aware of. 'There is' offence, 'much offence', as Hamlet emphasises – but not 'merely' between two beings that encounter each other, not as a result of inappropriate words. The offence touches, it concerns – as the Arden3 editors gloss again – the ghost, and more than that: the offence catches on,[10] it wants to com-municate itself. The change which Horatio notices in Hamlet indicates that a contagion has happened between Hamlet and the ghost. The apparently enigmatic formula, 'Touching this vision here', refers to this encounter. It strikingly resembles Marcellus's 'Touching this dreaded sight' (*Ham.* 1.1.24) discussed above: the verb 'to touch' again appears in an ambiguous participle construction, again followed by the demonstrative adjective 'this', expressing a relation of nearness to a noun denoting a visual perception (here 'vision' instead of 'sight'). The reoccurrence of the grammatical construction and of the paradoxical connection of two distinct sensual domains, the haptic and the visual, is too prominent to pass as mere coincidence. On the contrary, I would suggest that the wording of the two phrases characterises the encounter with the ghost in its defining particularity.

The participle construction produces the impression of serving as the beginning of a causal argument, the participle explaining the cause or reason for an action or an event that follows: 'because I touched the apparition, XY happened'. It thereby emphasises the focus on the effect that the encounter with the ghost brings forth. As a result, it also reinforces the particularity of the notion of touch worked out above: as illustrated by Shakespeare's use of the verb 'to unfold', touch carries in itself the double character of an action and a suffering, of active and passive, of initiating an encounter and of exposing oneself to becoming the object of one. Being bitten by the cold air – suffering a touch – requires exposing oneself to it (in itself a notion of touch) – and, conversely, exposing oneself to the cold air of the ramparts implies waiting for some sort of touch, no matter whether this is of a biting, nipping, or of a 'visual' nature. The paradoxical transfer from one sensual domain to the other which characterises the touch of the two phrases is even emphasised by the demonstrative adjective 'this'.[11] It allocates to the domain of nearness what is in fact absent and in itself untouchable: the past 'sight' or 'vision'. The actual impossibility of 'touching this vision' highlighted by the two formulas resonates with theoretical reflections on touch by Jean-Luc Nancy or Jacques Derrida. Reflecting on his friend's work, Derrida characterises this paradox of 'touching the untouchable' as the very core of the concept of touch itself:

> How to touch upon the untouchable? Distributed among an indefinite number of forms and figures, this question is precisely the obsession haunting a thinking of touch – or thinking as the *haunting* of touch. We can only touch on a surface, which is to say the skin or thin peel of a limit [. . .]. But by definition, limit, *limit itself*, seems deprived of a body. Limit is not to be touched and does not touch itself; it does not let itself be touched, and steals away at a touch, which either never attains it or trespasses on it forever. (Derrida *On Touching* 6)

Theatre's reflecting on its own mediality raises a question that latently accompanies all our touches: it is the convention of distance between audience and stage, between fictional and factual world, that suspends the illusion of the directness, the immediality of touch that makes suffering and initiating touches unproblematic in our everyday experiences. Theatre thus paradoxically intensifies touch by taking it its brute force.

Hans Blumenberg follows a path similar to Shakespeare's when trying to explain the 'permanent mediality of the subjective body [*ständige Mittelhaftigkeit des Eigenleibes*]' (*Beschreibung des Menschen* 659; my transl.). He reminds his readers of other media, like air, to which we have become so used that we forget of their existence as media. It is no coincidence that air, as shown above, happens to be of crucial importance for Shakespeare's metatheatrical reflections; both the mediality of the body and of the theatrical medium are involved in the production of theatrical affects.

The embeddedness of theatre in the actual real world of touches – its touch being one of many touches – grants it the possibility of being 'effective', of transgressing its own realm and of playing a role in the world. This is what Shakespeare stages with the insistence on the notion of 'offence'. One can be fatally offended in life – as has been the old king – one can be offended with words – as Marcellus thinks the ghost to be – and there is a line of transfer from one to the other – that is what Hamlet and his punning on 'offence' exposes. Shakespeare's *Hamlet* is dedicated to the communication, to the transfer, to the passing on of 'offences' – and thus comments on what theatre actually does. The old King's offence fights against its being forgotten. It is to be held in the world, it is to be proliferated, in order to be turned against its culprits.

'Offence' is, however, not to be understood as an abstract, as a moral concept merely indicating 'injustice'. '[T]he fundamental sense of "offence" is [. . .] tactile' (B. R. Smith *Phenomenal Shakespeare* 146). 'To offend' denotes literally a 'striking against' that in its Latin etymon *offendō* also transports the lethal consequences of striking, being a synonym of *interficiō*, 'to kill'. The etymological background of 'to offend' closely resembles the linguistic history of 'to touch': no matter whether it is the Vulgar Latin **toccāre*, from the onomatopoeic 'toc', suggesting the sound of two objects colliding, or a blending of the Latin *tundēre* and *tuditāre*, signifying 'to strike, to slaughter' that has to be counted as its etymological ancestor (cf. *Le Petit Robert*, 'toucher, *v.*'), 'touch', like 'offence', has its semantic roots in a rather violent movement which is both initiated and suffered. By grouping 'touch' and 'offence' together, their shared 'material', 'haptic' dimension is foregrounded. I would suggest that it is this 'material' level of transmitting impulses that plays a decisive role for Shakespearean theatre. In *Hamlet*, the serial movement of transmitted stimuli, of transferred offences, becomes thematic: Hamlet's famous hesitating exposes the impossibility of translating the received impulse, the initial offence into a rational, an intellectual scheme. As the protagonist of a tragedy, he cannot merely hear of an injustice, revenge his father and thereby set the world back in joint. He rather acts as a switch, a relay, a distributor through which the offence is channelled and by which it is spread in the world. As a result, Hamlet does not merely revenge an initial offence and thereby redeem his world from a wrong it suffered. On the contrary, he becomes himself the perpetrator of a series of offences which cannot be morally justified: he kills Polonius, and he is deeply involved in Ophelia's and Rosencrantz's and Guildenstern's death.

Let us return to the crucial early scene that sets in motion all the following. It is, as Freddie Rokem writes, '[t]he presence of the ghost [that] triggers the action of the play' (114). Hamlet is not so much informed by the ghost's words, he is contaminated by them. Hamlet himself introduces the notion of contagion in a later scene. His words intensely chime with the situation of the ghost's appearance:

HAMLET
[...]
'Tis now the very witching time of night
When churchyards yawn and hell itself breaks out
Contagion to this world. (*Ham.* 3.2.378–80)

The ghost's words touch Hamlet – from the Latin *con-tangere* – when they are poured in his ears as the venom has been poured into his father's. It is not so much a task he has been given, but a touch. Hamlet will pass on, will distribute this touch, will spread it in the world – and he begins this mission without delay. The 'wild and whirling words' he addresses at Horatio testify to Hamlet's contamination.

They literally continue the 'eager air' that 'bites shrewdly' to which Hamlet has been exposed while encountering the ghost. They 'offend' (*Ham*. 1.5.33), as the old king has been 'offended' (*Ham*. 1.1.49), intermitting/communicating the past and almost forgotten offence into the presence of a world which does not want to know of it. It is no coincidence that Hamlet's violent offending, that his 'wild and whirling words', take hold of the body via the very orifice that Claudius has chosen for his venom: the ears.[12] I agree with Thomas Rist that *Hamlet* 'embodies contemporary medico-religious theories', and that 'the metatheater of his response to the Ghost in Act 1 Scene 5 suggests a model for audiences' responses to theatrical affect' (151). The violence of words – and this implies that their effect is no less 'bodily' than that of Claudius's venom – is undoubtedly one of the major themes of Shakespearean theatre. As I have attempted to show elsewhere, Shakespeare elaborates in *The Tempest* on the analogy between theatrical speech and the forces of the weather in order to give an account of theatre's capacity to move and trouble the audience (cf. Ungelenk). Traces of this analogy can already be observed in *Hamlet*. In this earlier play, Hamlet's 'wild and whirling words' – which are in themselves always also associated with play-acting by the suspicion that his madness is not 'real' but 'feigned' – resonate with the advice he gives to one of the actors who have arrived at court:

> Nor do not saw the air too much with your hand, thus, but use all gently; for, in the very torrent, tempest and, as I may say, whirlwind of your passion, you must acquire and beget a temperance that may give it smoothness. (*Ham*. 3.2.4–8)

'O it offends me to the soul' (*Ham*. 3.2.9), Hamlet says, when actors overdo their art and thereby make fools of themselves. Theatre misses its goal when it is bad play-acting and not what is acted that touches its spectators. He instructs the players to temper their verbal and gestic 'whirlwind' because he wants to employ theatre's genuine, its irresistible, touch on the viewers.

The fact that the famous theatrical spectacle which Hamlet stages for the court – a paradigmatic play-within-a-play scene – is so prominent in the realisation of Hamlet's project indicates that theatre holds a special relation to touch. It is a privileged practice for spreading touch, for bringing into touch. In his explanation of the theatrical setting Hamlet himself comes to speak about theatre's touch:

> KING
> What do you call the play?
> HAMLET
> *The Mousetrap*. Marry, how tropically! This play is the image of a murder done in Vienna. Gonzago is the duke's name, his wife Baptista. You shall see anon 'tis a knavish piece of work, but what of that? Your majesty and we that have free souls – it touches us not. Let the galled jade wince, our withers are unwrung. (*Ham.* 3.2.230–6)

As its title suggests, *The Mousetrap* is thought to work as a test – or an 'experiment', as Howard Marchitello notes (152): it is to sift the guilty from the innocent and thereby verify the ghost's claims. The spectacular test is based on touch: as a coin is touched with a touchstone, the theatre performance touches its spectators – and Hamlet will closely observe their reaction in order to find out the one that is touched, the deceitful one with the false appearance. The trap springs: in the middle of the performance the 'king rises' (*Ham.* 3.2.258) and leaves the room. It is he who has been touched, he who is 'the stricken deer' (*Ham.* 3.2.264), as Hamlet says, continuing the haptic logic that characterises the whole scene. The play-within-a-play has from the beginning been concerned with him. It is not only 'the image of a murder done in Vienna' but also, rather, the exact image of Claudius's deeds, of his murdering his brother, of his marriage with the queen that the players bring on stage. For Claudius, the play must appear as a dreaded revenant, a revenant of the past which bursts into the seemingly shining present. He is 'the galled jade', because only he has fully experienced what the play depicts, he has already been touched by the depicted events 'in real life' – and probably carried away a wounded conscience. The play is therefore his personal spectral encounter – and it is him who is offended.

Touchability and Theatre – 'Who was so firm, so constant, that this coil / Would not infect his reason?'

The success of Hamlet's 'mousetrap' negates the scene's being what it is: a theatrical spectacle. As a theatre performance, *The Mousetrap* does not merely concern one single, because guilty, spectator. This is not how the theatrical touch works. Although apparently irrelevant for Hamlet's mission, the scene's theatricality plays a major role for the play as a whole. The scene is embedded in elaborate and lengthy metatheatrical reflections, which Hamlet shares with the theatre audience. Hamlet's thoughts revolve around one central observation. Although the actors are only 'in a fiction, in a dream of passion' (*Ham.* 2.2.487), they are capable of doing what the impassioned Hamlet does not feel able to do: they communicate their passions, spread them, affect others with 'their own' affects. Hamlet is fascinated by the actors' ability to touch – by their capacity to pass on touches, to convey the troubled harmony of humours they have produced in their own body.[13] Hamlet's plan to use the players' extraordinary ability for his mission is based on the indistinguishability, and therefore the functional replaceability, of authentic and feigned touches. The indifference for authenticity which Hamlet observes on the theatre's side of production sits rather uneasily with the apparent selectivity of its effect on the side of reception, with the individual reactions amplified by readings like Karim-Cooper's ('Touch and Taste' 229). Why should being touched by a theatrical performance depend on the authenticity of being the one who has suffered the very same touch in real life before? Hamlet's thought experiment of imagining an actor act out on stage the emotions he himself feels qualifies the idea of direct concernment via authenticity:

> HAMLET
> [. . .] He would drown the stage with tears
> And cleave the general ear with horrid speech,
> Make mad the guilty and appal the free,
> Confound the ignorant and amaze indeed
> The very faculty of eyes and ears. [. . .] (*Ham.* 2.2.497–501)

The effect which the actor's passions exercise on the audience does not depend on any preconditions: it is explicitly the 'general ear' which theatre's 'horrid speech' cleaves, which it touches violently. If there is any difference between 'the guilty' and 'the free', then it is a difference of degree: both are touched, the first rendered mad, the second 'only' appalled. However, the classification of effects which adds 'the ignorant' as a third category of watchers to the list does not aim at differences, but at the general effect which theatre produces: the last quality ascribed to the actor's craft sublates the specification of watchers. It concerns something we all share: 'the very faculty of eyes and ears' is 'amazed' – once again an allusion to Aristotle – and the power of theatre is thereby generalised. Theatre does not presuppose an indexical relation of play and watcher. The 'image of a murder' does not merely affect the murderer who is depicted.

The sentence, in which Hamlet comments on the effect, the 'touch', of the 'knavish piece of work' deserves close attention. Its complexity is easily overlooked: 'Your majesty and we that have free souls – it touches us not,' Hamlet tells King Claudius. The statement is highly ironic – the audience shares with Hamlet the knowledge that Claudius has probably murdered his brother. He certainly has no 'free soul' and therefore – this is what the statement implies – is likely to be touched by the following spectacle. The moment when this touch finally happens seems to decode Hamlet's message: it was a first, provocative verbal touch at the sore spot of Claudius's guilt. However, what about the 'we' that Hamlet talks of, including himself and others: do they have 'free souls' – and are they touched by the spectacle?

We do know that Hamlet 'is touched'. The offence his father suffered has taken hold of him. We have discussed Horatio's observation of Hamlet's 'contagion' after making contact with the ghost. His humours have obviously already been troubled before the performance begins. He is therefore no good test person to assess theatre's power to move the spectators. Instead of diagnosing – or rather speculating about – the rest of the stage audience's humoral reaction to the performance of *The Mousetrap*,[14] I would suggest turning the attention again to *The Tempest*.

Prospero, in the function of the stage director, asks his main actor, Ariel, the very question that we are about to examine. They meet after the spectacle of the shipwreck has ended and discuss the success of the performance:

PROSPERO
                        My brave spirit,
Who was so firm, so constant, that this coil
Would not infect his reason?
ARIEL
                        Not a soul
But felt a fever of the mad and played
Some tricks of desperation. [. . .] (*Tmp.* 1.2.206–10)

Theatre's touch is here negotiated not as a question of morals, of guilt and 'free souls', but – as we would today call it – as a question of physiology. It is medical knowledge of his time – and not merely a metaphoric field – that Shakespeare employs to make his characters discuss the effect of theatre. Infection was conceptualised as the effect of having been exposed to 'unwholesome', corrupted material, as contaminating contact with air, water, 'atmosphere' that passes on its own corrupted quality. In some of his curses Caliban gives us an idea of how this infection was thought to work in the early modern age – shared knowledge that would not have to be explained for Shakespeare's audience:[15]

CALIBAN
[. . .] A southwest blow on ye
And blister you all o'er. (*Tmp.* 1.2.324–5)

CALIBAN
All the infections that the sun sucks up
From bogs, fens, flats, on Prosper fall, and make him
By inchmeal a disease! (*Tmp.* 2.2.1–3)

The fact that 'not a soul' could resist the powerful impact of the spectacle which Prospero had staged is the result of simple natural laws. If the theatre company proves able to temper 'the very torrent, tempest and, as I may say, whirlwind of [their] passion' to produce an unwholesome atmosphere, the audience exposed to this troublesome theatrical weather will be contaminated, will be infected and catch the 'fever of the mad'. Theatre's touch is a 'material' one, one against which reason or knowledge is powerless.

Although the reach of Prospero's spectacle appears to be 'universal', this scene is only of limited validity for answering the question whether Hamlet's 'we', the party with presumably 'free souls', have been touched by the theatrical performance they attended. The 'souls' that Ariel speaks of, the souls who all 'felt the fever of the mad' are Prospero's intended audience. Prospero staged the spectacle for them, exactly as Hamlet organised the play for Claudius. Although Prospero's victims are not all tainted with obvious guilt – Ferdinand the king's son and future husband of Prospero's daughter and especially Gonzalo, the 'honest old councillor', are drawn as rather innocent, sympathetic characters – they become the objects of Prospero's rather violent dealings. They are more than merely the audience of a spectacle: they are closely involved in Prospero's project to re-establish the dynastic order; they are the subjects of the plot that he has designed. Prospero's spectacles thus also work as mousetraps: they sift the innocent (Gonzalo, Ferdinand) from the guilty and malevolent (Antonio, Sebastian, Caliban, Stephano). 'Theatre' is employed as a tactical means of reaching goals which are closely connected to the individual identities of its 'viewers' or, rather, 'victims'. From this perspective, as a tactical means, spectacle loses the specificity which characterises it as theatre. Prospero's manipulations could as well be read as the effect of his power as a magician. Theatricality comes to the fore when the double audience of the play-within-a-play is concerned: when the touch of the spectacle transgresses the intended audience and begins to affect both audiences, the one on stage and the one in the auditorium. Here, in this strange resonance between the internal and the external communication system, reflection ends and performance begins.

Shakespeare's *Tempest* gives an account of this theatrical process of transgression. A spectator discloses her theatrical experience, gives vent to her being moved by what she has just seen. A spectator, who merely happened to be present, whose attendance was not part of Prospero's tactical plans: Miranda. She represents on stage the anonymous spectator in the audience, who has watched the tempest scene from a certain distance, without having been involved in Prospero's strategic calculations. And yet, she complains to her father that she has 'suffered / With those that I saw suffer' (*Tmp.* 1.2.5–6). The 'tempest's' violent weather – which consists of both a heavy storm and the desperate 'howling' (*Tmp.* 1.1.35) of the shipwrecked human beings who are said to 'assist the storm' (*Tmp.* 1.1.14) – has literally hit Miranda. She is touched, although she is exposed to the tempest (*The Tempest*?) only as the audience in a theatre is to a play: 'O, the cry did knock / Against my very heart!' (*Tmp.* 1.2.8–9), she exclaims. Prospero's reassurances that the shipwreck was just a spectacle and that no one took any harm from it cannot revoke the bodily disturbance that Miranda has suffered:

> PROSPERO
> The direful spectacle of the wreck which touched
> The very virtue of compassion in thee,
> I have with such provision in mine art
> So safely ordered, that there is no soul –
> No, not so much perdition as an hair,
> Betid to any creature in the vessel
> Which thou heard'st cry, which thou sawst
>   sink. [. . .] (*Tmp.* 1.2.26–32)

The play clearly embeds Prospero's statement in the context of theatre. The effect of the two perceptions that dominate the reception of a theatre performance, seeing and hearing, are discussed. The dialogue from which this speech is taken is imbued with important keywords of Aristotelian drama theory: 'Be collected; / No more amazement. Tell your piteous heart / There's no harm done' (*Tmp.* 1.2.13–15), Prospero tells Miranda some lines before the passage quoted above. As in *Hamlet*, the Aristotelian concepts of τὸ θαυμαστὸν, *tò thaumastòn*, 'amazement/wonder', of ἔλεος, *éleos*, 'pity', and perhaps even of ἁμαρτία, *hamartía*, 'the tragic flaw', are alluded to. However, Prospero's soothing words slightly shift the semantic field that informs their speaking about the spectacle. Whereas 'pity' ('piteous heart'), the standard translation of Aristotle's *éleos*, is recognisable as a theatrical *terminus technicus*, 'compassion' rather invokes a different semantic context. Its Christian undertones are emphasised by being grouped together with the alliterating 'very virtue' that also transports a religious tinge. Replacing 'pity' with 'compassion' therefore attempts to transfer/convert Miranda's reaction from 'the affective' into 'the virtuous', from the realm of a bodily movement to the realm of intellectual or moral mastery. Prospero's verbal intervention tries to fend off or at least to make forget the bodily impulse, the *offence* that his daughter has suffered as a result of his conjuring up the tempest scene. It is significant that Prospero calls up his 'pro*vision*' to counter the 'knock[ing]' and 'beating' (*Tmp.* 1.2.176), the violent touches which Miranda experiences as effects of the spectacle she has observed. It testifies to the clash of two conflicting domains: the domain of rational and intellectual control and the domain of touch, of being exposed to forces whose contaminating contact cannot be avoided.

The domain of touch, which eludes intellectual or rational control, prevails. This is exposed in another play-within-a-play scene, the court masque which Prospero stages for the betrothal of his daughter to Ferdinand:

FERDINAND [*to Miranda*]
This is strange. Your father's in some passion
That works him strongly.
MIRANDA
                     Never till this day
Saw I him touched with anger so distempered!
  (*Tmp.* 4.1.143–5)

This time the emotional disturbance is no calculated effect achieved by theatrical means – it hits the stage manager, Prospero himself. Until now he had directed the emotionally 'offending', the troubling spectacles from a safe distance. In one scene he even literally watched the events from '*on the top*' (*Tmp.* 3.3.17 SD), towering over the spectacle like '[s]ome god o'th' island' (*Tmp.* 1.2.390). Now it is he who is 'touched'. The source of Prospero's distemper is not quite clear – probably Caliban's rebellion, although this appears to be well under Ariel's control; its function, however, is obvious: it disrupts the masque and brings it to a sudden end. It is significant that 'distemper' ends a stage spectacle which displays the very harmony of humours. The court masque can in many ways be understood as the tempest scene's opposite: whereas the latter performed a disturbing spectacle of violent and contagious humoral trouble, the masque presents an image of harmony; an abstract image, a piece of paradise which is to be gazed at and admired. This image is not moving, not troubling, not touching at all. It is, in Shakespeare's staging, a failure. Its sudden end can be understood as a biting commentary on the pompous stage practices of his rivals Ben Jonson and Inigo Jones – and it indicates that it is contagious distemper, not the ostentation of polished harmony, that Shakespeare's theatre is all about.[16]

Prospero does not (emotionally) remain '*at a distance*' (*Tmp.* 3.1.14 SD), does not direct and manipulate his surroundings as the unmoved mover of the others' humours. He is himself involved in the disturbance of the world. There is, to put it in Hans Blumenberg's words, no 'safe shore' from where to watch 'death and shipwreck' without being touched (*Shipwreck with Spectator* 32). 'Touchability [*Betreffbarkeit*]' – 'in the double sense of organic and optical exposedness' (Blumenberg *Beschreibung des Menschen* 777; my transl.) – is the name which Blumenberg gives to this fundamental condition of (human) being. 'Touchability' precedes all intellectual mediation and embeds the human in a world that he or she shares with others. Only the dead and the gods 'watch from the safe shore', from a sphere of 'untouchability [*Unbetreffbarkeit*]' (Blumenberg *Shipwreck with Spectator* 32). Whereas Miranda's emotional reaction to the tempest scene almost looks like a staging of Blumenberg's shipwreck-with-spectator-setting, Prospero's surprising distemper appears to illustrate another

Blumenbergian theorem – the human's back, which stands for the limits of human (pro)vision: 'The back is the unknown in and of ourselves; thereby at the same time the epitome of our touchability [*Betreffbarkeit*] for the unexpected' (*Shipwreck with Spectator* 204; my transl.). Touchability in its Blumenbergian understanding may also be used to give an account of the logic of touch on which the *Mousetrap* is based and which convicts Claudius of murder: 'It is the body that demarcates the spatiotemporal line that takes the deed as its starting point. The person responsible can be touched [*betroffen*] along this line and be held accountable' (Blumenberg *Beschreibung des Menschen* 783; my transl.). Shakespeare's theatre is undoubtedly intensely concerned with touchability. It examines, it probes, it 'touches on' touchability, as its own condition of possibility and reason for its emotional effectivity. There is, however, a fundamental difference between Shakespeare's and Blumenberg's understanding of touchability. Although Hans Blumenberg, the founding father of metaphorology (cf. Blumenberg *Paradigms for a Metaphorology*), can surely not be accused of being insensitive to the importance and the uncontrollable forces of semantic fields, Blumenberg's concept of touchability remains rigidly subjugated to a particular, metaphorical use. One of his rare definitions of touchability gives an explicit account of its conceptual dependence: he talks of 'touchability [*Betreffbarkeit*], which is founded on visibility and its consequences [*Folgen*] and which becomes conscious as such [*und als diese bewußt wird*]' (*Beschreibung des Menschen* 203; my transl.). Shakespeare's touch is not founded on visibility, and surely does not become conscious in the realm of the visible. On the contrary, his theatre can be understood as an extensive argument for the reverse relation.

In Blumenberg's oeuvre, touch supplements vision. Phenomenology's foundation on the visual perception of the subject inevitably causes a problem: How can I be sure that what I see with my own eyes can be seen by others in the same way? It is the 'possibility of objectivising my experience' (Blumenberg *Beschreibung des Menschen* 786; my transl.), as Blumenberg calls it, that is at stake. The introduction of touchability is necessary in order to find answers to the question of intersubjectivity and open phenomenological philosophy towards the social dimension of life.

Hamlet may be read as an indication that, in Shakespeare's theatre, touch is not merely an effect of vision and hearing. In a certain sense, it also precedes the two dominant medial channels. On the level of plot, it is the old king's offence and its transmission/proliferation that initiates and wheels the play, that 'gives to see'.[17] With regard to the external communication system, establishing the theatrical situation asks for a willingness of the audience to be touched. As the first words of the play indicate, the spectators have not only to expose themselves to the theatrical events ('stand still'), they also have to contribute their share – to 'assist the storm', according to *The Tempest* – even in order to hear and see. The empty platform stage, which has to be transformed into a lively scenery by the viewers' imagination, testifies to the cooperation demanded from the audience in the early modern theatre. The paradigm of visual or aural perception is not particularly suited to reflect on this cooperation taking place between stage and audience. 'Perception' establishes an asymmetry of active (actors) and passive (viewers) which forecloses the productive interaction in which the spectators get involved. Touch, in contrast, with mutuality at its conceptual core, allows us to trace the performative effects of seeing and hearing which define theatre – the vulnerability of the audience as well as the dependence of the theatre makers on their viewers' contribution to the performance.

Although Farah Karim-Cooper associates 'the inability to be touched' in Shakespeare with 'the inhumanity of being resistant to sensation' ('Touch and Taste' 236), touchability is not an 'anthropological' concept. It is not, as for Blumenberg, a quality which defines the human being's role in the order of the world. For Blumenberg, humanity took its start with the upright gait: a posture that decisively extends the field of view and at the same time exposes the human being to become the ('touchable') object of the perception of others (cf. *Beschreibung des Menschen* 777). In Shakespeare's world, touch is explicitly not a human affair, as *The Tempest* exposes, when Prospero notices that Ariel appears to be touched by the suffering of Prospero's enemies:

PROSPERO
Hast thou, which art but air, a touch, a feeling
Of their afflictions, and shall not myself
(One of their kind that relish all as sharply,
Passion as they) be kindlier moved than thou art?
   (*Tmp.* 5.1.21–4)

'By definition, an apparition or ghost cannot be touched,' writes Evelyn Tribble ('"O, she's warm"' 76). Nonetheless, Ariel is indeed sensitive to touch. He is but air and therefore invisible – and nevertheless not exempt from touchability. Although not human, 'one of the most damning judgements' (Karim-Cooper 'Touch and Taste' 246) does not concern him. This judgement is, of course, 'to be called "senseless"'. Blumenberg defines invisibility as the criterion that distinguishes the gods from the human being, the criterion that makes the gods untouchable. For Shakespeare, touch is neither mediated nor the abstract condition for mediation – it is itself the tangible medium, the medium which can be experienced with the own body.[18] As worked out above, it is the characteristic of touch that it combines action and suffering – Ariel, who is the main agent of distributing theatrical touches, must therefore himself be sensitive to suffering touch. Transmitting touch always involves both, acting and suffering, at the same time.

Touch is not the effect of a particularly human faculty – it is not intellectually mediated in any way. It is material touch.

Prospero's words give an account of the series of touches which is passed on from one agent to the other: Ariel has a 'touch' of the court party's 'afflictions', of their having been 'dashed', 'struck', 'knocked down' (lat. *affligere*) – the 'touch' Prospero has dealt via Ariel is transmitted to the court party, from them to Ariel and finally finds its way back to Prospero. The insistence of the very materiality of touch is no coincidence: it is not a dominant field of metaphor, but describes the way Shakespeare and his contemporaries conceptualised their embeddedness in the world.

Prospero provides us with the keyword that enables us to reconstruct the working of the early modern world of touch: 'passion'. 'Passions' in the early modern understanding can be literally 'moved' (cf. Raman 120): the balance of the four humours that were thought to flow through the microcosm of the human body was a fragile one. It stood in close communication with the elemental composition of the macrocosm that surrounded it, so that being exposed to 'external distemperances' like bad weather, unhealthy atmosphere, unfamiliar diet – or theatre! – could affect the temperance of humours, could cause 'distemper'.[19] 'Passion' is conceptually very similar to 'touch'. It implies a suffering – lat. *patior*, gr. πάσχω – that is not to be separated from a forceful, often violent action. 'The word *passion* [...] suggested that emotions seize upon and possess those who suffer them [...]' (Roach 28). When someone is 'in some passion', as Miranda's father is, 'distempered', 'touched with anger', he or she is not caught in passivity; on the contrary, we expect him or her to act, to pass on the offence, the touch he or she has suffered. 'Thus we move, because by the passion thus we are moved,' writes Thomas Wright in *The Passions of the Minde* (176), which appeared in 1604. The series of touches triggered in this way do not have to constitute a spiral of infinite violence. When Miranda hopes that 'Pity move my father' (*Tmp.* 1.2.447), she wants the touch to travel in loops and thereby establish a new balance. Her father has suffered an initial offence, the usurpation of the dukedom by his brother and he has given back the offence by exposing his brother to the spectacles. Being moved by others' sufferings, sharing their being touched, offers the chance of re-establishing a new humoral harmony. This is what the 'very virtue of compassion' is all about:

> What I am talking about here is compassion, but not compassion as a pity that feels sorry for itself and feeds on itself. Com-passion is the contagion, the contact of being with one another in this turmoil. Compassion is not altruism, nor is it identification; it is the disturbance of brutal contiguity [*contiguïté brutale*]. (Nancy *Being singular plural* xiii; transl. altered)

Nancy's words read like a wonderfully apt description of the early modern theatre space – despite of their having nothing to do with Shakespeare or early modern theatre at all. As part of an ontology of 'being-with' (cf. Heidegger *Sein und Zeit* §26) they challenge prevailing conceptions which base the world and its consistency on the self-sufficient subject and his subjugating vision. The resonance between Nancy and Shakespeare's theatre is, however, not a mere coincidence. The early modern theatre space can be understood as a prime example of Nancy's ontological reflections – because it is a special space of touch. As in Nancy's theories, touch in the Shakespearean theatre decentres and de-hierarchises relations of all kinds: in The Globe, spectators of different social background experience 'the disturbance of brutal contiguity'. This is not only an inevitable effect of a thousand people crowding in the narrow wooden structures of the public theatre, where contact (and probably also contagion) could hardly be avoided. Groundlings and aristocrats in the galleries share what Nancy calls 'com-passion': they co-experience the 'contact of being with one another in this turmoil'.[20] 'Turmoil' and 'disturbance' are theatre's productions: they are generated on stage and then spread in the auditorium. They are the reason why the spectators pilgrimage to this new cultural site. The joy of playgoing consists in exposing oneself to this theatrical turmoil. Theatre provides a reassuring and reliable frame for experiences which mean danger for life and limb in 'real life'. It gives its spectators the opportunity to cede control and be tossed about by theatre's stormy air. Theatre's state of emergency lasts only for two or three hours – this is, however, not the only reason why the touch of theatre can be enjoyed rather than has to be dreaded. The fact that one is not alone in and with this trouble is certainly equally important. Theatre is a space of com-passion in a profound and precise sense: 'being with one another' is not just the effect of experiencing the play as part of a crowd of watchers.[21]

The theatrical com-munity is constituted as a community by the very particular way that theatre affects its viewers – by the 'procedure' that I see at work in the formula 'Touching this dreaded sight'. Theatre does not establish a relation between two predefined, particular bodies. Theatrical community does not take place between entities (subject–object) that are linked for an intelligible reason. The spectators are moved by a spectacle that does not concern them personally, a spectacle whose fictionality erects an unbridgeable distance between itself and its viewers. Theatre's touch is characterised by its loss of direction: it *touches* the innocent bystanders for no reason at all and regard-less of their person or social standing. This is the ironic metatheatrical truth of Hamlet's famous words 'Your majesty and we that have free souls – it touches us not': theatre touches us because we do not have free souls. The theatrical community is not a community of humaneness, of a supposedly shared virtue of 'human' pity. It is a com-munity of 'brutal contiguity', of a shared neighbourhood, the neighbourhood of earthly, imperfect, radically dynamic and co-dependent life. As in Blumenberg, touchability is located in this mortal world.

Shakespeare's *Hamlet* can be read as an extensive reflection on the question of the 'free soul' – and of the radical incompatibility of this religious concept with earthly existence. As Stephen Greenblatt has so brilliantly worked out in *Hamlet in Purgatory*, the ghost embodies this complicated reflection. His spectral appearances, his (theatrical) entrances, his oscillating wanderings between purgatory and the earth have their origin, their condition of possibility in old Hamlet's lack of a free soul at the moment of his death. Hamlet's constant hesitation – and that is to say the play's main 'content' – is more than once fuelled by his relating his actions to the question of (moral) guilt and the free soul.

What Hamlet's behaviour gives to see – *zu sehen gibt / laisse voir* – is an unresolvable moral problem that governs the play's fictional world. The offence that his father has suffered cannot be redeemed. It is not an arbitrary impediment, located in the fictional world, that renders redemption impossible, but structural, even ontological reasons. Redemption is a privilege that is exercised the day after this, after our earthly world – as the ghost tells Hamlet with regard to his mother: 'leave her to heaven' (*Ham.* 1.5.86). The events proceeding from the offence suffered by the king are not framed by a higher 'moral' order. The offending, contaminating touch spreads itself, is transmitted and dispersed without any rationale fully controlling or coordinating its manifold paths.

The lethal duel between Hamlet and Laertes that initiates the play's catastrophe is explicitly characterised as an affair of 'touch' and 'contagion':

LAERTES
[. . .] I'll touch my point
With this contagion, that if I gall him slightly
It may be death. (*Ham.* 4.7.144–6)

The failure of Claudius and Laertes's plan, the fact that their stratagem heavily backfires – in the end, they all fall victim to the venom – exposes that the contagion of touch resists control and mastery. It cannot be instrumentalised for one's own ends. Laertes's offending 'touch' spreads; it contaminates without regard to plans or intentions. The radical indeterminateness of the *con-* of 'contamination' contradicts any manageable manipulative employment of touch. Although there may be exact plans whom the touch is to concern, whom it is 'to regard', touch remains indifferent to predefined directions. Its sole criterium is contiguity; it touches whatsoever its contamination can reach.[22]

With Claudius's dying of 'poison tempered by himself' (*Ham.* 5.2.312), the story appears to come full cycle. However, the production of poetical justice – at least Claudius has been 'punished' in the end – is superficial and weak. The play does not end in moral harmony; it ends in cruel devastation. Its touches have, as the finale exposes, eliminated themselves. Here something interesting and complex happens: the duel scene illustrates on stage how the formation of a (theatrical) community, that is, a community of contaminating compassion, works – and, at the same time, it brings this community to an end. The self-annihilation of touches performs the dissolution of the theatrical situation – the very moment when, as Prospero puts it,

> Our revels now are ended. These our actors,
> As I foretold you, were all spirits and
> Are melted into air, into thin air (*Tmp.* 4.1.148–50).

The theatrical situation collapses when the distance inscribed in the notion of touch is no longer upheld; when the offence destroys the touching contact, when it pierces – 'gall[s]', 'scratches' – the contact-surface. A tension had characterised the touching contact, a tension which held two (or more) 'bodies' together and at distance at the same time, articulating them against each other. The constitutive structures, writes Stephen Greenblatt, 'are themselves necessarily built up out of [. . .] friction' ('Fiction and Friction' 86). When the tension of touch is broken, the bodies which had been touching lose distinction and thereby cease to exist. This is what happens when Claudius, Hamlet, Laertes and Gertrude mutually kill each other: the tension between them had articulated Shakespeare's play; their death ends it.

Despite its illustrating the non- and therefore omnidirected contagion of touch, the final scene does not expose and metatheatrically reflect on stage the theatrical touch as so many scenes did before. Although it shows a sort of spectacle – the duel, which a stage audience watches – it may be among the least metatheatrical scenes of the whole play. It may be a surprising suggestion, but the fatal 'touches' which bring the play to an end are not metatheatrical at all. In fact, they work as a contrasting parallel scene to the initial ghost scenes. The one triggers theatre; the other makes it dissolve. The paradoxical 'Touching this dreaded sight' is replaced by the banality of lethal violence. Whereas the impossible sensual transfer of the first establishes a relation of fragile, but continuous, contact of contiguity, the latter's brutal corporeality destroys contact in a gesture of impatient annihilation. It is a banal 'touch', a 'touch' which does not bear in it the paradoxical tension, the distance and nearness, the acting and suffering, which characterises touch as touch and which makes touch so interesting for Shakespeare's theatre.

Hamlet's peculiar bearing in the last scene is a case in point for this contrast. Since his contaminating encounter with the ghost, Hamlet had been a precursor of Shakespeare's later *Tempest*. As worked out above, his 'wild and whirling words' offend. Despite their being hardly intelligible, they do not fail to exercise a strong effect on his interlocutors. No one really seems to be 'so firm, so constant', one could say, that Hamlet's 'coil / Would not infect his reason'. He touches others, in a theatrical way: 'Your behaviour hath struck her into amazement and admiration' (*Ham.* 3.2.317–18), Rosencrantz tells Hamlet about his mother's reaction to his odd demeanour – the choice of words again alludes to Aristotle's *Poetics*. According to his own testimony, Hamlet is 'essentially [. . .] not in madness / But mad in craft' (*Ham.* 3.4.185–6). There can be little doubt that this craft is of a theatrical nature, that Hamlet is literally 'acting' the ghost's 'dread command' (*Ham.* 3.4.105). I would suggest taking him by the word: he has not simply been infected with madness by the contaminating contact with the ghost, nor is he coolly putting into operation a plan that involves playing the lunatic. He has been contaminated with the theatrical touch – he is deeply moved, his passions are swelling and he distributes his being touched to the world. His madness is thus neither authentic nor fake. It is not even 'his' madness. It is theatrical: crafted, but beyond control. Hamlet becomes 'ghost' (and that is to say 'actor') – 'suggesting that ghostliness [or theatricality] is somehow physically catching', as Outterson-Murphy writes (258). He is not 'essential[ ]', but effectual, effectual as a result of his spectral, of his dubious 'ontological' (mad or not) status. This theatricality, this turmoil of passions is to be spread – this is the ghost's 'command'. Hamlet acts out this command. He has not chosen this task; the task has chosen, or rather contaminated, him.

In the final scene, however, Hamlet appears completely changed. At Ophelia's grave, in the scene before, Hamlet had exposed his having become ghost: 'This is I, / Hamlet the Dane' (*Ham.* 5.1.246–7), he had proclaimed, re-enacting the appearance of his father's ghost (cf. Gurr 'The Shakespearean Stage' 88), playing with the name he and his father share. He himself had called attention to the 'something dangerous' in him (*Ham.* 5.1.251), which the wisdom of the sane bystanders fear with good reason. Now, in the last scene, this 'something dangerous', Hamlet's incalculable, offending force, has suddenly disappeared. He is still effectively using his tongue, but in a different way than before. He outwits Osric, exposing the hot air of the latter's ornamented words. It is the intellectually superior position that Hamlet suddenly occupies – a position that no one, neither Horatio nor the audience, fears in any way, because it is not dangerous at all. Hamlet scores by getting the laughs, and it is the side of sovereign, well-controlled common sense that he personifies in this dialogue. What has become of his 'wild and whirling words'? Hardly any trace of them is left in the last scene. Hamlet has lost his characteristic theatricality, his being a forceful spectacle for the characters that share the stage with him. He has become an unambiguous, well-oiled cog in the play's plot. His surprisingly unhesitant embracing of the idea of the duel once and for all sets the play's course towards catastrophe.

At the same time, the last scene can be called the play's least didactic sequence. Here the audience is called upon to do what they have come for as a theatre audience: they stand 'unfolded', exposed to plain spectacle. There is no metatheatrical level, neither stage-audience nor a character embodying theatrical playacting, that shifts at least part of their attention away from the intensity of the play itself. The scene is not about theatre; it is theatre. It therefore structurally resembles the shipwreck scene of Shakespeare's *Tempest*. Whereas in the latter Shakespeare starts with providing the audience with a piece of intensive, unbroken theatrical experience in order to reflect on this experience in the following rest of the play, he does it the other way round in *Hamlet*: here he begins with extensive metatheatrical reflections and ends with intensive, unbroken spectacle.

As a consequence, the last scene is, in a sense, the most theatrical of the play. 'Touching this dreaded sight' – this is what happens in, or rather in contact with, this scene. However, it is not on the stage – as a character's encounter with some sort of 'ghostly' spectacle – but between the stage and the spectators that this '[t]ouching' takes place. The scene performs theatre's touch: it connects stage and audience; it binds together the theatrical space via the passions. It constitutes a contact which establishes the theatrical community by contamination, brings about a community of compassion.

'Give me that man / That is not passion's slave' (*Ham.* 3.2.67–8), Hamlet had told Horatio. We begin to understand that this apparently pessimistic sentence in fact exposes the very foundation of theatre. As admirers of theatre we are to affirm Hamlet's pessimism. It is our 'touchability' that makes us 'eligible' for compassion. It is neither a virtue nor a capacity we our endowed with as human beings, but an uncontrollability, an open door rather, which brings us into contact with one another and the world, which makes us enjoy both the 'disturbance of brutal contiguity' and the feeling of 'being with one another in this turmoil'.

Notes

1. Shankar Raman traces the critics' interest in the opening question back to Maynard Mack. He was 'perhaps the earliest to recognize that the question with which *Hamlet* begins – "Who's there?" (1.1.1) – is emblematic for its world [. . .]' (116).
2. In her cultural history of touch, Constance Classen makes us aware that moving in the dark was in itself a tactile affair: 'being able to find one's way by touch in the dark remained a useful skill well into the modern era' (11).
3. On the last pages of her 'Acting with Tact', Carla Mazzio gives a reading of the phrase 'Touching this vision' to which my chapter is indebted.
4. As we learn from Catherine Richardson, it would not only have been his 'elevated and authoritative verse' that 'marked him out from the others on stage', but also 'the costume of a scholar – probably the sober black of learning' (73).

5. Horatio's scholarly attitude and his following 'conversion' after encountering the ghost resonate with James Knapp's comparison of the attitudes of Hippolyta and Theseus in *A Midsummer Night's Dream*: 'Hippolyta offers an alternative to Theseus's reason; she urges an engagement with the phenomenal world that is embodied and invested rather than abstract and detached (a product of "cool reason"). Rather than seeking truth by bringing the world of apprehension under the control of reasoned understanding – making sense of what one has seen, or making what one has seen make sense – Hippolyta's reaction to the unfamiliar (the strange) is to remain open to the transformative power of experience' (383). The gendering of these attitudes – exposing oneself, affirming the transformational potential of vulnerability associated with the female – chimes with my readings in the subsequent chapters.
6. For the ontological implications of 'ghostliness' or 'spectrality', see Jacques Derrida, *Specters of Marx*. Many scholars, most prominently Stephen Greenblatt, have argued the connection of ghostliness and theatricality, on which my argument is based (cf. Greenblatt *Hamlet in Purgatory*; Outterson-Murphy; Carlson 4; Taylor 144; Anderson 5).
7. With good reason, James Knapp resorts to the notion of 'a constant source of wonder' when analysing the 'positive quality of images' – that is, the metatheatricality – in *A Midsummer Night's Dream*, emphasising 'our experience with them, our openness to their call', despite their being 'not comprehensible, able to be reduced to a concept' (383).
8. A similar physiological reference to theatre's effects can be found in Theseus's comments in *A Midsummer Night's Dream*: 'More strange than true. I never may believe / These antique fables, nor these fairy toys. / Lovers and madmen have such seething brains, / Such shaping fantasies, that apprehend / More than cool reason ever comprehends' (*MND* 5.1.1–6).
9. In reference to *King Lear*, Bruce R. Smith writes that 'The workings of speech are, then, no less tactile than the moving of arms and hands' (*Phenomenal Shakespeare* 165).

10. For Shakespeare's use of the medical notion of 'catching', see Michael E. Mooney's article on *Julius Caesar*.
11. The paradoxical crossing of senses that Jennifer Waldron associates with the 'effects of live theatre' (405) is a recurring topos in Shakespearean drama. Bruce R. Smith points us to different characters (Sly, Claudius, Leontes) having a 'desire to touch an illusion and to be touched by it' (*Phenomenal Shakespeare* 147); Farah Karim-Cooper reads the phrase 'This palpable-gross play' (*MND* 5.1.357) of *A Midsummer Night's Dream* literally, emphasising its tactility ('Touch and Taste' 226); Jennifer Waldron analyses the sensual crossing implied in St Paul's famous 'The eye of man hath not heard' (*MND* 4.1.209) passage of *A Midsummer Night's Dream* (412–14); Kevin Curran has dedicated a reading to a passage in *Macbeth* that negotiates the crossing between the visual and the tactile (395): 'Come, let me clutch thee. / I have thee not, and yet I see thee still. / Art thou not, fatal vision, sensible / To feeling as to sight? Or art thou but / A dagger of the mind, a false creation, / Proceeding from the heat-oppressed brain? / I see thee yet, in form as palpable / As this which now I draw' (*Mac.* 2.1.34–41). A similar crossing has been found by James Kearney in *King Lear* (459): 'Might I but live to see thee in my touch, / I'd say I had eyes again' (*Lr.* 4.1.25–6).
12. According to Shankar Raman, a passage from perception to vulnerability is associated with the ear, which has a 'defensive function' that 'equally evokes its status as a passage way laying the self open to the world (for good or ill), opening the possibility of changing, becoming other' (134).
13. For a reconstruction of the physiological way in which the early moderns thought about acting, which involved a bodily adaptation of the own humoral balance, see Roach.
14. An analysis of the effects of Hamlet's encounter with the ghost does not have to speculate. As Thomas Rist observes, the Ghost himself 'describes the potential impact of his words in physiological terms' (149).
15. In 'Shakespeare's Virginian Masque', John Gillies has connected the depiction of intemperance in *The Tempest* to

colonial discourse concerning the unwholesome climatic conditions in the British settlements in Jamestown.
16. For the relation of Shakespeare's masque-within-a-play and the cultural background of Stuart court masque, cf. Bevington; I. Smith; Gilman; Flagstad; Gillies; McNamara; Knowles.
17. 'In *Hamlet*, to take a case in point, Hamlet goes from being "touched" (or playing it) to being "touched" (and dead),' writes Carla Mazzio ('Acting with Tact' 183). He also distributes touches – one of which comes back to him in the end.
18. For a discussion of touchability which also refers to the medium of air, see B. R. Smith *Phenomenal Shakespeare*, 142.
19. Gail Kern Paster has introduced the material notion of 'the passions' into early modern studies, which has proved to be very fruitful for analysing the way Shakespeare and his contemporaries thought of the body and its interaction with its environment (cf. Paster *Body Embarrassed;* Paster *Humoring;* Paster *Reading*).
20. Michael Witmore makes a similar argument about the Greek *terminus technicus*, which is built analogously to *compassion*: 'the Aristotelian verb *sunaisthanesthai* (the activity of together sensing) names precisely the kind of distribution of sense and sensation that is the theater's stock-in-trade' (423).
21. Sarah Outterson-Murphy emphasises the 'collective response' (264) which the Ghost's command to 'remember me' (*Ham.* 1.5.111) demands from the audience, also pointing to the religious tradition it evokes.
22. Gilles Deleuze and Félix Guattari's thinking of 'contagion' can help understand the specificity of this concept, an important trait of which is the bringing into contact of radically heterogeneous bodies: 'We oppose epidemic to filiation, contagion to heredity, peopling by contagion to sexual reproduction, sexual production. Bands, human or animal, proliferate by contagion, epidemics, battlefields, and catastrophes. [. . .] The difference is that contagion, epidemic, involves terms that are entirely heterogeneous: for example, a human being, an animal, and a bacterium, a virus, a molecule, a microorganism' (Deleuze and Guattari *A Thousand Plateaus* 241–2).

CHAPTER 2

TOUCHING THE DEPTH OF THE SURFACE: *RICHARD III*

'Grim-visaged War hath smoothed his wrinkled front'

Richard, the Duke of Gloucester, enters the stage – '*alone*' (*R3* 1.1.1 SD). With its 'opening solo entry for a play's title-character', the first scene of *Richard III* is 'unique in Shakespeare's work' (Holland 17–8). The famous soliloquy with which the play begins serves not only the function of the 'prologue to a play' (Day 149), it also situates the play in the historical situation depicted by the preceding three plays of the tetralogy. However, besides its informing the audience about the triumph of the York party in the Wars of the Roses, Richard's soliloquy mainly elaborates on a theme that his entrance exposes in a performative way: the protagonist's 'essential solitude', as I would like to call it, using a concept I have purloined from Maurice Blanchot's *The Space of Literature* (cf. 19–33).

The historical situation in which Richard finds himself at the beginning of the play is expressed in one particularly evocative sentence of the soliloquy, a sentence which I would like to take as a point of departure for my reading: 'Grim-visaged War hath smoothed his wrinkled front' (*R3* 1.1.9).

The Wars of the Roses over, Richard's brother Edward has been crowned England's king. Richard describes the contrast between the time of war and the period of peace, which has just begun. A series of parallelisms spills into the highly metaphorical sentence quoted above:

RICHARD
Now are our brows bound with victorious wreaths,
Our bruised arms hung up for monuments,
Our stern alarums changed to merry meeting,
Our dreadful marches to delightful measures.
Grim-visaged War hath smoothed his wrinkled
    front; (*R3* 1.1.5–9)

Richard presents the change effected by his family's triumph in artful words. The two lines which embrace the three anaphorically constructed lines in the middle of the passage provide us with keys with which to understand the passage. The parallelism opposes war and peace and allocates each of them half of the verse. In other words, each of the three central lines re-performs the change which Richard is obviously bothered about. The lines' first syllables speak of the past war, the final syllables of the new peace. This antithetical organisation culminates in the rigid oppositions of lines 7 and 8, in which 'stern alarums' / 'merry meeting' and 'dreadful marches' / 'delightful measures' form binaries that expose the stark contrast between the two states of worldly affairs. The parallel antithetical construction of the lines finds support in additional structures of similarity that strengthen both central isotopies from within. The terms constituting the isotopy 'war' show a striking aural resemblance; they each include the sound /ar/: 'bruised *ar*ms', 'stern al*ar*ums', 'dreadful m*ar*ches'. With regard to the isotopy 'peace', it is the bilabial consonant *m* which reoccurs in all the terms: '*m*onu*m*ents' '*m*erry *m*eeting', 'delightful *m*easures'. The line which concludes the passage merges and reconciles the two semantic and phonetic series: with 'Grim-visaged W*ar*', Richard not only introduces the personification of the notion around which one of the two isotopies is grouped; he also refers us to the aural centre that resonated in the linguistic material of the w*ar*-series. The bilabial /m/ is also prominent, right at the centre of the passage's last verse: 'Grim-visaged War hath s*m*oothed his wrinkled front'.

The line does not, however, continue the juxtaposition of war and peace which the preceding lines appeared to erect. Peace does not emerge as War's eternal antagonist – in the concluding line, the '*m*onuments', '*m*erry *m*eeting' and 'delightful *m*easures' of peace merely resound in a verb – to s*m*ooth –; a verb that expresses a temporary modulation rather than the triumph over the opposing force, a modulation whose subject remains the personalised 'War'. It is no coincidence that the epithet '[g]ri*m*-visaged' also incorporates the bilabial stop. The line thus exhibits an important asymmetry: in contrast to the preceding antithetical parallelisms, it is not bifurcated but encloses the current, peaceful 'expression' of the world in the description of War's actual, his 'original' face. 'Grim-visaged War' and his 'wrinkled front' not only build the frame, constitute the alpha and the omega of the verse, but are the material basis, the ontological foundation of which peace is but a particular state, a modulation without substantial reality on its own. War is not a state of exception; it is the foundation of the world that can disguise – that is, 'smooth' – itself, and take on a mild appearance in times of peace.

The line's phonetic structure supports its semantic articulation: 'Grim' at the beginning and 'wrinkled' at the end of the line assonate, and are connected by the fricative /r/, whose frequency of occurrence is a striking characteristic of the whole passage. The verb 'smooth' contrasts with its surroundings, both in its vocal colour and its onomatopoetic 'silkiness'. The careful aural elaboration of the metaphor – War's smoothing his 'wrinkled front' – indicates that this image is not mere ornament. It refers us to thinking about 'surface' and its modulations, about how 'semblance' and 'reality' may be understood differently when read as effects of dynamic processes of surface-(de)formation.

Shakespeare's *Richard III* exhibits these surface-processes and their power on different levels, and also makes them a subject of discussion. As we will see, these processes stand in close proximity to the practice of theatre. In a certain sense, theatre consists of a manifold manipulation of surfaces: 'wrinkling' phonetic surfaces, roughening them with roaring fricatives or 'smoothing' them with sonant stops; clothing the actors on stage in different fabrics; coordinating their movements and gestures – staging conflict or harmony. All this turns out to be a production of sense, constituting a (fictional) world of its own. In the theatrical constellation, substantiality (the question 'What is real, substantial and what is just fake?') is suspended. It is suspended in favour of touch: the audience comes to the theatre in order to expose themselves to the touch of theatre's elaborate surfaces.[1] Nevertheless, this cultural practice does not have to be shallow – on the contrary. Shakespearean theatre cannot be reduced to the evocation of intense affects – which certainly exceed the emotional routine of everyday life – since, at the same time, it negotiates complex existential and philosophical questions, though certainly not in the way a philosophical treatise would do. It does not lecture and present answers but involves its audience in these questions, infects them with a fundamental uncertainty, abducts them into a realm of fascination.[2]

In the passage we began to analyse, the theme of surface-modulation takes on the depth and reach of an existential and philosophical question. It provides the key for the functioning of the asymmetry that also defines Richard's position in the world. At first, the situation appears to be simple. In contrast to all the others, Richard is not made for 'this weak piping time of peace' (*R3* 1.1.24):

> RICHARD
> But I, that am not shaped for sportive tricks,
> Nor made to court an amorous looking-glass;
> I, that am rudely stamped, and want love's majesty
> To strut before a wanton ambling nymph;
> I, that am curtailed of this fair proportion,
> Cheated of feature by dissembling Nature,
> [. . .]
> Have no delight to pass away the time. (*R3* 1.1.14–25)

This contrast is expressed by the prominent and emotionally charged 'But I' that appears to single Richard out, to distinguish him from the rest. However, the series of three parallel sentences anaphorically beginning with an 'I' does not distinguish Richard from the collective of a universal 'they'. Being 'rudely stamped', Richard cannot smooth his 'grim face', his disproportionate outward appearance. He lacks the physiognomic means to dissemble in the way that War does. Obviously, the others can. They are able to smooth their wrinkled fronts.

The series of three parallel, anaphoric sentences beginning with an 'I' echoes the tripartite series which describes the changes coming along with peace analysed above. In their consonance, the two series tell their own story of change, and the repeated 'Our' of the time of war turns into Richard's 'I': he becomes an outsider in 'the weak piping time of peace'. Despite his deformed body, Richard is not born an exception. He had not been physically or socially handicapped for as long as war has reigned.[3] He had been well integrated in a devoted collective – this is what his anaphorical insistence on the 'Our' ('Our bruised arms', 'Our stern alarums', 'Our dreadful marches') emphasises. In Richard's soliloquy, there is no counterpart to this collective for the time of peace – the collective 'Our' which opens the lines fades away in the striking impersonality of peace's 'victorious wreaths', its 'monuments', 'merry meeting' and its 'delightful measures'. The formal symmetry of the antithetical structure exposes the lack of social collective that, according to Richard, distinguishes war and peace. As we will analyse in greater detail, the first scene of the second act supports Richard's analysis: the peaceful unity which the dying king establishes at his court is based on dissembling. It is superficial, in a literal understanding of the adjective: it relies on simple, ritualised gestures of touch that modulate the deep rifts between the rivalling parties, so that they form the temporary appearance of smooth peacefulness.

The fact that Richard is denied this 'smoothing' modus makes him embody the foundational, 'substantial' nature of war. He is a consequent reminder of the luring superficiality of peace, because he embodies the forces that bring forth peace's smooth surface: the forces of war.

The passage analysed at the beginning exposes peace as only a fleeting moment, a temporary modulation that veils its origin in forces of war ('War hath smoothed his wrinkled front'). The emblems of the new, triumphant peace, the 'victorious wreaths', speak of this material origin in war. Although symbols for the fact that the bloody conflict has ended and that a glorious victor has been found, the signifier 'wreath' betrays its close connection to the signifiers to which it is supposed to establish a binary opposition. Phonetically, '*w*reath' and '*w*rinkled *f*ront' clearly form a group, sharing the conspicuous phonetic sequence of /w/ (or /f/) and /r/. Semantically, 'wreath' and 'wrinkle' can be synonyms ('A fold, crease, or wrinkle' (*OED*, 'wreath, *n.*'; 4.a.)). Now, in this new period of peace that has begun, the brows are no longer 'wrinkled' in the gesture of frowns, and it is no longer 'wounds' that have to be bound up (cf. *R3* 5.3.177). Victorious wreaths bind the winners' brows and mark the transition to a new order of the world. However, these 'wreaths' are but a modulation of the ancient 'wrinkles'; like bandages that cover wounds, these wreaths veil War's 'grim-visaged' face, they dissemble his 'wrinkled front' – and, at the same time, these wreaths are nothing but a particular arrangement of wrinkles that produce the smooth surface of peace.

It is wrinkles that bind the loops of repetition, whirls and folds that make the surface (re)encounter itself and thereby produce structures of sense, of belonging and identity. As I have tried to show, the few lines I quoted from Richard's soliloquy expose this process on the level of the signifiers, of the entangling play in-between meaning and phonetics. There is a last phenomenon of this kind to which I would like to direct our attention before moving on to elaborate on the relevance of these observations for the play as a whole.

The first line of the passage establishes a striking assonance on the sound /ow/ that issues into the anaphora 'Our', shaping lines 2–4: 'N*ow* are *our* br*ow*s bound [. . .]', '*Our* bruised arms', '*Our* stern alarums'. This phonetic group is characterised by a strong tension: whereas 'our' and 'brows' are clearly delegated to the semantic field of personalised War (the past period that Richard bemoans), the adverb of time 'now' demarcates the new era of peace that has just begun. In the theatrical setting, the temporal deixis of 'now', however, opens up an additional layer of meaning, a layer that criticism has discovered to be among Shakespeare's almost conventional sources of theatrical wit: the playwright frequently plays with the reference of the shifter 'now' to the theatrical situation as such, to the here and now of the performance that is established by the bodily co-presence of actors and audience.

The fifth line echoes the very beginning of the play, which employs the shifter 'now' to its maximum impact: '*Now* is the winter of our discontent / Made glorious summer by this son of York' (*R3* 1.1.1–2). With Richard standing alone on the empty platform stage, the reference 'Now', the first word of the play, is as undetermined as can be. This effect is even heightened by the fact that the 'reality' that is established – 'Now is the winter of our discontent' – is crossed out again by the second line and apparently turned into its opposite: winter 'is made' summer by an agent to which another undetermined shifter, 'this', refers. The logic of the seasons that Richard uses as an image for the change from war to peace emphasises the temporality and the fragility of the situation: victory and peace cannot, once and for all, banish war. The following two lines continue the metaphor of season and weather: 'And all the clouds that loured upon our house / In the deep bosom of the ocean buried' (*R3* 1.1.4–5). It will be another son/sun of York that will re-raise these clouds, attract their watery substance from the bottom of the sea and thereby change the surface of the world once again. This sun/son is Richard. He embodies the force that connects depth and surface. He embodies, in Gilles Deleuze's words, the 'becoming subversive of the depths' ('Plato and the Simulacrum' 258) that all the others try 'to repress [. . .] as deeply as possible, to shut it up in a cavern at the bottom of the Ocean' ('Plato and the Simulacrum' 259). He exposes the processes of which the current moment, as stable as it might appear, are but a temporary modulation. There are no smooth objects, in contrast to others that are sharp or rough – there are but processes of smoothing and wrinkling which endlessly create the textures of the world.

It is no coincidence that Shakespeare opens his play with a 'Now' that is defined as a moment of change. At this critical point, the movement of 'smoothing' becomes perceivable or at least reconstructable, as Richard shows in his soliloquy. The transition from war to peace summarised by Richard is, however, not the only change to which he asks the audience to direct their attention. He prepares them for yet another, more important transition: as 'the troubler of the poor world's peace' (R3 1.3.220), he will disrupt the current world's smoothness, he will reintroduce holes and wrinkles. These surface-manipulations which come from an agent of the repressed warring depths will shape the play that the audience are about to experience. The shifting 'Now' describes the moment in which these transitions are performed – in which the tension between what is and what could be is given room to unfold, to become productive. This moment is deeply theatrical – a moment to which the audience exposes themselves willingly, more than that, for the thrill of which we – the audience – have come to the theatre. In *Richard III*, Shakespeare exposes our involvedness as viewers in the temporary 'trouble' that we are confronted with in the plays we see. Richard's odd expository soliloquy makes us his accomplices, his partners in crime (cf. McNeir 172). No matter whether it is Richard's thirst for revenge and power or the viewer's thirst for stories – we both want something to happen, now, in the limited time of our co-presence. The theatrical 'Now' thus re-establishes, on a different level, a form of collective that we encountered in Richard's soliloquy: *our* brows are not supposed to be smoothened in theatre – we expect them to be either convulsed by comic laughter or distorted by tragic fear. Therefore, we are secretly looking forward to Richard's manipulations – and they will touch us as deeply as his fictional victims.

Touches of Peace and War

When the sick King Edward senses his end is near, he pursues a last wish: he wants to make '[his] friends at peace on earth' (R3 2.1.6). In other words, although the triumph of the House of York has been duly celebrated and peace proclaimed, 'the blessed period of this peace' (R3 2.1.44) is still to be realised. The king himself voices obstacles to this project: the members of the king's party 'have been factious one against the other' (*R3* 2.1.20); it is their 'unity' (*R3* 2.1.31) that has to be ensured.

King Edward attempts to ensure that his peers 'continue this united league' (*R3* 2.1.2) by summoning them to a sort of pacification ritual that establishes the longed-for peace. According to early modern custom, the contractual speech acts that King Edward demands from his subjects are supported by gestures of touch which enact the unity declared by the words spoken:

> KING EDWARD
> – Hastings and Rivers, take each other's hand;
> Dissemble not your hatred. Swear your love.
> RIVERS
> By heaven. My soul is purged from grudging hate,
> And with my hand I seal my true heart's love. (*R3* 2.1.7–10)

Further 'reconciliations' follow this pattern: the king asks his wife to let her arch-enemy, Hastings, kiss her hand (*R3* 2.1.21), Dorset to embrace Hastings, and Buckingham to embrace the Queen's 'allies' (*R3* 2.1.30). They all obey and perform what the king, acting like a stage manager, directs them to do – only Buckingham wittily evades a contractual, declarative speech act. However, he, like all the others, enacts his part of the king's charade of social touches. The whole measure appears desperate: the king is well aware that these social touches are in danger of remaining shallow. He repeatedly expresses his anxiety of 'hidden falsehood' (*R3* 2.1.14) that may continue to lure behind the smooth surface of public show. However, there is nothing he can do about these doubts.[4] On the contrary, the imperatives he directs at the court members testify to their foundation. The king's imperatives are haunted by the paradoxical structure that Niklas Luhmann has discovered for the semantics of love (cf. Luhmann *Love as Passion* 70; 166): analogue to the appeal 'Be authentic!' that Luhmann elaborates on, the king's 'Dissemble not your hatred' (*R3* 2.1.8) or 'do it unfeignedly' (*R3* 2.1.22) prompts what cannot be prompted. He knows that the different factions hate each other, and it is this situation that motivates his intervention. The members of court are called to act against their hearts and perform a romance of reconciliation. At the same time, this acting out of the king's wish is to be done without dissembling and 'unfeignedly': a typical double-bind situation that demands play-acting while calling for authenticity.

In fact, the king's helplessness exposes the impossibility of constituting a 'united league' of peace. It confirms the diagnosis Richard presented in his initial monologue, when the collective of war did not find a counterpart in times of peace – a Schmittian insight, one might say.[5] It is only two closely related 'instances' that can fully meet the king's paradoxical demand: theatre and Richard, both rather belligerent and not at all embodiments of peaceful harmony.

The theatrical situation solves the king's paradox by introducing a conventional agreement: although the audience know that what they see is play-acted, 'feigned', they have accepted to take it as if it was authentic. Theatrical speech is not to be confused with lying or dissembling – even though, outside the theatrical situation and its silent contract, it would have to be regarded as exactly these two.

Richard, I would like to argue, is authentic: he exposes his essential being only when dissembling, when feigning. To me, Joel Elliot Slotkin is correct when speculating that Richard has 'no essential identity in himself apart from performance' (14). In a certain way, he embodies theatre.[6] Whether his lack of stable identity singles him out, or whether 'his mode of being' (Siemon 247) 'reflects [the] common nature' of those surrounding him (Siemon 245), is hard to tell. The awareness he creates for the potential lack of a trustworthy, 'genuine' 'non-dissembling' (non-fictional) core certainly distinguishes him from the rest, and contributes to the fascination he radiates.

His role in the king's ceremony of reconciliation speaks volumes. He is the only person in the feud who manages to evade both the contractual speech and the ceremonial touches the king enforces upon the quarrelling courtiers. He feeds the illusion of his involvement in an all-encompassing peace by plain lies. However, although it is highly uncertain that the others' oaths of harmony and peace are more honest than Richard's manipulative words, his 'feigning' and 'dissembling' follow a different mode. This is indicated by his not becoming part of the community of touch that the others have joined. Richard does not adapt and subject himself to the king's superficial, ceremonial mode of touch, a mode which only the authority of the king has at its disposal. Richard's lies 'touch deeper' than the courtiers' submissive gestures of ceremonial reconciliation. As he himself tells the audience right at the beginning, his 'lies' are 'well steeled with weighty arguments' (*R3* 1.1.148). As we will see, his touch is an existential one. It penetrates the surface of courtly conduct; it is violent, always potentially fatal. It has the depth of war, whose touches are not slyly submissive but negotiate the question of life and death.

Richard himself elaborates upon his being different, which excludes him from the courtly community and its particular 'touch'. His tirade precedes the scene of reconciliation:

RICHARD
By holy Paul, they love his grace but lightly
That fill his ears with such dissentious rumours.
Because I cannot flatter, and look fair,
Smile in men's faces, smooth, deceive and cog,
Duck with French nods and apish courtesy,
I must be held a rancorous enemy.
Cannot a plain man live and think no harm
But thus his simple truth must be abused
With silken, sly, insinuating jacks? (*R3* 1.3.45–53)

Although Richard's words can be pitted against his actual behaviour/performance two scenes later, true, trenchant analysis and plain lie can hardly be kept apart, with regard to his self-description. It proves to be correct that Richard, unlike the others, does not '[d]uck with French nods', he does not partake in the 'apish courtesy' of kissing hands and embracing his foes, as directed by his majesty the king. And yet Richard is far from being a 'plain man', whose social interaction would be characterised by 'simple truth'. He does (nothing but) 'deceive and cog'. He has divulged the secret of his evil machinations to the audience at the very beginning of the play, so that we can observe him lying without any embarrassment. However, there is 'truth' woven into his lies – this is what makes them 'well-steeled', gives them their violent, piercing strength.

A dimension of 'honest' self-revelation continues the discourse of surface quality – 'wrinkled' and 'smooth' – that Richard has established in his initial soliloquy. He now elaborates on the lack of a capacity for peaceful times, which can already be found in his first words. The phrase 'I cannot flatter' may serve as a case in point. On the surface, it looks like a plain lie. We have seen Richard 'beguile or persuade with artful blandishments' (*OED*, 'flatter, *v.1*'; 5.), he is a master in that. However, the verb 'to flatter' is connected to the field of surface quality via its complicated etymology: it probably derives from the old French *flater*, 'to flatten down, smooth', hence 'to stroke with the hand, caress' (cf. *OED*, 'flatter, *v.1*'; etym.). In early modern England, *flatter* could still be used in 'French sense', signifying 'to touch or stroke lightly and caressingly' (*OED*, 'flatter, *v.1*'; 1†b.). Richard himself adduces the synonym 'to smooth' in the triad 'smooth, deceive and cog', which explains what he understands by flattering. The notion of smiling also alludes to the constellation that Richard's early soliloquy sketched out: as

Richmond will explicate eventually, it is 'smooth-faced peace' (*R3* 5.5.33) that brings along 'smiling plenty' (*R3* 5.5.34) – and thus stands in binary opposition to 'Grim-visaged War' and its 'wrinkled front' (*R3* 1.1.19). Paying attention to the semantics of surface quality, we can discover a layer of parrhesiastic truth (cf. Foucault *Fearless Speech*) in Richard's words: he is, indeed, not capable of 'flattering'; his touch is not 'silken'; he cannot operate in the 'light', the 'smooth' modus of peace's surfaces.

The reason for this incapacity is indeed 'plain': Richard cannot 'look fair'; he is a 'plain man', an overtly unattractive person (*OED*, 'plain, *adj*.2'; 17.). As he has told us in his initial soliloquy, he is 'curtailed of this fair proportion', 'rudely stamped', 'not shaped for sportive tricks', 'cheated of feature by dissembling nature' (*R3* 1.1.14–19). Richard's outward appearance is the exact opposite of 'fair'; it is not at all 'free from roughness or irregularities; smooth, even' (*OED*, 'fair, *adj*.'). He embodies the cross-grained crookedness that makes others expect the 'rancorous enemy' that he is. In contrast to other Shakespearean villains like Iago or Edmund, from the beginning, (almost) everyone is well aware that Richard, as a person, poses a serious threat. '[I]t is a mistake to overemphasize Richard's success in fooling other characters,' writes James R. Siemon (245) with reference to Robert C. Jones (cf. 37). His 'interior hatred' is well known, and not only because it is exposed by Richard's 'outward action' against parts of the royal family, as Queen Elizabeth claims (*R3* 1.3.65–7). The early modern audience, who experienced their world as held together by resemblances and analogies (cf. Foucault *The Order of Things* 17–44), would have inferred this 'interior hatred', this interior deformity, from Richard's outward appearance: 'Richard epitomizes the union of outer appearances and inner truths' (Slotkin 7).

In his famous soliloquy at the end of *Henry VI, Part 3*, Richard himself explains his machinations with this analogy:

RICHARD
The midwife wondered and the women cried,
'O, Jesus bless us, he is born with teeth!'
And so I was, which plainly signified
That I should snarl, and bite and play the dog.
Then, since the heavens have shaped my body so,
Let hell make crook'd my mind to answer it.
I have no brother; I am like no brother.
And this word 'love,' which greybeards call divine,
Be resident in men like one another
And not in me: I am myself alone. (*3H6* 5.6.74–83)

Richard 'shapes' his mind according to the body in which he has been born – so that they correspond in their being 'crook'd', that is, 'not straight', 'not fair', 'uneven'. The natal teeth play an important symbolic role in this process: they demarcate Richard's 'fate' from the very moment of his birth. They are responsible for his 'dissembling': they make him *dissimilar* (cf. lat. *dissimilis*) from the rest (cf. *OED*, 'dissemble, v.2'). He has 'no brother', because he is 'like no brother'; there is nobody who matches his odd, deformed appearance. At the same time, they make him *dissemble*, 'simulate by imitation' (*OED*, 'dissemble, v.1'; 5.d.): The natal teeth mean that he should '*play* the dog'. It is important to note that Richard is not born evil, he is not born a dog. A sentence from his initial soliloquy confirms this: 'since I cannot prove a lover', Richard says, 'I am determined to prove a villain' (*R3* 1.1.28–30). Richard is born with a restricted set of capacities. He admits to 'have neither pity, love nor fear' (*3H6* 5.6.68); he knows that he lacks the mode of smoothness: 'Why, Love forswore me in my mother's womb: / [. . .] for I should not deal in her *soft* laws' (*3H6* 3.2.153–4; my emph.). He has been born, nevertheless. As a result, with Richard, a sharp piece of war, of death, a piece of brutal 'chaos', of 'disproportion' and 'deformity' (*3H6* 3.2.158–61; my emph.) protrudes into the apparently 'smooth', loving and peaceful world of the living. '[L]ike one lost in a thorny wood, / That rents the thorns and is rent with the thorns' (*3H6* 3.2.174–5), Richard embodies an existential mode of touch that the prevalent 'soft laws' of humanist and/or Christian pedigree are not used to represent. However, as Richard's simile spells out, there are thorns in the world that he, the epitome of thorns, encounters.

'I am myself alone.' Michael Thalheimer took this sentence as a motto for his 2017 production of *Richard III* at the Residenztheater Munich. The production does not focus so much on the protagonist's psychic disposition as one might expect, but rather explores Richard's theatricality, his capacities as actor and stage manager. By following traces that Richard has left in his soliloquies from *Henry VI 3*, Thalheimer suggests an understanding of the title hero's exceptionality, which reaches deeper than a phenomenology of psychological pathology. It is a commonplace in criticism to recognise 'Richard's narcissism' (Slotkin 22), and reconstruct how 'the stage Machiavell's self-love' (Siemon 244) has slowly developed into '[s]chizophrenia' (McNeir 184) by the fifth act. However, 'the actor [...] exposed without his masks' (McNeir 184), which Waldo F. McNeir discovers in Richard's late 'schizophrenic' soliloquy, resembles what others have found to be present on stage from the beginning: theatricality somehow short-circuits the attempt at seeing in Shakespeare's play a psychopathological case study. Thalheimer's production therefore takes a different approach, focusing directly on theatricality. His strategy is similar in outline to Vance Adair's Lacanian reading: it refrains from identifying Richard's psychic illness – that is, categorising Richard as sick and explaining the reasons for his problems – and analyses the play as the elaboration of a greater, structural problem which concerns us all. According to Adair, the deformed Richard embodies what Lacan has called the 'anamorphic stain' (cf. Adair 54). This stain is not a pathology of subjectivity, but its unconscious foundation. Richard refers us to a layer that is situated before or beyond the closing of the 'symbolic order', beyond the realm of commensurability, stable meaning and oneness. His 'ineffectuality of one who has lost all cohesion as an individual', his being 'potentially anyone and at the same time no one' (McNeir 184) refers us to the starting point of subject formation, where play-acting appears to hold a constitutive function.

Like Michael Thalheimer, I would suggest that Richard's 'I am myself alone' can be understood against the theatricality located at the degree zero of subject formation. Richard's 'loneliness' is not 'the complacent isolation of individualism', as Blanchot (20) calls it. The 'standard', the 'measure' for his 'loneliness', is not merely the others – it is also, and primarily, himself: 'I am *myself* alone.' He is alone to himself; he is not even alone with himself. His incapacity to love affects the very foundation of personhood and individuality. Richard is not only unable to form loving (or any kind of) bonds to others; he exposes a protopsychic layer – a layer preceding his apparent pathological narcissism – on which he is not even capable of developing a relation to himself. On this level, 'he' and 'himself' are 'all one' (*OED*, 'alone, *adj.*'; etym.), a mere grey dot, without a stabilised interior distance (a differentiation into at least two instances) to itself. His state may perhaps be said to resemble what Freud calls primary narcissism, a state which precedes the formation of the ego and any libidinal object-cathexes (cf. Freud 'Zur Einführung des Narzißmus').

It is this proto-individual, pre-personal neutrality, this absence of any definitive binding and therefore stabilising structure, that makes Richard, in my opinion, embody Maurice Blanchot's notion of 'essential solitude' (19–33). For Blanchot, 'essential solitude' does not signify a subject's social situation, it does not denote a feeling of loneliness; it does not belong to the subject at all. On the contrary, it demarcates the transcending of the very limits of subjectivity.

In Blanchot's understanding, 'essential solitude' is the condition of possibility for the writer's 'access' to what he calls 'œuvre'; the realm of writing – a realm that will always remain mysterious, and that knows neither domination nor domesticity. It is an a-personal realm, a realm of 'neutral, impersonal presence', of 'the indeterminate They [*On*], the immense, faceless Someone' (Blanchot 32), a realm which we as individualised persons cannot experience in everyday life, although it touches us essentially, as mortal beings that have 'come' from 'somewhere' and will 'go' 'somewhere', some day:

> Here lies the most hidden moment of the experience. That the work must be the unique clarity of that which grows dim [*s'éteint*] and through which everything is extinguished [*s'éteint*] – that it can exist only where the ultimate affirmation is verified by the ultimate negation – this requirement we can still comprehend, despite its going counter to our need for peace, simplicity, and sleep. Indeed, we understand it intimately, as the intimacy of the decision which is ourselves and which gives us being only when, at our risk and peril, we reject – with fire and iron and with silent refusal – being's permanence and protection. (Blanchot 45)

With Richard, what Blanchot calls 'work' [*œuvre*] enters the stage. Shakespeare, in one of his typical metatheatrical strategies, constructs a *mise-en-abîme* structure: staging the (literary) 'work' within a 'work', exposing its literary effect and functioning. Luhmann would call this the staging of a re-entry: the re-entry of the literary form into the literary form (cf. Luhmann *Social Systems* 167).

As Thalheimer emphasised in his production, the 'form' that Richard embodies is overtly theatrical. He thus literally 'performs' the 'essence' of Blanchot's 'essential solitude': 'in it dissimulation appears [*qu'en elle la dissimulation apparaît*]' (Blanchot 33; transl. altered). Richard's theatricality is a theatricality of (dis)simulation:

> RICHARD
> I can add colours to the chameleon,
> Change shapes with Proteus for advantages,
> And set the murderous Machiavel to school. (3H6 3.2.191–3)

But what is it that Richard's art of dissimulation, of camouflage and deceit, what is it that it dissembles? His hunger for the crown? The Machiavellian 'advantages' he speaks of indicate that his theatrical art merely serves the purpose of empowerment. However, is power really the root motive of Richard's project?

> RICHARD
> Then, since this earth affords no joy to me,
> But to command, to cheque, to o'erbear such
> As are of better person than myself. (3H6 3.2.165–7)

The motive of power drives his quest – it is, however, as Richard explicitly notes, a secondary effect: it takes the place of something else. Is it 'other joys'? The 'joy [...] to command, to cheque, to o'erbear' serves compensatory purposes. As a psychological structure which Richard has fabricated for his own stability as an individual, this hunger for power is an epitome of Nietzschean 'resentment' (cf. Nietzsche *Genealogy of Morals* 17–21). It is a reactive, negating, annihilating force that aims at the destruction of others, because they are 'of better person'. By shifting the focus from the 'self' to the others, this psychological structure masks, it 'dissembles', the actual problem: the problem of Richard's personhood. We are very quick in accepting Richard's compensatory, sadistic joy because it follows the libidinal economy that we ourselves identify with. However, if we are to take seriously what

Richard has told us, his own psychological explanation loses cogency. It may turn out to be a mere 'screen-explanation' (cf. Freud 'Über Deckerinnerungen'), since sadistic joy clearly belongs to Love's 'soft law'. If Love has really already 'foresworn' Richard in his 'mother's womb', the force driving his actions must lie beyond his subjective, libidinal economy.

In the beginning was Richard's body, its deformity, its disproportion – its teeth.[7] This is what Richard cannot conceal – and he will not even try to dissemble his abnormality. On the contrary, as we have seen, it is his deformity that 'dissembles'. In the beginning were the teeth – and an appeal to play: 'Play the dog!' This dissimulation dissembles 'nothing', it dissembles the mystery of birth, the 'nothing' that we were and through which we pass before making our entrance on the stage of this world.

'Play the dog!' follows the same logic of double bind that we encountered in the king's imperative to 'play the role and do not dissemble'. However, it is located differently, on a different level. Here, the imperative initiates the primal scene of play-acting that happens to be, at the same time, the primal scene of a being's being. The equation: 'Be yourself! = Play yourself!' does not dissemble, does not conceal or cover up anything, except the abyss of being. All the other roles that Richard, as the dog, the villain, takes on to realise his project are secondary; they are part of his first role, in that they are located on the same level as the roles the king forces on the courtiers. However, Richard's secondary roles reach deeper. They do not merely function as a superficial costume that one throws on to meet external requirements, while one's 'true', inner essence/being secretly remains untouched. Richard's dissembling, his 'changing shapes with Proteus', is always in touch with his first, his existential role – it serves his original histrionic project of playing the dog.

In other words, Richard's 'flattering', his 'smiling', is a mode of 'biting' – it goes back to his natal teeth and their appeal to play. Play-acting is thus associated with a particular mode of touch: a violent, an existential touch that reaches deep, that does not know the difference between surface and inner essence: a touch of war which touches at life and death.

It is this 'truth' about his deep dissembling that Richard, between the lines, tells his brother Clarence, shortly before commissioning his death. It is again 'lies well steeled' (*R3* 1.1.147) that speak of the connection of play-acting and touching deeply:

RICHARD
Were it to call King Edward's widow 'sister',
I will perform it to enfranchise you.
Meantime, this deep disgrace in brotherhood
Touches me deeper than you can imagine. (*R3* 1.1.110–13)

Richard will perform a 'reconciliation' with Queen Elizabeth. He will, however, make sure that Clarence is already dead when this scene of reconciliation takes place. As it turns out, Clarence would have been set free, if he were still alive. The 'deep disgrace in brotherhood' does not only 'touch' Richard; it will also touch Clarence 'deeper' than he had hoped for. The depth of this touch is the depth of play-acting; of a performance whose 'authentic', 'honest', non-performative 'foundation', its strategic motivation, can only be guessed at. And what if there was 'no such [non-play-acting] substratum'? If there was 'no "being" behind doing, working [*Wirken*], becoming'? If '"the doer" [was] a mere appanage to the action' – and 'the action'/*acting* were everything (Nietzsche *Genealogy of Morals* 28; transl. altered)?

Richard – A 'deep dissembler'

Although its protagonist is a master of surface manipulation who claims to be able to 'add colours to the chameleon',

Shakespeare's *Richard III* is a play about depth. The bare figures speak for themselves: the adjective *deep* occurs eighteen times; by way of comparison, *Hamlet* has four, *King Lear* five. The entry in the *OED* gives quotations from *Richard III* for seven different meanings of the adjective 'deep'. The play apparently sounds the semantic 'depth' of this concept – and, as I would like to suggest, it links its reflections on depth to the question of theatrical manipulations of surfaces: it is about theatre's 'touching upon the deep'.

It is Richard who introduces the adjective 'deep'. We have quoted him speaking of a 'deep disgrace in brotherhood' that 'touches him deeper' than his interlocutor, Clarence, could imagine. For Clarence, 'deep' signifies a certain, enhanced intensity here – something that 'comes from or enters into one's inmost nature or feelings; that affects one profoundly' (*OED*, 'deep, adj.'; 9.). This is the way he himself, according to the *OED*, uses 'deep' three scenes later, when he, in 'dialogue with God', refers to his prayers as 'deep' (*R3* 1.4.69). As with Anne's 'deep exclaims' of mourning (*R3* 1.2.50), the intensity of their 'acts' testifies to their authenticity: it is not just a superficial stylisation, no costume, but their 'inmost nature' that exposes itself as touched. However, Richard undermines the authenticity connected with the adjective *deep* early in the play. In an instance of dramatic irony, the audience notices that Richard's comparative 'deeper' does not merely further intensify the intensifier 'deep', but introduces a false bottom. What here happens to the intensifying adjective 'deep' does not happen to it 'from without': Richard merely activates one of its central semantic dimensions. The fact that one has to touch *deeply* in order to reach 'one's inmost nature' means that this inmost nature is '[h]ard to fathom or "get to the bottom of"' (*OED*, 'deep, adj.'; 6.a.). Deep is what does not show on the surface – which is both the reason for its authenticity/truth and its secretiveness.

In other words, when Richard divulges his 'deep intent' (*R3* 1.1.149) to us, we cannot be sure to have reached a bottom that is, once and for all, secure. This is not due to the fact that Richard is the sort of friend, '[d]eep, hollow, treacherous and full of guile' (*R3* 2.1.38), who only suits as a punishment and should never be trusted.[8] Richard is, for once, certainly not lying when he shares his plans with us. However, it remains doubtful whether a person's 'intent' may resolve the 'secrets of the deep' (*R3* 1.4.35) with which Richard is 'playing', whether it may stop the ambiguous forces at play . . .

Richard and Buckingham consciously conjure up the depth of the deep – they trust in their having it at their disposal. Richard himself obviously believes in his 'deep intent'. Together with Buckingham he relies on the fact that the helping hands they are using are 'sworn as deeply to effect what we intend / As closely to conceal what we impart' (*R3* 3.1.158–9). Here again, the semantic doubleness/duality of 'deep' emerges: it combines 'trustworthy authenticity' and 'secretiveness'. At the same time, Richard and Buckingham use the effect of 'authenticity' produced by deepness for their manipulative stagings. It is Richard's 'meditating with two deep divines' (*R3* 3.7.74) that makes him (appear) an adequate personality for the 'deep designs' (*R3* 3.7.66) of appointing a new king – that is, for heaving Richard on the throne. Buckingham picks his words carefully and calculates with the persuasive force of 'deepness'. However, all these 'deeps' are instances of dramatic irony: the audience has been made aware of the false bottom of this deepness. Furthermore, the adjective 'deep' carries in itself the semantic tinge of sin, crime and guilt. The cardinal's 'so deep a sin' (*R3* 3.1.43), Clarence's being 'in sin as deep as I' (*R3* 1.4.213) and the Duchess of York's speaking of 'deep vice' (*R3* 2.2.28) actualise this semantic dimension of 'deep', its being used '[a]s an attribute of moral qualities or of actions in which sinking or abasement is present' (*OED*, 'deep, *adj.*'; 8.).

When Buckingham and Richard re-raise the warring 'clouds that loured' on the house of York, raise them from their being 'buried' in 'the deep bosom of the ocean' (*R3* 1.1.4–5), they are not aware that they are actively accelerating their own abasement. Their own rise on the wheel of fortune is doubled by a simultaneous movement downward, their continual sinking on moral grounds. They unleash the power of the deep, they attempt to exploit it for their own project – and they even come to embody it. However, despite the almost godlike mastery they must feel while successfully pursuing their plans, they have no idea what it is that they are operating with. This is hardly surprising. According to Maurice Blanchot, '[t]he deep does not surrender itself directly [*en face*]; it only reveals itself by dissembling itself [*en se dissimulant*] in the work' (170; transl. altered). Although it is Richard, as suggested above, who embodies what Blanchot calls work and who reveals the deep by dissembling, the deep also hides from/eludes him. The abyss of the deep inevitably breaks open and will swallow him, along with anybody else. Murdering his young nephews, the '[t]wo deep enemies' (*R3* 4.2.71) as he calls them (he obviously believes in the intensity of their hostility), is a desperate attempt at impossible rescue. Margaret's curse finally seizes him: in Buckingham and Stanley, he takes 'deep traitors' for 'dearest friend[s]' (*R3* 1.3.223) and dies all alone. Buckingham falls prey to the deep as well: his 'reward' for the 'deep service' he has provided for Richard (*R3* 4.2.117) is no less fatal.

It is others who gain insight 'in the secrets of the deep' (*R3* 1.4.35). Strikingly, they – Clarence and Hastings – are both doomed to die. While staring death in the face, they get a glimpse of – the deep!

Although the clouds that Richard sets out to raise are 'buried' in 'the deep bosom of the ocean', he does not fully realise that he is playing with death. The vivid hope for a worldly rise covers the existential backside of his 'deep' project. Death is certainly present in the notion of war that Richard affirms – it is, however, only the death of others that Richard literally touches upon. As with anyone else, the reality of his own death remains repressed. Unlike Hastings, when on the brink of death, Richard is not aware that human existence and its megalomaniac thirst for power, especially in the warlike situation that he fosters, resembles the drunken sailor on the mast, 'Ready with every nod to tumble down / Into the fatal bowels of the deep' (R3 3.4.99–100). The deep of which Richard thinks himself to be the master, the deep, which he exploits for his ends, turns out to be 'fatal': the deep is the deep of death.

This is why both for Richard and for us (us living mortals), 'insight' into the deep is impossible.[9] One would have to be 'in the time of death / To gaze upon these secrets of the deep' (R3 1.4.34–5), as the Keeper trenchantly remarks. In a certain way, Richard, as the one incapable of mourning, is the furthest away from the 'time of death'. It is this trait that distinguishes him from the play's female figures – the widows Anne, Margaret, Elizabeth and the Duchess of York. Lady Anne or Queen Elizabeth do not fall for him or his charms. They willingly accept him as what he is: death. They have come in touch with death – they have lost dear ones – and having nothing to lose except for their lives, they willingly comply with the inevitable.[10] Refusing to fight their fate and '[a]ssuming their tragic roles as pitiable victims' (Howard and Rackin 106), Lady Anne or Elizabeth appear to be weak characters in a tragedy.[11] However, their refusal to resist testifies to a superior 'knowledge' of the essence of mortality. Paradoxically, what they do by preferring not to play the tragic heroine is affirm the (non)essence of existence. As women, they appear to have particular access to the mysterious limits of the human being: giving birth and losing (one's) life.[12]

The 'female knowledge' of mortality, however, does not provide direct insight into the secrets of the deep. The impossibility of mortals to form an idea of or even pre-experience their death subsists. Different, 'medialised' modes of experience are necessary to circumvent this impossibility. The play exposes one such mode: the dream.[13] It provides Clarence with a dreadful opportunity to live through 'the time of death' and 'gaze upon these secrets of the deep' shortly before his murderers enter his cell:

> CLARENCE
> [. . .]
> Methoughts I saw a thousand fearful wracks,
> A thousand men that fishes gnawed upon,
> Wedges of gold, great anchors, heaps of pearl,
> Inestimable stones, unvalued jewels,
> All scattered in the bottom of the sea.
> Some lay in dead men's skulls, and in the holes
> Where eyes did once inhabit, there were crept –
> As 'twere in scorn of eyes – reflecting gems,
> That wooed the slimy bottom of the deep
> And mocked the dead bones that lay scattered
>   by. (*R3* 1.4.24–33)

What is it that characterises 'the deep'?[14] Its 'secret' appears to reside in a verb: the deep *scatters*. It dissipates, dispels, disperses, so that disparate 'things' – corpses, anchors and jewels – come to lie next to each other. More than this, they intermingle and build grotesque formations.[15] As an effect of this grotesqueness, the abject and the invaluable question each other in their very essence: skulls become parts of precious, almost artistic arrangements and the invaluable is tinged by the corpses' vanity. The 'fascination' that undoubtedly issues from the deep 'is fundamentally linked to neutral, impersonal presence' (Blanchot 32): 'a thousand' human bodies 'form' the 'indeterminate They, the immense, faceless Someone' of which Blanchot speaks (32). This fascinating neutrality is produced by a primordial natural force, by the deep's scattering.[16] Sometimes this force appears to reach over into the world of living beings, drawing them into its abyss, as the Messenger reports having happened to Buckingham:

> MESSENGER
> The news I have to tell your majesty
> Is that by sudden floods and fall of waters
> Buckingham's army is dispersed and scattered,
> And he himself wandered away alone,
> No man knows whither. (*R3* 4.4.509–13)

It is certainly no coincidence that it is the watery, the oceanic element, the abyssal 'fall of waters' that scatters Buckingham's army and conveys him into a state of essential solitude: 'wander[ing] away alone' with nobody knowing where, Buckingham dies a kind of first death that prefigures his second and final one, which will follow shortly, when he is taken by Richard's men and executed.

Buckingham's fall, his falling prey to the scattering of the deep, foreshadows Richard's own end – as did Clarence's dream. The editors of the Arden3 edition have made a striking observation: some of the 'proceedings' taking place at the bottom of the deep, the 'wooing' and 'mocking' in particular, are reminiscent of Richard's main activities. As we will see, scattering (dissolving fundamental boundaries) is, indeed, his business. However, the paradigms that Clarence's dream exposes as dissolved, as neutralised,[17] are exactly those that lend stability to Richard's very person and project. He works on nothing but the separation of dead bodies from the crown jewels: he sends his opponents down into the deep of death in order to adorn his living head with the golden ring. '"A crown, or else a glorious tomb, / A scepter, or an earthly sepulcher"' (*3H6* 1.4.15–16), his father had heard him shout on the battlefield. What at first looks like Richard braving death turns out to be the opposite: his project aims at 'earthly' rewards – crown, sceptre, sepulchre – no matter whether Richard will survive the battle or not. The tomb he speaks of is not the abyss of death, but the worldly monument representing Richard's glory to the living. Clarence's dream therefore collapses the very foundation of Richard's braveness and hope. The bottom of the deep is not the dead counter-world of the living. It is its basis, its bottom, the place where all ends and from which all emerges[18] – there is no earthly escape. It is the place that does not distinguish, where all distinctions are extinguished, the place of the absolute dissembling. It neither cares for individual heroics nor knows of glory or representation. At the bottom of the deep, the particular ceases to exist. Any difference of own and other dissolves – a thousand faceless bodies are scattered and it is faceless skulls – not heroic brows – that are terribly adorned with jewels, for no reason at all.

All these neutralising operations happen in the grounds of the deep's 'slimy bottom'. This bottom does not provide the ultimate foundation, but causes slippage. It scatters and disintegrates. If it founds anything, it founds the deep and its abyssal force – on mucous.[19] The deep thus turns out not to be an additional vertical dimension that would supplement the horizontal dimension of the everyday world, qualifying it as superficial. 'The deep' is itself a surface phenomenon. Its 'slimy bottom' is of an absolute smoothness: not the smoothness of 'smiling plenty' that promises eternal stability, but a smoothness that brings together fish gnawing on corpses and polished 'reflecting gems'. A smoothness that does not know an opposite, because it extinguishes, it neutralises all opposites. It is biting and polishing at the same time.[20] Richard embodies this absolute, this biting, de-forming smoothness of the deep. He not only brings the deep to the world (where it has always been, but repressed and hidden), but he exposes, exhibits it in the world – and on stage.

The idea of connecting Richard with the notion of the deep was not Shakespeare's. He found it in one of his principal sources, in Thomas More's *History of King Richard III*. 'Hee was close and secret, a deepe dissimuler' (37), writes

More about Richard, and it is this sentence, I would suggest, that Shakespeare's play sets out to explore.

As we have shown, Richard's project of pursuing the crown, his thirst for worldly power and glory, is driven by a desperate impulse to defeat death, to escape its depth, a human impulse he shares with all of his adversaries. At the same time, he embodies the very forces of the deep. We may learn from Maurice Blanchot that what looks like a problematic contradiction turns out to be the key to Richard being the theatrical character that he is:

> This in itself indicates that if men in general do not think about death, if they avoid confronting it [*se dérobent*], it is doubtless in order to flee death and hide from it [*se dissimuler à elle*], but that this escape [*dérobade*] is possible only because death itself is perpetual flight before death, and because it is the deep of dissimulation [*la profondeur de la dissimulation*]. Thus to hide from it [*se dissimuler à elle*] is in a certain way to hide in it [*se dissimuler en elle*]. (Blanchot 94)

Death is 'the deep of dissimulation', the 'slimy bottom' of all hiding and dissembling, its slippery, non-foundational ground. A hiding that does not preserve what it hides – a hiding that is 'the essence' of all hiding – making disappear, dis-figuring, deforming, for ever. As the 'deep dissimuler', Richard embodies death. He embodies its extinguishing forces as well as the 'perpetual flight before death' – that is, death. His being a deep dissimuler or dissembler indicates that he does not merely dissemble something. His dissembling reaches deeper than King Edward fears when he, for example, tells Hastings and Rivers not to '[d]issemble' their hatred (*R3* 2.1.8). The deep that Richard dissembles is an 'empty deep [*profondeur vide*]' (Blanchot 43; transl. altered), 'an indistinct plenitude which is empty' (Blanchot 26). Dissembling becomes 'deep' when it reaches the point of intransitivity, when it ceases to dissemble something and just dissembles. It is here that Shakespeare discovers the theatrical potential of the historical figure of Richard III: theatre practises pure, intransitive 'dissembling'; it exposes it, puts it on stage. Its simulation is 'deep dissimulation': theatre dissembles; it play-acts, without a 'true essence/core' in the background, without anything to hide – except for its own dissembling.

It is therefore only consequent that More's formulation makes an appearance in Shakespeare's text with a crucial displacement. Buckingham, talking to Richard, voices what I would suggest to be the centre of the play:

BUCKINGHAM
Tut, I can counterfeit the deep tragedian,
Speak, and look back, and pry on every side,
Tremble and start at wagging of a straw,
Intending deep suspicion. (*R3* 3.5.5–8)

More's 'deep dissimuler' has become 'deep tragedian'. Although it is Buckingham who claims this 'epithet', it is, at the same time, surreptitiously attributed to Richard. The latter has triggered Buckingham's claims with a question: 'Come, cousin, canst thou quake and change thy colour [. . .]?' (*R3* 3.5.1)

When Buckingham, only seconds later, proves indeed capable of joining Richard in play-acting their being chased by imaginary enemies, he 'counterfeit[s]' one particular 'deep tragedian': his master Richard. He 'changes colour' like Richard, who, as quoted above, boasted of being capable of 'add[ing] colours to the chameleon' and '[c]hanging shapes with Proteus' (*3H6* 3.2.191–2). At the same time, the explicitly theatrical vocabulary that Buckingham employs introduces a decisive shift. In contrast to More's choice of words, 'dissimuler', which focuses on Richard's veiling of his 'secret project', Buckingham's 'tragedian' draws attention to Richard's dissembling itself, to the play-acting, to the histrionic productions Richard brings forth. The deep of the 'tragedian' does not conceal anything. The tragedian is all surface. Nevertheless, his art is an art of depth. As Buckingham's voicing of 'deep suspicion' emphasises, the tragedian must be a master of creating intense affects. Hamlet will marvel at exactly this phenomenon when encountering the players in the second act: for creating its emotional power, theatre does not need any foundation on true, authentic grounds. Buckingham exposes the gaping of the (theatrical) abyss, the slimy bottom of theatre, so to speak, by applying theatre's characteristic operation to itself. This is what happens when he claims to be able to 'counterfeit the deep tragedian'. He claims more than and something different from being able to imitate someone who is pursued by an enemy and who fears for his life. The 'tragedian' embodies imitation having become intransitive. Buckingham therefore boasts of being able to (dis)simulate pure (dis)simulation, to 'counterfeit the deep tragedian'.

The paradox that Shakespeare – with an ironic wit that surpasses that of his characters – puts into Buckingham's mouth indicates the paradox that is inherent in the 'deep tragedian' as such: the paradox of the depth of a surface. By definition, the 'tragedian' does not have an 'inmost nature or feelings' – nevertheless, he is probably more than anyone else capable of affecting 'profoundly': he is deep without being deep (cf. 'deep, *adj.*'; 9.). Does he reveal the deep as (mere) simulation? Yes and no. The frightening groundlessness of theatre, its kinship to the pre- or post-figural, the shapeless realm of 'the deep bosom of the ocean' reaches over to 'our' world. It contaminates the world as we imagine it. It shakes our belief in the stable grounds of authenticity and truth, in the unchanging and timeless foundations of being. Here, we encounter the issue that Stanley Cavell has identified as central to Shakespeare's works: 'how to live at all in a groundless world' (3). Theatre's intensity undermines the hierarchised distinction of 'the real, the grounded, the "material" world' and 'mere appearance, simulation, shadows of imitation'. It testifies to the profound reality of the deep, the bottomless, the paradoxical, slimy abyss of (dis)simulation.

Theatre's ungroundedness is not only spoken about; it is also performed. When Richard and Buckingham enter the stage '*in rotten armour, marvellous ill-favoured*' (R3 3.5 SD), the audience is made to believe – for some seconds – in a turn of events. Although the stage characters' dialogue quickly restores the superior awareness of the spectators and reveals the 'rotten armour' to be a carefully considered costume, the scene unleashes an intense theatrical affect. This is not so much due to the fact that the audience, for a short moment only, is taken in by Richard's dissembling and comes to share his victims' position; the scene 'touches more deeply': it touches upon the slimy bottom of theatricality.

We should not forget that it is a 'tragedian' who speaks Buckingham's words; an actor, who lives and breathes in the same world as the audience. As a tragedian, the actor (also) – in a case of dramatic irony – talks about his own art, which, in the surrounding of flourishing theatre business and prominent, competing actors, certainly entails 'counterfeiting' histrionic role models, adapting to a certain style of play-acting. Hamlet's famous instructions to the players can be read as a commentary on this question of 'counterfeiting the tragedians'. However, the scene does not merely crack a theatrical joke. What makes it a typical instance of Shakespearean metatheatre is the fact that it operates on the very boundary of theatre and reality.

When Buckingham, the stage character, 'counterfeits the deep tragedian', something strange and complex happens: the role/part plays its actor. The relations of material basis (actor) and ephemeral effect (the stage character) are inverted, or rather perverted. As a result, the boundary of theatre and world collapses in a double movement. On the one hand, theatre appropriates, it 'eats up' the world: the materiality of the actor on the stage, theatre's material conditions of possibility, are drawn into theatre's ephemeral realm; they become the objects, the effects of play-acting. On the other hand, theatre's material conditions of possibility, the tragedian, the theatrical machinery, appropriates, 'eats up', the actual theatrical 'production': when the role/part plays its actor, there is just 'actor' left on stage – an actor who does not play anything, except for his playing the actor that he emerges to be.

In a fascinating parrhesiastic moment that transgresses the fictional framing, the actor is given the opportunity to speak truly about himself. For a very short moment, he bails out of the conventional 'lies' of the theatrical setting. He does not dissemble his being someone else while performing a role on stage. He is not a shallow 'dissimuler', who, on the surface, dissembles what he actually 'is' in his inner inmost. For a moment, he does not cloak his true intents. He becomes a 'deep dissimuler': he exposes his costume as a costume. More than this, he exposes himself to *be* nothing but a costume – a chameleon – the costume of costumes.

However, what is it that this actor acts, what is it that he stages – what has become of the theatrical communication whose project it has been to make a fictional world appear on stage? In publicly play-acting nothing but its material foundation, theatre shows literally nothing. It is exactly this gesture that deeply affects the viewers – an affect that Maurice Blanchot calls 'fascination' (cf. 31–2). In his metatheatrical moments, Shakespeare entangles his audience in a particular sort of communication, a sort of communication that Maurice Blanchot characterises as 'literary': 'In this communication it is obscurity that must reveal itself [*se faire jour*] and night that must dawn. This is revelation where nothing appears, but where dissimulation becomes appearance' (198; transl. altered). Although theatre, as its name indicates, consists of 'putting something before our eyes', it is acquainted with the obscure secrets of the deep. In fact, it might, especially in its Dionysian origins, be closer to these secrets of the deep than we might today imagine. This is what Friedrich Nietzsche aims at when speaking of the 'great history' of a 'delight in dissimulation' (*Nachlaß 1880–1882* 474; my transl.).

Literary criticism has certainly contributed to the fact that we probably do not (primarily) associate theatre with this delight in dissimulation. The original delight has been tamed, if not eradicated, by our interest in 'political' or aesthetic intentions, in the 'actual' message 'behind' – dissembled by – the play or its 'mimetic' connection to the 'real', the historical world. Both project a vision of theatre that is founded on non-theatrical, stable 'entities' of our world. Theatre represents intentions or events/state of affairs that we are familiar with, or that we can decode. However, as many thinkers have noted, equalling *mimesis* with imitation or representation is grievously mistaken. 'Imitation presupposes the abandon of an inimitable, *mimesis* on the contrary expresses the desire for it,' writes Jean-Luc Nancy ('The Image' 75). As Nancy again emphasises with reference to Blanchot, this desire longs for 'the inimitable, the obscure ground [*fond*] of the thing in itself' ('The Image' 75): 'That which resounds and that which moves (us), is [. . .] the desire to get to the bottom [*aller au fond*] of things, or even, which is nothing but another way of saying it, the desire to let this ground rise to the surface' (Nancy 'The Image' 80). This is exactly what happens when Richard, the 'deep dissimuler', enters the stage and plays theatre, 'play[s] the devil' or 'counterfeit[s] the deep tragedian'. The 'ground rise[s] to the surface', because Shakespeare makes his audience encounter theatre's paradoxical, its abyssal, structure:

> This abyssal structure is a non-fundamental structure, at once superficial and bottomless, still and always 'flat,' in

which the proper-ty [*propre*] sends itself to the ground, sinks in the waters of its own desire, without ever encountering, rises and is swept away – of itself. It passes into the other. (Derrida *Spurs* 117; transl. altered)

Theatre, as an art of (dis)simulation embodies this 'non-fundamental structure'. It is in the moments when theatre does not show anything, when its production of illusions is suspended for seconds only, that we get the opportunity 'to gaze upon these secrets of the deep'. We do not have to gaze into the theatrical abyss for long to experience it gazing back into us:[21] the abyss fascinates us, it touches upon us, it draws us into its depth. '[A]rt always makes us founder,' Jean-Luc Nancy writes, 'and the shipwreck is in this sense assured' ('The Image' 80).

It is therefore not only the dream that possesses the mysterious power to provide us with an experience of the unexperienceable, of the 'slimy bottom of the deep' – theatre does so as well.[22] And as Shakespeare's play exposes for the dream, the experiencing of the unexperienceable is no process of pure and distant recognition. The audience does not merely watch the 'passing into the other', the processes of Protean changes, being performed on the stage – the 'passing into the other' reaches over to the spectators, seizes them, contaminates them; 'the line separating spectator from player is stretched so thin that the demarcation becomes precarious', writes Waldo F. McNeir (174).[23] For Richard's victims – and also for himself – this is a violent process. It is therefore no coincidence that Nietzsche, in his fragment that ends on the 'delight in dissimulation', associates the name 'Shakespeare' with someone 'who wants to do violence to the reader with his fantasy' (*Nachlaß 1880–1882* 474; my transl.)[24] Richard's brutality transcends the limits of fiction. It is the brutality of the 'deep dissimuler' that touches upon us as theatre's affective power:

Touching the Depth of the Surface: *Richard III*

> [T]he delight in dissimulation erupting as a power that pushes aside, floods, and at times extinguishes the so-called 'character'; the inner longing for a role and mask, for an *appearance* (*Schein*); an excess of capacities for all kinds of adaptation that can no longer be satisfied in the service of the nearest and narrowest utility: all that perhaps does not pertain solely to the actor in himself? (Nietzsche *The Gay Science* 225–6; transl. altered)

Shakespeare, Blanchot and Derrida expose Nietzsche's question as rhetorical. Richard embodies the forces of theatre. He is a pure and therefore highly dangerous affirmation of the delight in dissimulation which drives theatre as a cultural and artistic practice. However, it is exactly this abyssal delight – the accomplice of the secrets of the deep – that links theatre with the world. Transgressing, 'overflowing' 'the nearest and narrowest utility' and everything else that is 'in the service' of the human, intentional being does not solely pertain to the 'deep tragedian' Richard. As the protagonist voices right at the beginning of the play, he is himself the result of an event of dissembling – 'performed' by nature herself: nature is 'dissembling Nature' (*R3* 1.1.19). Her unfathomable processes of forming and de-forming, of making emerge and drawing back into nothingness, of giving birth and bringing death are driven by the same, abyssal force of dissembling as Nietzsche's actor. Theatre provides an experience of this deep, existential surface by exposing its audience to its (violent) intensity.

Spurning Touches: Richard – 'plain man' and 'shallow woman'

Richard is an artist of surface-manipulations: a Protean chameleon, as well as an extraordinarily skilled knifeman. The two 'capacities' differ significantly. The one fashions surfaces that generate effects as '*action at a distance*' (Nietzsche *The Gay Science* 71); the other destroys surfaces in the absolute nearness of penetration. In this difference, a difference of gender emerges: Friedrich Nietzsche regards the power of dissimulation, its '*action at a distance*', as '[t]he magic and the most powerful effect of women' (*The Gay Science* 71). 'Woman' 'plays at dissimulation, at ornamentation, deceit, artifice, at an artist's philosophy. Hers is an affirmative power,' writes Jacques Derrida in his reading of Nietzsche (*Spurs* 67). The knifeman's penetrations, on the other hand, obviously follow a male phallic imaginary. How do these two 'capacities' go together? Do they go together? And which one is characteristic of Richard, which is the one responsible for his success (and downfall)?

They are both closely related to touch. In fact, they demarcate the two opposing poles that are necessary to define the notion of touch: touch takes place 1) when something 'strikes' or 'hits' something (Old Occitan *toccar*), when there is physical contact that has a certain effect (cf. *Le Petit Robert*, 'toucher, *v.*'); and 2) when, at the same time, the two (or more) that touch remain separate, when they do not lump together and form a new entity, but hold a certain distance all the way through their touching. The latter is the reason why Nietzsche, in one of his earliest reflections on the topic, notes: 'Pythagoreans: [. . .] Touch. Actio in distans' (Nietzsche *Nachlaß 1869–1874* 572; my transl.).[25]

The fact that these two defining poles of touch are split by the divide of sexual difference – one actualising and visualising a male, the other a female imaginary[26] – leads to the disturbing disintegration of Richard's capacities. Thomas More's labelling him 'a deep dissimuler' takes sides with the female pole of artifice and deceit – and, as we have shown above, it is this trait that renders Richard a fascinating metatheatrical character. However, although Shakespeare was certainly inspired by the theatricality associated with Richard, he did not forget about the latter's male, his penetrative, capacities. On the contrary, Shakespeare takes up the natal teeth attributed to Richard and employs them to characterise Richard as a person. He is not only the 'yonder dog' of whom Queen Margaret warns: 'when he fawns, he bites: and when he bites, / His venom teeth will rankle to the death' (*R3* 1.3.288–90). He is also drawn as a 'hedgehog' (*R3* 1.2.104), to borrow a word from Lady Anne. Shakespeare associates him with all sorts of sharp spikes, pricks and quills against which one should be on guard.

I would, however, like to suggest that it is the complex interplay of Richard's two capacities – 'hedgehog' and 'dissimuler' – a particular mode of touch, penetrative and distant – that is held responsible for Richard's remarkable power. This interplay may best be observed in a scene paradigmatic for Richard's histrionic capacities, in the 'spectacle of Gloucester's seduction of Lady Anne', as Stephen Greenblatt calls it (*Hamlet in Purgatory* 168).

The scene begins with a rather violent and obviously phallic encounter of two aggressive males. Richard stops the funeral procession of King Henry VI's corpse with a harsh command that one sole halberdier, protecting the cortege, is courageous enough to disobey:

RICHARD
[. . .]
Advance thy halberd higher than my breast,
Or by Saint Paul, I'll strike thee to my foot
And spurn upon thee, beggar, for thy boldness. (*R3* 1.2.40–2)

Richard's use of the unusual verb 'to spurn upon' attracts attention. The Arden3 editors paraphrase its meaning with 'trample contemptuously' (cf. 'spurn, *v.1*'; 5.), which is certainly what Richard's words 'signify'. However, whereas 'trampling', that is, hitting with the sole and heel of one's shoes, describes an impact of blunt force, the etymology of 'spurn' points in a different direction: the sharp, pointed spur is a paradigm of penetrating force. 'Spurning' is Richard's, the hedgehog's 'style': as Lady Anne tells us only seconds later, Richard has '[s]tabbed' (*R3* 1.2.11) King Henry VI, her father-in-law, as well as her husband, Edward. His is the 'selfsame hand' (*R3* 1.2.11) that has fatally penetrated the two bodies, 'that made these holes' (*R3* 1.2.14).

Jacques Derrida has made the spur the key term around which his reading of Nietzsche revolves. As his text resonates strongly with Shakespeare's *Richard III* – it is dedicated to the power of dissimulation – I will come back to Derrida's writing repeatedly, in order to open up Shakespeare's text from this perspective.

As Derrida's title indicates – *Spurs. Nietzsche's Styles* – it is not one spur, but at least two – it is spurs in the plural – that make styles and spurs mutually 'define' each other. Two spurs also characterise Richard's encounter with the halberdier. Richard answers the threatening gesture of the halberd, a sharp weapon, with a second threat of 'spurning/spurring'. The doubling of the 'phallic agency' might make the scene less phallic than one might think. Although it negotiates (male) authority and exposes the phallic insignia of power, the absence of the thorn's smooth counterpart, the absence of the plain, unguarded (female!) flesh which might be penetrated undermines the simple logic of phallic power. Two pointing spurs attack each other – from a distance. The halberdier's boldness in turning his weapon on a superior, who has the phallus via his social position, creates a situation that does not permit the distinction between an active and a passive part. As the situation is not one of rivalry – the halberdier is no peer – fighting it out is not an honourable option, and another solution has to be found. Richard simply mirrors the phallic threat. As the hedgehog that he 'is' (or, rather, that he plays), he does not even have to draw his sword in order to counter the threat of penetration. He fends off the attack with mere words, which are figurative and rather unusual, but nonetheless prove to be 'penetrating'. His superior authority is indicated (or rather produced) by the fact that he can successfully play, or dissimulate, his penetrating forces even without using the 'prop' of a weapon.[27]

The coincidence of attack and defence, of activity and passivity, of action and reaction, that characterises the scene follows the logic that Derrida associates with the way a spur advances: 'Like the prow, for example, of a sailing vessel, its *rostrum*, the projection of the ship which surges ahead to meet the sea's attack and cleave its hostile surface' (*Spurs* 39). In this image, the sea is not a passive victim – it is itself 'hostile' and on the 'attack'. It is not destroyed or eliminated either: what Derrida calls 'spurring operation (*opération-éperonnante*)' (*Spurs* 107; transl. altered) does not aim at oneness.[28] This is not only indicated by the fact that the two 'opponents', ship and sea, outlive their conflict; the actual, the interesting, result of the operation is the 'twoness' of the water, its being cleft into a difference to itself, creating a trace, what the Germans call a *Spur*. This trace draws the outline, the contours, the shape, the *eidos* of the ship, whose oneness turns out to be an effect of spurring operations. The cleaving of a surface is the moment of birth of another surface. In fact, oneness does not play a significant role in the whole process. The spurring operation is fuelled by a whole series of twonesses: the difference of ship and sea; of wind (and helm); the difference of air pressures ... This series does not refer to a stable bottom; it is abyssal. It is not held together by the organising 'oneness' of origin or end. If one had to assign a sex to it, it would surely be female.

The encounter of Richard and the halberdier, marginal as it is, prefigures the spectacular encounter of Richard and Lady Anne that follows. In doing so, it indicates that this encounter will be fuelled by the encounter of penetrative, 'phallic' forces; forces, however, that cannot be located in predefined gender roles. On the contrary, these roles have to be played – in an overtly theatrical sense, as we will see. Furthermore, the cast even changes parts during the scene. The 'phallic' forces – or 'castration's effect', as Derrida calls them (*Spurs* 61) – are generated in-between the roles, and cannot be fully appropriated. They always exceed an instrumental use. The overall effect of the phallic forces' 'touch' escapes intentional control.

The 'spectacle of Gloucester's seduction of Lady Anne' is organised around the penetrating touch of the sword. It is no coincidence that Richard enters the stage while Anne is bemoaning the deadly wounds of her father-in-law. Richard appears on the scene as the man of the sword, as the one who is renowned for stabbing. His short skirmish with the halberdier emphasises Gloucester's aggressive inclination to penetrating violence. The threat this directs towards the simple soldier reverberates through the whole scene and surpasses its actual addressee. The halberdier's provocative gesture has merely prompted Richard to express, in words, what his aura alone transports to anyone who knows about his past deeds.

It is these past deeds that dominate the first part of his conversation with Anne. The widow reads Richard's character from the very beginning. She is not deceived at all – she 'falls undeceived', as Joel Elliot Slotkin notes (20): to her, Richard does not 'seem a saint' (*R3* 1.3.335), not for a second. Even before he has spoken a single word, Anne identifies him as the 'fiend' (*R3* 1.2.34), the 'devil' (*R3* 1.2.34; 1.2.50; 1.2.73) that he is – or, rather, that he 'plays', as Richard tells the audience a scene later (cf. *R3* 1.3.335–7).

According to his own, misogynistic standards, Richard '[p]lay[s] the maid's part' (*R3* 3.7.50) in the first sentences that he exchanges with Anne: he mimes the 'shallow, changing woman' (*R3* 4.4.431); he lies, changes strategies, contradicts himself. However, this all proves to be to no avail.

Anne masterfully sifts truth from lie: 'In thy foul throat thou liest' (*R3* 1.2.95), she exclaims, when Richard denies the murder of Anne's husband; 'O wonderful, when devils tell the truth!' (*R3* 1.2.73), when Richard admits his lack of pity. If we decide to conclude for Richard, as Jean E. Howard and Phyllis Rackin do, that 'the woman's part has been included in the master showman's repertory from the very beginning' (109), we would have to come to a similar conclusion about Lady Anne: she knows how to play the man's part of having truth's unambiguity at his command.

However, feminist readings like Howard and Rackin's, which reconstruct the scene as a competition of the sexes, face one decisive problem. They presuppose what the scene negotiates. Who says that Richard's 'original' part is 'the man's' part? Does he represent 'masculinity'? Shakespeare's play does not expose the simple, 'naturalistic' model of 'warlike masculinity' (Howard and Rackin 109) opposing 'womanly', 'virtuous' femininity (Rackin 79). The seduction scene shows that one cannot know which trait, 'masculine' or 'feminine', will prove powerful or even useful in a certain situation. Neither Richard's initial attempt at deceit and dissimulation nor Anne's clear-sighted command of truth bring about an effect. The abstract appropriation of (gendered) capacities that Howard and Rackin evaluate – the more capacities, the better – is obviously no suitable indicator of concrete power relations. On the contrary, it is not appropriation, but the ceding of a gendered role that changes the game. Richard, the man of the sword, hands his weapon over to Anne:

RICHARD
[...]
I never sued to friend, nor enemy;
My tongue could never learn sweet smoothing word.
But now thy beauty is proposed my fee,
My proud heart sues, and prompts my tongue to speak.
She looks scornfully at him.

> [...]
> If thy revengeful heart cannot forgive,
> Lo, here I lend thee this sharp-pointed sword,
> Which if thou please to hide in this true breast
> And let the soul forth that adoreth thee,
> I lay it naked to the deadly stroke
> And humbly beg the death upon my knee. (R3 1.2.170–81)

Quite against his intentions, Richard speaks truly when he tries to seduce Lady Anne with a lie. As Anne's reaction indicates, Gloucester's 'tongue' is indeed not capable of 'sweet smoothing word'. Instead of 'smoothing' her face into a smile, he provokes a scornful frown.[29] It is this rhetorical defeat – some lines earlier, he had already attempted to persuade Anne '[t]o leave this keen encounter of our wits' (R3 1.2.118) – that makes Richard proceed to other means. He supplements his verbal skills with theatrical, bodily performance, with play-acting (cf. Slotkin 15; Olk 8). It is no longer the maid's verbosity that he plays – he now 'counterfeit[s] the deep tragedian'.

As a result, Anne suddenly finds herself involved in a melodramatic scene that is triggered by a rapid instance of gender trouble. In the blink of an eye, she touches upon 'the instrument of power'; she has the penetrating touch at her disposal. However, as soon as she has the sword – the phallus (cf. K. M. Smith 154) – her agency apparently shrinks to nothingness. She does not only appear to be incapable of using the sword and stabbing her enemy: even her sound judgement about Richard's person seems to have suddenly left her, even though Richard now frankly admits that he has 'stabbed young Edward' (R3 1.2.184):

> ANNE
> I would I knew thy heart.
> RICHARD
> 'Tis figured in my tongue.
> ANNE
> I fear me both are false.

RICHARD
Then never man was true.
ANNE
Well, well, put up your sword. (*R3* 1.2.195–9)

With Anne's 'sparing' Richard, which the latter wittily connects to her consent to marriage, the battle is over – and there is little doubt who comes off the victor: 'Richard holds his own against Anne and eventually gains rhetorical mastery over her,' writes Dorothea Kehler (118). However, the way that Richard comes out the winner contradicts Kehler's very phrasing. Richard does not 'hold his own'; he rather mimes 'the other' and carries away the prize. His victory is a victory of Protean gender trouble. The 'power' that earned him the victory has been identified as 'female': Kristin M. Smith calls it 'Richard's feminine linguistic power' (154), while Howard and Rackin speak of 'the female power of erotic seduction' (109). With reference to Nietzsche, one could also add the 'female' 'theatrical power and agency', of which Howard and Rackin think 'the women' in Shakespeare's Histories to be 'deprived of' (108). However, as we will see, Richard has not 'appropriated' this power, as Howard and Rackin claim (108).

The power at work in the seduction scene is the power of spurring touch. It cannot be appropriated, because it is generated between at least two 'agents' and it takes its effect from a distance. It is not the possession of the sword that grants the power, however. The phallic sword is nevertheless the necessary (and necessarily dangerous) 'prop' that provides (part of) the theatrical impact that the scene distributes. It is also not the bloody, the fatal, use of the sword. Although it would have been possible for both, neither Richard nor Anne take the chance to stab their opponent. It is not brute violence but a different, a more sophisticated and more sustainable form of power that is at play here.

Both Richard and Anne play with what Jacques Derrida has called 'castration's effect'. In psychoanalysis, the castration complex describes the dynamic that is generated when the phallus begins to circulate – when the positions of having and not not-having start to communicate (in both directions, as penis envy and castration anxiety) (cf. Freud 'Drei Abhandlungen zur Sexualtheorie'; Lacan). This energetic dynamic is constitutively a phenomenon of distance: both envy and anxiety are only directed towards their 'objects'. If their 'objects' were reached (the penis appropriated for ever or castration irreversibly and universally executed), the dynamic would abruptly come to a standstill.[30] The penis would cease to be of any value. This is what Richard's handing over his sword to Anne simulates. Once the constitutive distance vanishes, once touch (as *actio in distans*!) is replaced by appropriation, all that remains is death: stabbing Richard and probably being executed for the deed. One could say that this would have been the 'masculine', the 'heroic' solution, that this would have shown the 'warlike masculinity' which Howard and Rackin so desperately miss in the play's female characters. However, Richard and Anne prefer to defer their ends – and rather choose to play. They are theatrical; they are 'woman': 'Unable to seduce or to give vent to desire without it, "woman" is in need of castration's effect. But evidently she does not believe in it. She who, unbelieving, still plays with castration, she is "woman"' (Derrida *Spurs* 61).

Strikingly enough, feminist critics appear to believe more readily in the truth of castration, that is, the stable basis of the distribution of gender roles and gender hierarchy, than Anne herself. '[I]t is the male protagonist who opposes the patriarchal project.' write Howard and Rackin (106–7). But what about Anne? Which part does she play?

Seeing her in one of the 'typically female' 'roles of helpless victims' (Rackin 79) indicates that one may have fallen prey to the melodramatic spectacle which Richard has staged. The part he made Anne play is calculated to expose 'her' as weak, as incapable of using the phallic instrument of power. It is not unreasonable to conclude, as Rackin does, that the 'phallic incapacity' that Richard attempts to attribute to Anne also affects her 'female' capacities of seduction and play-acting:

> Would a woman be able to hold us (or 'enthrall' us, as they say) if we did not consider her able under certain circumstances to wield a dagger deftly (any kind of dagger) *against* us? Or against herself – which in certain cases would be the more severe revenge (Chinese revenge). (Nietzsche *The Gay Science* 74)

However, are the 'circumstances' that Richard has created in manipulative intent suitable for taking the scene as a litmus test which decides over Lady Anne's capacities in general? And does she, indeed, prove incapable of wielding 'any kind of dagger'? Lady Anne sees through Richard's theatrical ruse and abruptly stops the melodramatic intermezzo:

> RICHARD
> [. . .]
> Take up the sword again, or take up me.
> ANNE:
> Arise, dissembler; though I wish they death,
> I will not be thy executioner. (*R3* 1.2.186–8)

It may have been Richard's borrowing his phrasing from Thomas Kyd's *The First Part of Ieronimo* that enables Anne (and probably also parts of Shakespeare's audience) to unmask his histrionics. Strikingly, in Kyd's play, the scene does not revolve around the sword, but a different 'kind of dagger': 'Take vp thy pen, or ile take vp thee' (2.3.28) Ieronimo tells his sun Horatio. Richard's rephrasing exposes the exchangeability of sword and the stylus, the instrument of word, which plays a decisive role in the scene.

By calling Richard a 'dissembler', Lady Anne shows that, in contrast to the mayor or most of the male characters, she is not the naïve victim that Richard assumes her to be. Similarly to Richard, Lady Anne is 'woman': she embodies 'scepticism and veiling dissimulation' (Derrida *Spurs* 57). It is especially the latter that one tends to forget when evaluating the role she plays in the seduction scene. Why does no one seem to think her capable of playing a role, of dissembling her 'true intents'?

Lady Anne is made a 'pitiable victim[ ]' by anyone thinking her unable to wield a woman's dagger. In fact, she has been masterfully handling one all the while – but it is of a 'kind' that successfully dissembles its efficacy.

Anne not only puts an end to Richard's melodramatic play, but also immediately starts her own. The 'second act' of their spectacle, which is now secretly directed by Lady Anne, is based on a 'phallic weapon' as well; a 'phallic weapon' that Lady Anne, symmetrically to Richard's handing over of his swords, passes on to her enemy: language/the power of the word.

At the beginning of the seduction scene, Anne directs the audience's attention to an incident between Queen Margaret and Richard:

> ANNE
> [. . .] Queen Margaret saw
> Thy murderous falchion smoking in his blood,
> The which thou once didst bend against her breast,
> But that thy brothers beat aside the point.
> RICHARD
> I was provoked by her slanderous tongue (*R3* 1.2.95–9)

The scene exposes a central correspondence that plays a crucial role in the whole play: 'murderous falchion' matches 'slanderous tongue'. Although the one seems to carry masculine, the other rather feminine associations, 'the point' is the *tertium comparationis* which connects the two: both have the (phallic) power to penetrate and hurt, to touch upon their opponent.

Shakespeare employs the character of Queen Margaret to establish this symmetry of sword and word. Margaret is 'a most worthy opponent to the chameleon king, Richard III', note Naomi C. Liebler and Lisa Scancella Shea (79). Margaret and Richard both hold aggressive outsider positions, which are exposed by their physiognomy. A 'wrinkled witch' (*R3* 1.3.163), as Richard calls her, she is, like the deformed protagonist, not a character of smooth peace; she shares sides with 'Grim-visaged War' and his 'wrinkled front' (*R3* 1.1.9).

The harsh label that Richard assigns to her indicates that she is to be feared. Her war is, however, not fought with weapons of steel – her 'power is entirely linguistic' (K. M. Smith 153). 'Can curses pierce the clouds and enter heaven?' (*R3* 1.3.194), she asks. The outcome of Shakespeare's play can be interpreted as a positive answer to this question.

Margaret even acts as an expert, informing others on how to achieve the penetrative verbal touch for which she appears to be famous:

QUEEN ELIZABETH
My words are dull. O quicken them with thine.
QUEEN MARGARET
Thy woes will make them sharp and pierce like mine.
   (*R3* 4.4.123–4)

The expert of sharpening the metal blades corresponding to Margaret's linguistic ones is Richard: 'No doubt the murderous knife was dull and blunt', Queen Elizabeth tells him, 'Till it was whetted on thy stone-hard heart' (*R3* 4.4.227–8).

The two corresponding 'phallic' instruments, the sword and the tongue, do not come to touch very often on a thematic level in the play. However, when they do, we are provided with insights in the structure which shapes the play as a whole. Apart from the seduction scene, this happens in a marginal sequence often cut in productions, a scene which turns out to be a comment on the seduction scene: Gloucester's conversation with the two little princes. Like the seduction scene, it centres on Richard's phallic weapon: 'I pray you, uncle,' York exclaims, 'give me this dagger' (*R3* 3.1.110). When Richard is reluctant to hand over the dagger (which he himself appears to value as a symbol of power) to his nephews, they entangle him in a rhetorical skirmish that exposes Richard's (verbal) vulnerability.[31] The fact that the legitimate heir to the throne, still a child of nine years, can rhetorically challenge Richard worries the latter's right hand: 'With what a sharp-provided wit he reasons' (*R3* 3.1.132), Buckingham notes in an aside. Having the brute force of dagger and sword at one's command obviously does not render one untouchable. There are other kinds of pointed, penetrating 'daggers'. Power is a question of styles:

> In the question of style there is always the weight or *examen* of some pointed object. At times this object might be only a quill or a stylus. But it could just as easily be a stiletto, or even a rapier. (Derrida *Spurs* 37)

In the seduction scene, Richard's 'sharp-pointed sword' encounters a pointed instrument of language, a stylus, or rather a quill, of a special kind: 'sweet smoothing word'. It is no coincidence that Shakespeare positions the two four-syllabled word combinations of similar morphological structure at corresponding positions, the end of their lines. Their juxtaposition exceeds the characters' use of these terms: they provide us with the two weapons with which the conflict of the scene is fought out, or rather the two instruments with which the protagonists play, in a symmetrical fashion. We have already analysed the first act's exchange of sword – the second act is dedicated to the power of 'sweet smoothing word'.

Critics agree that Richard plays the (female) part of the seducer and successfully wins Anne with the power of his love-talk. However, Lady Anne does not naively fall for Richard: it is she who stages his surprising 'success' as a lover. Has not Richard himself admitted that he is 'not shaped for sportive tricks, / Nor made to court an amorous looking-glass' (*R3* 1.1.14–15)? Anne casts him in this surprising and odd role – as he had cast her in the role of the master over life and death only moments before. Like many feminist critics, Richard believes that he has appropriated the feminine power of erotic seduction – but, in fact, the first act of melodrama is followed by a romantic comedy into which Lady Anne has secretly entangled her adversary. It is she who 'play[s] the maid's part': she abandons her witty resistance and counterfeits the seduced victim. Hers is perhaps the sharpest, certainly the most perfidious of weapons: it is 'sweet smoothing word' that touches with the backside of the quill, with the smoothest of all surfaces. Lady Anne plays the mirror: 'a mirror all the purer in that it knows and is known to have no reflections. Except those which man has reflected there' (Irigaray *Speculum of the Other Woman* 134).

Has she fallen in love with Richard? We do not know, and we have no evidence for it. Her 'since you teach me how to flatter you' (*R3* 1.2.226) only indicates the ambiguity of the 'affection' that she shows towards Richard.

Has Richard fallen in love? Yes, he has. We do know because there is evidence for it. As soon as he is alone on stage, he confides his love to the audience:

RICHARD
Upon my life, she finds, although I cannot,
Myself to be a marvellous proper man.
I'll be at charges for a looking-glass
And entertain a score or two of tailors
To study fashions to adorn my body;
Since I am crept in favour with myself,
I will maintain it with some little cost. (*R3* 1.2.256–62)

Richard has 'crept in favour', he has fallen in love – with himself! As he concludes, it has been Lady Anne that has given him the feeling 'to be a marvellous proper man'. 'Maintaining' this feeling means buying 'a looking glass', which replaces the role that Lady Anne has played with a permanent object of the same function. Richard's narcissistic love does not testify to a new, healthier relation to himself – he has simply fallen prey to his own skills of seduction, which he admires all the more for the difficult starting situation that he thinks them to have overcome:

RICHARD
And I, no friends to back my suit withal
But the plain devil and dissembling looks?
And yet to win her? All the world to nothing? (*R3* 1.2.238–40)

Unlike Narcissus, Richard is not spectacularly carried off by his self-love. On the contrary, winning Anne is one of his great triumphs, and it is Anne who will pay for this triumph with her life: it is she who soon 'withers' away and dies a silent death offstage. However, she does not leave the stage without her own style of taking revenge: by playing the maid, by exchanging 'sweet smoothing words' with Richard, she contaminates him with the slow poison of human feelings. Certainly, Richard does not immediately perish from them. His ascent still continues and eventually leads him onto the English throne. However, Anne's mirroring intervention does not remain without consequences. Richard will not be touched by pity, but by a growing egomania that is accompanied by an almost paranoiac anxiety and need for control. These affects increasingly determine his actions and limit his former capacities.[32] Although Shakespeare's play depicts the rise and fall of King Richard III, it tells a story of decline: the 'plain devil' that appears onstage in the first act gradually turns into the 'plain man' (*R3* 1.3.50) that he detested so much.

Whereas the 'plainness' of the devil paradoxically signifies the maximum deepness of dissimulation, the infinite depth of the surface, the 'plainness' of man stands for the banality of the human existence that is characterised by following one's all-too-human goals: above all, self-preservation. The deep dissembler, gradually, becomes one of us.

Richard's decline can be observed as a decline of his capacity to touch. The more he thinks himself capable of controlling 'the touches', the less they work for him. It is paradigmatic that when he briefs Buckingham at the end of the third act on how to manipulate the London people with a public speech studded with lies, the result turns out disastrously. 'Yet touch this sparingly, as 'twere far off' (*R3* 3.5.93), he had instructed Buckingham, and comes back to this order when the latter returns to report on the people's reaction:

RICHARD
Touched you the bastardy of Edward's children?
[...]
BUCKINGHAM
Indeed, left nothing fitting for your purpose
Untouched or slightly handled in discourse. (*R3* 3.7.4–19)

Nevertheless, feeding the folk a plain lie and hoping for their enthusiastic support – crowning Richard their king – backfires terribly. Moreover, this trivial stratagem is not worthy of the 'deep dissembler' we encountered at the beginning of the play. Significantly, Buckingham has to intervene and advise Richard to '[p]lay the maid's part' (*R3* 3.7.50). He carefully stages a small scene in which Richard is seen praying 'between two churchmen' (*R3* 3.7.47), and pretends not to be easily won over to the request of the crown. Buckingham's reminding the former chameleon Richard of the power of play-acting proves successful: it is theatricality that heaves him on the throne.

However, Richard has irretrievably lost his touch. His 'delight in dissimulation' that had been responsible for his exercising 'theatrical power and agency' – the capacity of touching at a distance – is gone. The demonic incalculability of Richard's deep, abyssal surface is replaced by its very antidote: a compulsion to control, a compulsion to determine the 'true nature' of his surroundings. It is not a theatrical, not a playful kind of 'touch' that he 'plays' when testing Buckingham's loyalty: 'Ah, Buckingham, now do I play the touch / To try if thou be current gold indeed' (*R3* 4.2.8–9). In contrast to the devil or the maid, the touchstone has not the power to seduce or tempt, its touch does not 'magically' transform its counterpart. It lacks the power of (dis)simulation; it is essentially anti-theatrical. It merely indicates the present material composition of a thing – and it does so by its 'simple truth' (*R3* 1.3.51) of staying the same itself. More and more, Richard shows this trait that the touchstone and the 'plain man' share. The deep dissembler has become a man of plain words: 'Shall I be plain?', he tells Buckingham, 'I wish the bastards dead' (*R3* 4.2.19).

The weakness of Richard's new 'plainness' is showcased in the late counterpart to the seduction of Lady Anne. This time, it is Queen Elizabeth whom Richard attempts to win for his purposes. For dynastic reasons, he wants her to marry her daughter to him. Like the first seduction scene, Richard seems to have seduced his female conversation partner in order to meet with his wishes at the end of their talk:

QUEEN ELIZABETH
Shall I go win my daughter to thy will?
KING RICHARD
And be a happy mother by the deed.
QUEEN ELIZABETH
I go, write to me very shortly,
And you shall understand from me her mind. (*R3* 4.4.426–9)

As he is alone on stage, Richard celebrates his triumph. He does obviously not doubt his having, again, fooled 'the female sex':

KING RICHARD
Bear her my true love's kiss; and so farewell.
Exit Queen [Elizabeth]
Relenting fool, and shallow, changing woman.
   (R3 4.4.430–1)

However, this time, Richard's assessment of the situation does not find unreserved approval among the audience and critics. 'The scene inverts the pattern of Act I, scene 2, by turning courtship to self-defence,' writes Gillian M. Day. 'Elizabeth leaves, equivocating her decision as did Anne, but fooling Richard with an ambiguity which, for the first time, he misreads' (Day 153). The assessment of the scene is rendered difficult by the fact that Richmond's successful rebellion prevents the realisation of the marriage plans. Stanley's message that 'the Queen hath heartily consented / He [i.e. Richmond!] should espouse Elizabeth her daughter' (R3 4.5.7–8) does not help to clarify the situation. It can either be read as a confirmation of Richard's statement – the queen is 'changing', in her decision she again follows the new male power hierarchy – or as evidence of her having fooled Richard all along.

The doubts that accompany Richard's 'triumph' are mainly caused by the course of the conversation itself. As Dorothea Kehler writes, 'in this second debate the preponderance of stichomythic responses are Elizabeth's, hers the sarcasm and greater dramatic force' (Kehler 118). Elizabeth emanates an astonishing 'delight in dissimulation' – she 'plays the fox' (Kehler 118). She wittily creates and balances on double meanings; 'it is she who now prosecutes the duplicity of words' (Day 153). While Richard tries hard to fix the plain meaning of what is said – 'What do you think?' (R3 4.4.258);

'Be not so hasty to confound my meaning' (*R3* 4.4.262) – Elizabeth's artful eloquence seems to overcharge her opponent. Richard clearly becomes defensive:

> KING RICHARD
> Be eloquent in my behalf to her.
> QUEEN ELIZABETH
> An honest tale speed best being plainly told.
> KING RICHARD
> Then plainly to her tell my loving tale.
> QUEEN ELIZABETH
> Plain and not honest is too harsh a style.
> KING RICHARD
> Your reasons are too shallow and too quick.
> QUEEN ELIZABETH
> O no, my reasons are too deep and dead,
> Too deep and dead, poor infants, in their graves.
>   (*R3* 4.4.357–63)

Structurally, the situation resembles Clarence's conversation with Richard. This time, however, Gloucester finds himself in the position of the petitioner, whose future depends on the goodwill and the verbal skills of others. 'I will deliver you, or else lie for you' (*R3* 1.1.115), Richard had promised Clarence. In contrast, Elizabeth refuses to use her eloquence for Richard's request – and rather continues to deploy it against him. By introducing the opposing notion of 'plainness' to Richard's attempt at appropriating her eloquence, Elizabeth builds Richard a verbal trap that exposes his project as dishonest at heart. More than this, with 'eloquence' and 'plainness', Elizabeth also exposes the binary pair of roles, the 'styles' of communication, which distinguish Richard's and her part in their current conversation. Her witty words thus also provide us with a kind of metacommentary of rhetorical strategies and their limitations. The 'style' that Elizabeth appears to suggest to Richard is exactly the one that characterises Richard's weak, almost helpless performance in the scene. He is '[p]lain and not honest' – his words are of very limited effect; they do not seduce or fascinate at all. The 'plain man' Richard encounters a woman, meaning someone 'playing at dissimulation, at ornamentation, deceit, artifice' (Derrida *Spurs* 67).

Elizabeth's wordplay indicates that her rhetorical battle with Richard negotiates the question of the sexes. By playing with the homonymy of Richard's 'loving tale' / *tail* – 'Sexual member; penis' (*OED*, 'tail, *n.1*'; 5.c.) – Elizabeth connects the question of the power of words with the 'phallic' power of penetrating touches. However, things are more complicated than the conventional binary of 'warlike', 'powerful' masculinity and weak, 'virtuous' femininity that Phyllis Rackin attempts to apply to Shakespeare's *Histories* (cf. 79). Richard's is at the same time too plain and 'too harsh a style'– stylus, thorn, spur, pointed instrument – to perform effective touches. It is all a question of surfaces. In this scene, his 'style' does not seduce, because it is too obviously 'disagreeably hard and rough to the touch' (*OED*, 'harsh, *adj.*'; 1.), it is too 'smoothly', too honestly and too directly phallic. Richard speaks with the unambiguous and non-playful authority of the king – his non-dissimulating plainness is brutal but it does not touch; it does not 'act at a distance'. And this is exactly what his project of wooing the queen's daughter would have required!

As Richard himself taught us at the beginning of the play, the warlike is never 'plain', it is not 'free from roughness, wrinkles' (*OED*, 'plain, *adj.2*'; †3.a.). However, in order to be effective, it must not be exclusively 'harsh' either. The 'female power of erotic seduction', the 'theatrical power and agency' that Richard had embodied as the deep dissembler, paradoxically combines both: smooth surface and penetrating touch. In this late scene, it is not Richard's but Elizabeth's 'style', her rhetorical strategy of playing the fox, that exerts this kind of fascinating power. Richard says more than he is aware of by calling Elizabeth's witty statements

(*OED*, 'reason, *n.1*'; 1.a.) 'shallow' and 'quick'. They are, in a way, 'superficial' and 'hasty': in contrast to Richard's, they are improvised and do not communicate any plain, 'deeper' intent that would have preceded their utterance in any way. However, Richard does not realise the danger his words speak of. Elizabeth's reasons may be 'shallow', but they are 'quick'. The 'ground' she is standing on might not be well founded, but it is exactly this quickness, this being 'mobile, shifting, readily yielding to pressure' (*OED*, 'quick, *adj.*'; 18.), that poses a threat to her conversation partner. In contrast to Richard's allusive remarks to Clarence, Elizabeth explicitly elaborates on why Richard's request 'touches her more deeply' than he seems to imagine. Her children are 'dead', and she knows that Richard has 'whetted' 'the murderous knife' (*R3* 4.4.227–8) against them. More than this, it is her children's being dead that 'quickens' Elizabeth's words, that accounts for their piercing sharpness (cf. 'quick, *adj.*'; 17.). '[S]orrow' not only offers the women in Shakespeare's play 'a unique opportunity for speech in the hard, masculine world', as Joseph Campana claims (24), as we have already seen, 'woes' also 'quicken' the women's linguistic weapons – 'make them sharp and pierce' (*R3* 4.4.123–4).

Richard is right: Queen Elizabeth is, indeed, a 'shallow, changing woman', though this does not signify a weakness, but a powerful capacity: 'Women are considered deep – why? Because you never get to the bottom of them. Women aren't even shallow' (Nietzsche 'Twilight' 159). Richard is taken in by Elizabeth's abyssal, witty quickness, as he will be deceived by Stanley only shortly later. It is deep surfaces, keen, artistic play-acting – Richard's own weapon! – that save their (step)children's lives and thereby lay the foundation of a new dynasty of English royalty.

Richard's fall is not the result of a lack of wariness; it does not follow from a tragic flaw he commits as an act of individual weakness. It is significant that whenever the word 'shallow' passes someone's lips in a disparaging way, a fatal 'mistake', a deadly error of judgement, looms in the air. Richard's is certainly the most prominent case. He does not only attribute the adjective to Elizabeth, but also to his future killer, whom he calls 'shallow Richmond' (*R3* 5.3.219). Richard's tragic misjudgement of 'shallowness' is prefigured by the fate of Hastings, who dismisses Stanley's prophetic dream about Richard's threatening brutality as 'shallow' fears:

HASTINGS
His honour and myself are at the one,
And at the other is my good friend Catesby,
Where nothing can proceed that toucheth us
Whereof I shall not have intelligence.
Tell him his fears are shallow, wanting instance: (*R3* 3.2.20–4)

Hasting's explanation of why he thinks Stanley's fears 'shallow' is indicative. He claims a superior position that renders him untouchable, that grants him control over 'the touches'. Being crowned England's king, Richard finds himself in such a position of authority that implies an attitude towards touch that differs from the one he had before. Instead of playing with the uncontrollable, wild power of touch (which is the privilege of the outsider position), the authoritative position demands shielding oneself against touch.[33] Paradoxically enough, the position most exposed to being touched upon, the position of honour and authority, is the one that holds the most defensive relation to it. It thereby constitutively loses contact to a considerable source of power and inevitably remains vulnerable on this flank. The intelligence, the prevision of touches that Hasting claims, is an illusion. The male eye of authority must be blind to the deepness of the 'shallow' – however, it will nonetheless feel its fatal intensity.

'The question posed by the spurring-operation (*opération-éperonnante*) is more powerful than any content, thesis or meaning,' writes Jacques Derrida (Derrida *Spurs* 107; transl. altered). It can, however, not be appropriated and employed for one's own intents or personal projects:

> The stylate spur (*éperon stylé*) traverses the veil. It rents it not merely in order to see or produce the thing itself, but in fact undoes the opposition itself, the opposition that has folded over on itself, bringing forth the veiled/unveiled (sailed/unsailed), the truth as production, the unveiling/dissimulation of that which is produced in the presence. (Derrida *Spurs* 107; transl. altered)

The stylate spur is no touchstone that informs us about the 'true' composition of the present world. On the contrary, it does not leave the opposition of 'true' and 'fake' untouched, of friend and foe, of you and me and the whole mechanics of hierarchy that organise the negotiations of power and influence. Its power is not political but anarchical, its reach incalculable and therefore inescapable: 'It touches you, my lord, as much as me' (*R3* 1.4.261), as Dorset says, 'For emulation who shall now be nearest / Will touch us all too near' (*R3* 2.3.23–6), a wise citizen adds.

Although the title might suggest otherwise, Shakespeare's play is not dedicated to the spectacular story of an exceptional individual. As Jan Kott has convincingly shown, its object is history (3–46). It depicts and explores a pair of antagonistic forces, whose interplay shapes the course of history. Both are embodied by Richard at different stages of his life: the deep dissembler's anarchical spurring-operations and the apotropaic authority of the status quo.

The spurring-operation, the deep dissembling, is operated from the margins, from the peripheries of the established power structure. It is, constitutively, 'a womanly' intervention.

Shakespeare's play does not expose this intervention as weak or powerless or ineffective, however. On the contrary, one does not do justice to the early modern play when projecting the 'modern dilemma' of 'womanly or warlike' onto it (Rackin 79). Shakespeare's *Richard III* suggests the exact opposite: the 'womanly', deep dissembling, the 'female' erotic seduction and theatrical agency – in short, all the 'touching at a distance' – are associated with the warlike and exposed to be powerful. Richard fascinates the audience and is successful when he plays the woman's role. He fails, one might say, because he 'is not feminine enough' ('Conceiving Tragedy' 99), using words that Tanya Pollard found to reference Hamlet. He fails when attempting to exercise the classical, male authority of the throne.[34] 'Richard is perhaps the only tragedy by Shakespeare in which women have, on their own behalf [*pour leur compte*], relations of war,' writes Gilles Deleuze ('Un manifest de moins' 90; my transl.), and he is right. One repeats Richard's mistakes of the second half of the play – the structural failings of patriarchal authority – when declaring the play's women to be 'powerless', 'helpless' (Rackin 79) or even 'pitiable victims' (Howard and Rackin 106). They might be 'shallow', but we should be warned!

The play's women are not victims. They are outsiders – and Richard, at least in the beginning, is one of them. The 'lamenting widows in *Richard III*' (Rackin 79) hold a particular status. They are remainders of a past world. Unlike their husbands, fathers and sons, they have survived a change of regime. It is, however, only their bare lives that subsist – as 'widows', they do not find a place in the new world. They are socially outlawed but, in a certain sense, also untouchable (cf. Agamben): Richard's brothers stop him when he bends his murderous falchion against Margaret's breast (cf. *R3* 1.2.95–9).[35] Their place out of touch with the system of worldly power renders any direct political intervention impossible. They exist apart, and all that remains to them is the authority over their tongues – 'their speech acts of complaint' (Shortslef 120).

In fact, it is their isolation and their being cut off from any means of political power that grants them a licence to speak freely. This is what they do in Shakespeare's *Richard III*: they act as parrhesiastes (cf. Foucault *Fearless Speech*) who call the cruel things by their name; they prophesy and curse. Their roles may be traditionally 'womanly', but this does not mean that they are powerless. On the contrary, their curses can 'pierce the clouds and enter heaven' (*R3* 1.3.194) and may prove as effective as Richard's 'deep dissimulating'. It is the insubstantial, shallow, apparently only superficial and empty sources of power that Shakespeare explores with his play. It is these deep, anarchical, spurring-operations, not backed by any agency of worldly power, feeding only of the deepness of words, that he exposes onstage. He shows that they form a constitutive part of 'the poetic or tragic structure of history', of the 'secret structure', which, according to Stephen Greenblatt, 'fascinated Shakespeare' (*Hamlet in Purgatory* 173).

With the play, he also argues on his own account. Shakespeare is all too familiar with the position of the lamenting widows, at society's margin, far away from worldly power, free only to use their tongues and at the same time completely dependent on them: it is theatre's position that the play's women embody. As so often, Shakespeare makes his plays argue theatre's case themselves. Theatre has the power to affect by touching at a distance, in a 'female', seductive way. Its insubstantial touches may even touch 'more deeply', more intensely, than what we are used to accepting as real and effective – this is what Richard tells us when waking from a dream:

KING RICHARD
By the Apostle Paul, shadows tonight
Have struck more terror to the soul of Richard
Than can the substance of ten thousand soldiers
   (*R3* 5.3.216–18).

Richmond's triumph not only brings the anarchic spurring-operations of Richard, Margaret, Anne and Elizabeth to an end – it also terminates the 'deep dissimulating' of Shakespeare's play. I would therefore suggest reading it as a disguised epilogue, which mediates between the fictional world and its extra-fictional frame. The play had started with Richard's plan to prolong War's frowns, and resist the smooth smiles of the 'weak piping time of peace' (*R3* 1.1.24). It ends with Richmond's bidding God for 'smooth-faced peace, / With smiling plenty and fair prosperous days' (*R3* 5.5.33–4). There can be little doubt that the early modern playgoers, living in turbulent times still haunted by England's having 'scarred herself' (*R3* 5.5.23), shared Richmond's wish for the world into which these words dismissed them. However, the 'civil wounds are stopped' for a short time only, because many of the viewers would probably be looking forward to coming into contact with theatre's deep surfaces soon. Then, when the actors enter the stage, 'the new-healed wound of malice' will 'break out' (*R3* 2.2.125) again: although always remaining at a distance, their warlike spurring touches will certainly not fail to have their deep effect.

Notes

1. In his article 'Honeyed Toads: Sinister Aesthetics in Shakespeare's *Richard III*', Joel Elliot Slotkin refers his readers to a passage in Philip Sidney's *Defence of Poetry*, which chimes with theatre's particular relation to surfaces (cf. Slotkin 9): 'And truly even *Plato* who so ever well considereth, shall finde that in the body of his worke though the inside & strength were Philosophie, the skin as it were and beautie, depended most of Poetrie. For all stands upon Dialogues, wherein he faines many honest Burgesses of *Athens* speak of such matters [. . .]' (Sidney B2v). A few pages later, Sidney emphasises that it is the surface perfected by poetry that is responsible for the affective power of a text or the rendering of a thought: 'the Philosopher bestoweth

but a wordish description, which doth neither strike, pearce, nor possesse, the sight of the soule so much, as [the Poet] doth' (D1v). The haptic quality of *striking* or *piercing* words or images distinguishes poetry – poetry proves, according to Sidney, capable of touching from a distance, also in a material, physiological sense.

2. At least since Sigmund Freud's 'Einige Charaktertypen aus der psychoanalytischen Arbeit' (1916) Richard has been associated with an ambivalence of repulsion and attraction, which is often referred to by the term 'fascination'. This is not limited to the psychoanalytical tradition of reading *Richard III* ('[Richard is] endowed with a deadly power of fascination' (49), writes Vance Adair inspired by Lacan); Linda Charnes notes his 'fascination that always underlies revulsion' (*Notorious Identity* 38), Joel Elliot Slotkin speaks of 'demonic power and fascination' (25), Majorie Garber links the 'very fascination exerted by Richard' (81) to his deformity. My use of the term 'fascination' is indebted to Maurice Blanchot, who relates this term to solitude, an existential state of uncertainty which touches on notions of life and death, and which brings them into contact with the incommensurable (32).

3. Kristin M. Smith's claim that 'Richard is not "shaped" for the purely masculine world of the battlefield' (156) and therefore doomed to be defeated by Richmond does not do justice to Richard's past and the beginning of the play, which explicitly refers to his martial merits. Smith appears to be guided by an intuitive division of gendered spheres, which opposes war and femininity. As we will see, *Richard III* undermines those (very modern) segregations.

4. As William C. Carroll has shown (1992), *Richard III* diagnoses a desacralisation of the ritual order which transcends the king's desperate attempt of reconciliation and characterises the early modern historical setting.

5. For an extensive reading which links *Richard III* to the ideas of Carl Schmitt, especially his political theorem of the state of exception, see Rebecca Lemon (1992). Carl Schmitt plays a major role in the closing chapter of this book dedicated to *Troilus and Cressida*.

6. Richard's 'self-conscious theatricality' (Slotkin 14) has become a commonplace in criticism. 'The hero's play-acting forms the only real subject of at least the first three acts,' writes Thomas F. Van Laan (72), while Claudia Olk notes that 'Richard emphatically adopts theatricality to create himself and to direct others' (8), to give only two examples.
7. For Richard's deformity and its role in the play's reflections on history, see Garber.
8. Hastings curses himself with this punishment in *R3* 2.1.32–40.
9. '[E]vents or phenomena, such as one's birth or death, never show themselves,' writes Ken Jackson (473), referring to the philosophy of Jean-Luc Marion. As a consequence, sight does not seem to be the proper mode with which to approach such 'events or phenomena'. Touch might prove to be a more promising candidate, as a paradoxical mode that oscillates between the impossibility of reaching what it touches and the nearness which it nonetheless establishes.
10. In *Mothers in Mourning*, Nicole Loraux assigns the mother a 'preeminent position alongside the dead', which she owes 'to the unconditional privilege given once and for all by the bond of childbirth' (38).
11. Unlike Jean E. Howard and Phyllis Rackin, Tanya Pollard suggests moving away from male heroics as the standard for tragic action. Referring to *Hamlet*, she writes: 'The ideal protagonist, then, should be a woman, and one who has been pregnant' ('Conceiving Tragedy' 93). From this perspective, many of the female characters in *Richard III* cannot be called weak at all.
12. In 'Women's Time', Julia Kristeva contrasts different concepts of time, which she aligns with male and female subjectivity. She identifies 'two types of temporality (cyclical and monumental) [which] are traditionally linked to female subjectivity' (17). Both are associated with maternity (one via 'repetition', the other via 'eternity'). However, Kristeva emphasises that these two principles 'are found to be the fundamental, if not the sole, conceptions of time in numerous civilizations and experiences, particularly mystical ones' (17). These two female concepts of temporality clash with the prevailing male concept of time, which Kristeva characterises as 'time as project,

teleology, linear and prospective unfolding; time as departure, progression, and arrival – in other words, the time of history' (17). Against this background, Jean E. Howard and Phyllis Rackin's interpretation of the women's role in *Richard III* can be understood. Their feminist strategy pursues the goal which Kristeva ascribes to the first feminist generation, the women's movement, which 'aspired to gain a place in linear time as the time of project and history' (Kristeva 18). In other words, it is in terms of (male) history that the women in *Richard III* may be called 'pitiable victims'. However, instead of bemoaning their failure of securing a successful place in (male) history, I would suggest following Kristeva's feminist strategy and affirm the peculiarly female concepts of temporality which the women in Shakespeare's play embody and read their resistance to heroic (male) roles as a critical intervention.

13. Maurice Blanchot exposes another mode: 'the [literary] work itself is by implication an experience of death' (92).
14. Steve Mentz's *At the Bottom of Shakespeare's Ocean* is an important reference for this question. His emphasis on change and instability resonates with my reading of the depths in *Richard III*.
15. For a historical setting of the notion of the grotesque, see Neil Rhodes, *Elizabethan Grotesque*.
16. The Shakespearean notion of 'scattering' is reminiscent of Jacques Derrida's concept of 'dissemination' (cf. Derrida *La Dissémination*).
17. Starting from a reading of Maurice Blanchot, Roland Barthes has elaborated on the concept of neutrality, which is, for him, defined by the suspension or even dissolution of (semantic . . .) paradigms: 'I define the Neutral as that which outplays [*déjoue*] the paradigm, or rather I call Neutral everything that baffles the paradigm' (Barthes *The Neutral* 6).
18. When describing a force that '*distinguishes the ground of things* [fait *distinguer le fond des choses*]', Jean-Luc Nancy (with Maurice Blanchot as his reference) characterises the 'ground' involved in this operation in the following way: 'this ground presents itself at the same time, moreover, as the

ground *of* forms held outside of it in their *status nascendi* as well as vibrating at the same time in the correlative imminence of a *status moriendi* by which they slide back anew to ground' (Nancy 'The Image' 78). To me, Shakespeare's reflections on theatre's power of dissembling appear to be dedicated to the same (de)formative ontological force.

19. Luce Irigaray associates the notion of mucous with the feminine 'ground', or matrix, out of which the notion of stable sameness and the masculine subject rise – and whose existence is disavowed by a belief in the originality of stable sameness: 'Eternal mediators for the incarnation of the body and the world of man, women seem never to have produced the singularity of their own body and world. The originality of a sameness that would relate to incarnation. Before and after the advent into the light of day. Before and after the movement outward into the brightness of the outside of the body, of the inside of a world. This *sameness*, quite apart from everything that can be said about it from the outside, has a way of relating to its appearance which cannot be equated with that of the masculine world, as a result of the way it lives in *mucous*. [. . .] [T]he mucous has no permanence, even though it is the 'tissue' for the development of duration. The condition of possibility for the extension of time? But only insofar as it is made available to and for a masculine subject that erects itself out of the mucous. And which believes it is based on substances, on something solid. All of which requires the mucous to blur in its potency and its act (in its potentially autonomous *hypokeimenon*?) and to serve merely as a means for the elaboration of the substantial, the essential' (Irigaray *An Ethics of Sexual Difference* 93).

20. Viewed more closely, the difference between biting and polishing is a difference only in scale – a difference in intensity, not in quality.

21. Cf. 'And if you gaze for long into an abyss, the abyss gazes back into you' (Nietzsche *Beyond Good and Evil* 68).

22. For the kinship of dream, ghosts and theatre, see Greenblatt (esp. *Hamlet in Purgatory* 164–80).

23. Lady Anne may testify to this contamination of Richard's deep dissembling when she claims, at the end of the seduction scene, that Richard 'teach[es] me how to flatter you' (*R3* 1.2.226) and performs this very flattering by accepting his ring and returning his farewell wishes.
24. Nietzsche's passage reads: 'Or, as with Heinrich Kleist, who wants to do violence to the reader with his fantasy; Shakespeare, too' (*Nachlaß 1880–1882* 474; my transl.).
25. 'Pythogareer: [...] Berührung. Actio in distans' (Nietzsche *Nachlaß 1869–1874* 572).
26. Luce Irigaray is certainly the thinker of these two imaginaries and their relation to touch. In her famous 'This Sex Which is Not One', the 'touch' of male penetration interrupts the female touch of the labia, which embody and perform the actual, paradigmatic notion of touch.
27. The scene's phallic encounter could be described with recourse to what Bruce R. Smith has called the topical 'analogy between tongue and penis' (*Phenomenal Shakespeare* 167). However, whenever activated, the analogy undermines the phallic regime by contaminating it with the tongue's 'slipperiness', with potential falsehood, dissimulation – all associated with 'the female' in Shakespeare's plays.
28. For Luce Irigaray, this aiming at oneness is actually the phallic characteristic. When she asks, '*Perhaps it becomes phallic through this relationship to the one?*' (*Speculum of the Other Woman* 229), the question is rhetorical.
29. The pair of facial expressions, or rather sur-facial qualities – smooth smile and grim frown – form a key metaphor that frames the play. We had already analysed it in Richard's initial soliloquy, and it re-emerges in Richmond's monologue at the end of the play: 'Smile heaven upon this fair conjunction, / That long have frown'd upon their enmity! / [...] And let their heirs, God, if Thy will be so, / Enrich the time to come with smooth-faced peace, / With smiling plenty and fair prosperous days' (*R3* 5.5.20-34).
30. For the dynamic of circulation which is connected to having and not having, see Jacques Lacan, 'Seminar on the "Purloined Letter"'.

31. On Richard's being 'vulnerable to the "pricking" accusations of others' (125) and the early modern physiological background for this vulnerability, see Shortslef.
32. This is in part compensated for by Buckingham's assistance, who continues the devilish capacities that Richard shows in the beginning and who is, in a large part, responsible for Richard's gaining the crown.
33. To put it gendered terms, Richard joins the hegemonic, patriarchal project of 'undermining female tactility' (Karim-Cooper *The Hand* 167) in the authoritative position of the king – and thereby deprives himself of his major capacity.
34. In *A Thousand Plateaus*, Gilles Deleuze and Félix Guattari associate Richard with what they call the 'war machine', that is, nomadic, anarchical forces opposing the stability of the 'state apparatus': 'Richard III comes from elsewhere: his ventures, including those with women, derive more from a war machine than from a State apparatus. He is the traitor, springing from the great nomads and their secrecy' (*A Thousand Plateaus* 126).
35. Only when Lady Anne's outsider status ends by marrying Richard does she seem to be in the position to become a victim of his brutality. Is it the same 'law' that protects the outsider Richard when Lady Anne points his sword at him?

CHAPTER 3

CARESSING WITH WORDS:
MUCH ADO ABOUT NOTHING

'There's no true drop of blood in him to be *truly* touched with love' (*Ado* 3.2.17–18; my emph.), Don Pedro says about Benedick in Shakespeare's *Much Ado About Nothing*. His sentence forms part of a challenge: Don Pedro and his comrades have decided to test Benedick's apparent immunity to love and set him up with Beatrice. Is there really 'no true drop of blood in [Benedick] to be truly touched with love'?

Shakespeare's play acts out this very question. The capricious challenge conceived to manipulate Benedick and Beatrice into love is one of two parallel storylines in *Much Ado*. There is, however, another love story, between Claudio and Hero, which also becomes the focus of a third party's intervention – this time a malicious one, which almost leads to a tragic catastrophe: Claudio is (deceitfully) made to believe his beloved unfaithful and openly humiliates her with the harshest words. Nevertheless, in the end, the two couples marry, and the conventions of comedy are met.

The relation of the two plotlines raises an important question that has left its traces in the scholarly discussions of the play as well as in its stage history. Is the Beatrice–Benedick story merely 'a light-hearted parallel to the more serious deception in the main plot,' as Brian Vickers suggests (172)?

His claim confirms an observation that Claire McEachern voices in her introduction to the Arden3 edition. Whereas, in her opinion, literary studies tend to focus on the more serious proceedings around Hero and Claudio, the Beatrice–Benedick plot exhibits a 'tendency to upstage' it in the concrete theatre performance (McEachern 4).¹ As a result, the apparently light-hearted parallel shifts the centre of dramaturgic decisions and acquires an attention that it only rarely enjoys in the academic discourse.

Scholars have, however, identified an overarching theme that unites the two contrasting plotlines, a theme to which the play as a whole is said to be dedicated: the power of words. '*Much Ado* as a whole, is [...] a play of signification,' writes Anthony B. Dawson (221), and, in a similar vein, Maurice Hunt reads the comedy as a dramatisation of 'the potential of speech' (165). As we will see in greater detail, the two plotlines comment on each other with regard to the working of language. Both amorous unions are initiated and finally achieved by verbal power.² However, a closer look at how this power of words actually functions in Shakespeare's play returns to the division of the plotlines that the focus on the theme of language attempted to overcome. At the latest, since John Langshaw Austin's epochal *How to Do Things with Words* we have become aware that the power of words is not restricted to the dimension of signification, that is to say of producing representational meaning. Identifying the play's focus on divorcing the sign from the real (Crunelle-Vanrighe 257) and on the 'fears about never getting to "the real"' (Howard 176) in my opinion overlooks the decisive dimensions of the power of spoken words that *Much Ado* exposes on the stage. If Maurice Hunt is right, and 'what we are accustomed to call the truth' is '[a]t stake' in Shakespeare's play (Hunt 166), then it is surely in a more radical way than he envisions it to be. His longing for representational stability, for a 'control' (Hunt 171) that he sees restored in the final 'beneficial results of freezing unreliable, unconfirmable speech by writing it down [in the lovers' sonnets]' (Hunt 184) can hardly be supported in *Much Ado*. The fact that Hero's alleged dishonour is discovered to be apparently untrue marks the only instance where this constative dimension of truth comes to the fore. The role it plays for the power of words is, however, minimal: Claudio's slander obviously causes disastrous effects even though his words turn out to have had no foundation in 'truth'.

With regard to the Beatrice–Benedick story the linguistic dimension of signification and constative truth is of even less relevance. By expecting language to 'convey [...] feelings' (189) and to deliver 'unambiguous, trusted words of affection' (173) Maurice Hunt has to degrade the 'inevitable ambiguity of Beatrice's and Benedick's dialogue' (173) to 'subversive, irrelevant jests' (172). Although in a less explicit manner, the majority of scholars surprisingly joins Maurice Hunt's strategy and qualifies the witty couple's linguistic practices as either aberrations of language that has to be repaired (Magnusson) or as latently complicit with the patriarchal pattern that governs Hero's tragic experiences: 'Different as they are in style from Claudio and Hero, Benedick and Beatrice are of a piece with their world,' writes Carol Cook ('Sign and Semblance' 200) in an article whose indebtedness to the notion of signification is already betrayed by its title.[3]

Against these readings I would however suggest that Shakespeare's *Much Ado* stages more than a depiction of patriarchal order, more than a general 'masculine prerogative in language' (Cook 'Sign and Semblance' 186). It is the restriction of the power of words to the dimension of signification and of 'true' meaning that forecloses the view on the spectrum of powerful linguistic practices that *Much Ado* exposes. Besides the question of representational truth, dominant in the event of slander but rather marginal for the play's love affairs, it is a question of pragmatics,[4] of what words do in certain contexts, that Shakespeare's comedy explores. With regard to pragmatics, a fundamental difference emerges between the

Caressing with Words: *Much Ado About Nothing* [151]

linguistic strategies that the two loving couples deploy in the play. The question raised with regard to Benedick thus has to be answered against the background of the contrasting use of language of the two plotlines. It spreads to and contaminates the other characters as well: what does it mean 'to be truly touched with love'? As we will see in the following sections, the notion of touch decisively touches on the notion of truth – a contamination that shifts both concepts and provides evidence of the creative potential of Beatrice's and Benedick's linguistic prowess.

Claudio and Hero – Declarations

Claudio approaches Hero in the classical, the conventional way: by speaking 'truly'. He confesses his love – not to Hero directly, but first to Benedick and then to Don Pedro. His word is heard and passed on to the two pairs of ears that matter for the realisation of this love: to Hero's and, more importantly, to her father Leonato's. Claudio woos by proxy, not in his own voice – and he quickly wins Leonato's consent:

> LEONATO
> Count, take my daughter, and with her my fortunes. His grace hath made the match, and all grace say amen to it.
> BEATRICE
> Speak, Count, 'tis your cue.
> CLAUDIO
> Silence is the perfectest herald of joy; I were but little happy if I could say how much. Lady, as you are mine, I am yours, I give away myself for you, and dote upon the exchange.
> BEATRICE
> Speak, cousin, or, if you cannot, stop his mouth with a kiss and let not him speak neither. (*Ado* 2.1.277–91)

Now, in the presence of father and daughter, Claudio repeats his confession: 'as you are mine, I am yours,' he declares. However, Beatrice's linguistic interventions signal that Claudio's speaking 'truly' is not as sincere or authentic as one might think. As Harry Berger writes, Beatrice 'manages the scene' ('Against the Sink-a-Pace' 304): by reminding Claudio and Hero of their 'cue[s]' she lays bare the ceremonial character of this exchange of words. The 'truth' of the scene does not lie in the sincere expression of '[one's] own love's strength' or 'might' (cf. Sonnet 23, ll. 7–8) – it is the correct acting out of the pre-scripted text that renders this betrothal ritual 'true', that is to say valid and legitimate. As a result, 'Beatrice's facetious putting of words in silent, obedient Hero's mouth' does not merely 'serve[ ] [. . .] to stress the verbal dependency of Claudio's beloved in a patriarchal society,' as Maurice Hunt claims (175). As a pseudo-mistress of protocol, Beatrice wittily expresses the bias that is inherent in the conventional way of declaring one's love. By giving Hero the chance not to speak 'if [she] cannot' and instead 'stop [Claudio's] mouth with a kiss' she discloses the patriarchal structure of social reality: Hero indeed cannot speak in her own voice; as the audience knows, her answer has been dictated to her by her father and her uncle. Maurice Hunt might thus be right in suggesting that Beatrice's 'witty, mutinous protest in no way liberates Hero's *speech*' (176; my emph.) – he, however, fails to see that the intervention works in a different, no less empowering way: Beatrice creates an option of non-scripted action for Hero. Her breach of protocol, interrupting the conventional exchange of words with a mute gesture, achieves two things: 1) it exposes the structural silencing of the woman – Hero does not speak a word in this scene; 2) it gives Hero an opportunity to escape the patriarchal protocol and express her consent with a gesture that subverts the illusory 'truth' of the betrothal ritual and brings its rhetorics to an abrupt end: 'let not him speak neither.'[5]

As there is no stage direction, it is a dramaturgic decision whether Hero kisses Claudio or not – I would, however, read Beatrice's comment that Hero 'tells [Claudio] in his ear that he is in her heart' as an ironic testimony of intimate body contact. Whatever the case may be, if anyone is 'truly touched with love' in this scene, then it happens outside the betrothal ritual, outside the 'perfect ceremony of love's right' (cf. Sonnet 23, l. 6). The 'truth' of this touch is not to be judged by the legal standards of ceremony or protocol. It is 'true' because it somehow goes beyond the contractual force of conventional speech acts.

The scene of their final reunion exhibits how much Claudio's relation to Hero is established by the rhetorical strategy of declaration – and that is to say of speech acts stabilised by (patriarchal) convention. Claudio has discovered that he has slandered his innocent beloved Hero for no reason at all. In order to allay her father Leonato's fury, he has accepted the latter's request to marry whomsoever Leonato wishes. A marriage ritual is celebrated and Claudio presented with a veiled bride:

LEONATO
[. . .] I do give you her.
CLAUDIO
Why then she's mine. [to Hero] Sweet, let me see your face.
LEONATO
No, that you shall not till you take her hand
Before this friar and swear to marry her. (*Ado* 5.4.54–7)

The scene mirrors the betrothal ceremony – and reduces it to its defining parameters. Claudio marries his beloved Hero – but Leonato insists that he does so without knowing. Love is thus absent from this ceremony. It is obviously no necessary ingredient of the 'true', that is, valid marriage ritual. Instead of a marriage of 'true minds' (cf. Sonnet 116, l. 1), the ceremony's solemn declarations perform a transaction. The speech acts of declaring and swearing enforce a contract whose partners are all male. Hero is not present as a person – she is veiled and thus not recognised by Claudio; she is the object of a bargain that transfers property between two men (cf. Rubin).[6] As Janice Hays has written with regard to the slander scene: 'Hero is for [Leonato and Claudio] little more than a pawn on the masculine chessboard' (87); she is simply 'to be traded to Claudio' (Berger 'Against the Sink-a-Pace' 304).

The extreme, the minimalist conditions that Leonato imposes on this marriage ceremony retroact also on the initial betrothal scene. The mutual declarations of love, the apparently mutual giving of oneself to the other, are retrospectively unmasked as rather misleading decorum. It is not love that touches when the declarations are spoken, but the force of contract. Far from a mutual and spontaneous gesture like the shared contact of the lips that could be an expression of an 'inly touch of love' (*TGV* 2.7.17), the contract binds with forces that come from without. As an effect, the dénouement of the Claudio–Hero plot, their apparently miraculous marriage, not only finally realises their love – it at the same time questions its true foundation. If we want to accept their love as 'true' love, we must accept it as a given that is hardly – if at all – performed within Shakespeare's play; in any case, the *linguistic* strategy of declaration on which Claudio's and Hero's relation is based does not enable the two 'to be truly touched with love'.

Beatrice and Benedick – Caresses

Benedick enjoys the reputation of being different. Don Pedro's provocative statement cited at the beginning of the chapter reflects this reputation: 'There's no *true* drop of blood in him,' he claims, and thus ascribes a humoral disposition to Benedick which differs significantly from that of the normal courtier. His less liable, firm or constant nature disqualifies him for the declarative, contractual mode of love that Claudio represents:

> BENEDICK
> [...] But it is certain I am loved of all ladies, only you excepted; and I would I could find in my heart that I had not a hard heart, for *truly* I love none.
> BEATRICE
> [...] I had rather hear my dog bark at a crow, than a man swear he loves me. (*Ado* 1.1.118–26, my emph.)

Like Claudio, Benedick begins his liaison with a confession, with an act of speaking 'truly': 'for truly I love none.' His is, however, a confession that categorically precludes all love – or, rather, all love that works in the contractual, confessional mode of 'truly': 'for truly – I love none.' It is in this aversion to a certain kind of love (speech) that Benedick and Beatrice meet. As Beatrice asserts some lines later, she is immune to the speech act of one's swearing love to her, which obviously sets her off from her fellow ladies. Like Benedick, she is different. She has 'no true drop of blood' in her as well – speaking 'truly' is not her talent either: 'I beseech your grace pardon me,' she bids Don Pedro, 'I was born to speak all mirth and no matter' (*Ado* 2.1.303–4). 'The bond between Beatrice and Benedick is something genuine,' writes Steven Rose (148) and thereby voices an impression that the majority of viewers share. The similarity in nature, in humoral disposition, that somehow couples Benedick and Beatrice manifests itself primarily as a shared inclination to an unconventional, to a provocative and unsettling, use of language: 'Through their language, and in their wit, Beatrice and Benedick recognize each her and his match, or likeness. Their repulsion is epiphenomenal to a deeper attraction, a paradoxical gravity that attracts by repelling' (Shoaf 160). Despite their high rank, they both play the role of the fool or jester in their respective social environments.

Given their linguistic inclinations it is all the more astonishing that Don Pedro expects a 'dumb-show' from the trick he and his confederates play on 'Lady Tongue' (*Ado* 2.2.252) and her equally talkative Gentleman. The plan is to make them both believe that they are incredibly loved by the other and see what happens once their love is kindled:

> DON PEDRO
> [...] The sport will be when they hold one an opinion of another's dotage, and no such matter. That's the scene I would see, which will be merely a dumb-show. (*Ado* 2.3.208–11)

The scenes that not only Don Pedro and his confederates but also the audience in the theatre witness with great pleasure are anything but a 'dumb-show'; in contrast to Claudio and Hero who barely talk to each other, Benedick and Beatrice act out their intensifying love in their usual manner: as a witty exchange of words.

The initiating impulse of their flirtatious tête-à-tête must look familiar to us:

> BENEDICK
> I do love nothing in the world so well as you. Is not that strange?
> BEATRICE
> As strange as the thing I know not. It were as possible for me to say I loved nothing so well as you. But believe me not – and yet I lie not. I confess nothing, nor I deny nothing. (*Ado* 4.1.267–72)

By supplementing only a few words, Benedick transforms his initial 'truly I love none' into an apparently conventional declaration of love: 'I do love nothing in the world – so well as you.' Beatrice's surprising response is, however, quick to distort the conventional pattern that a declaration of love invokes. Instead of following the expectations of the lovers' discourse and responding with a reciprocal confession of her love, she fends off Benedick's declarative speech act. Beatrice, who, as we remember, 'had rather hear [her] dog bark at a crow, than a man swear he loves [her]', faces the rhetorical challenge to neutralise the conventional, the contractual performative power of Benedick's loving confession. But how does she manage to do so?

It is this art of giving quick and witty responses that characterises the couple and the play as a whole: 'The use of repartee in *Much Ado* is the most brilliant in Shakespeare,' writes Brian Vickers (175), adding that 'repartee is more than a linguistic device here: to Beatrice and Benedick it is a way of life, a mutual witty antagonism' (176). Vickers is certainly right that the couple's verbal 'fencing is so brilliant as to almost resist criticism' (175) – I do, however, think that there are some theoretical reflections available that Vickers did not have in mind for his study of style – reflections by French thinkers such as Roland Barthes and Jacques Derrida that enable us to move a step closer to what is happening in this art of repartee.

Beatrice proves to be a master of what Roland Barthes has called 'Beside-the-Point Answers [*Réponses à côté*]' (*The Neutral* 109). Beatrice 'frighten[s] the word out of his right sense' (*Ado* 5.2.52–3), as Benedick once puts it. Beatrice unhinges the reference of Benedick's confession by indicating the instability of Benedick's comparison – how well he loves Beatrice cannot be determined, because, as Benedick himself inadvertently claims, there is no thing available in this world to measure his love. His words are thus discovered by Beatrice to be empty. Without the risk of being bound by contractual forces issuing from her speech act, Beatrice could even reply using the very words that are expected from her; she could give back the identical formula, and nevertheless 'confess [. . .] nor [. . .] deny nothing'. The speech acts of reciprocal declarations of love are hollowed out, deprived of their conventional, of their contractual power.

Beatrice's linguistic intervention is, however, not merely destructive; it does not work as a reactive move of defence –

the neutrality she achieves is not the empty grey of a world immune to love. She does not 'deny' Benedick's advances – on the contrary, she reciprocates them! She affirms them by shifting the linguistic environment of their loving discourse towards what Bruce R. Smith has called 'a "linguistics of touch"' (*Phenomenal Shakespeare* 171). It is by suggesting this shifting of the linguistic environment that my reading departs from the feminist analyses of the play that read it as representative of the inescapability of patriarchal structures, studies which argue that '[t]he women in *Much Ado* demonstrate in their different ways their entrapment within the contradictions of this system of difference' (Cook 'Sign and Semblance' 190).

Benedick's and Beatrice's 'witty, erotically charged sparring' (Greenblatt 'Fiction and Friction' 89) actually undermines well-known, general claims like Carol Cook's regarding 'language as the domain of masculine privilege and masculine aggression' ('Sign and Semblance' 186) or 'speech as phallic and capable of violent penetration' ('Sign and Semblance' 189). As pertinent as these assertions are for an analysis of patriarchal society, they somehow miss the point with regard to what Shakespeare puts on stage with the Benedick and Beatrice plot. Beatrice is surely not a good example for a 'masculine prerogative in language' (Cook 'Sign and Semblance' 186), and as a detailed analysis of the couple's complicated mode of confessing love to each other shows, the two do not simply 'take up their places within that gendered order [. . .] [w]hen led to confess love for one another' (Howard 180). Moreover, despite their finally obeying to the conventional comic end in marriage, Benedick and Beatrice can hardly be said to act 'as subjects of a love discourse in which a role for each to play is clearly marked, the role of the "normal" male and female' (Howard 178) – one has to close one's ears to all of their famous witty fencing to arrive at these conclusions.

'Claudio and Hero are better suited to the currently popular study of patriarchy,' Marta Straznicky suggests (150), and her observations are confirmed by the strategic trajectory that studies of patriarchy in *Much Ado* follow. It is the broad premises themselves – language as phallic, penetrating and essentially male – that lead scholars like Carol Cook to qualify Beatrice's linguistic prowess as merely 'usurp[ing] the masculine prerogative of language and wit' ('Sign and Semblance' 190) and instead celebrate Hero's 'silence and the exposure of vulnerability that are the real threats to Messinan men' ('Sign and Semblance' 191). In contrast, I would like to claim that when more attention is paid to Beatrice's and Benedick's actual language use different results are disclosed. This approach discovers verbal expression that is, in a very precise way, not 'phallic', speech that is characterised precisely by evading 'violent penetration' and that develops a different kind of power or force.

Beatrice's intervention is directed against the discursive regime of speaking 'truly' that automatically converts love into truth – loving *contact* into *contract*. Hers is 'a verbal [. . .] act of decontextualization [*un acte verbal [. . .] de dé-situation*]' (Barthes *The Neutral* 121) that opens up an opportunity to answer lovingly in her own voice and avoids merely repeating the conventional part of the 'perfect ceremony of love's right'.

Beatrice's neutralisation of the contractual force of love declarations does what every resistance against discursive rules has to do. According to Roland Barthes, it 'needs to be accompanied by a connotation, by a theatre (it's a "gesture") that will transform it into something active (putting an end to the image of coward-passive) and unexpected (leaving the contender speechless, and a bit ridiculous?)' (*The Neutral* 118).

Beatrice definitely represents this image of the active, the unheard of. In contrast to Hero, she does not remain passively subjected to the patriarchal regime of 'true' speech and contract. As we have seen, her intervening in Hero's betrothal ritual has supplemented the verbal ceremony with a haptic gesture – a loving touch – that allowed Hero to escape the pre-scripted role and act out her own love. The gesture with which Beatrice lives out her own inclinations towards Benedick is purely verbal. It suspends the 'truth' of speaking: 'But believe me not – and yet I lie not. I confess nothing, nor I deny nothing.' Language is stripped of its referential function and thus also loses its performative power. However, it is thereby not rendered useless. On the contrary, Beatrice's unheard-of reduction of language might foster a linguistic capacity that has been prevented by its dominant, its more violent contractual powers. Once language ceases to contractually codify one's love, it might begin to make love – once it ceases to serve for confessing it or promising it, for expressing it or representing it with words – it might begin to establish 'a warm, perhaps heated relation of proximity' (Loxley and Robson 125) and become a loving gesture itself.[7]

Shakespeare's *Much Ado* is about *Nothing*: confessing *Nothing*, denying *Nothing*.[8] It is not about how to do things with words – which is always a contractual affair. It is about the fragile operation of how to do nothing – and thus make love – with words. But what does this mean? How does Beatrice's verbal strategy work?

Beatrice and Benedick provide the audience with further instances of their witty love that promise to help us find answers to these questions.

> BENEDICK
> [. . .] I protest I love thee.
> BEATRICE
> Why then, God forgive me.
> BENEDICK
> What offence, sweet Beatrice?
> BEATRICE
> You have stayed me in a happy hour; I was about to protest
> I love you.
> BENEDICK
> And do it, with all thy heart.

BEATRICE
I love you with so much of my heart that none is left to protest. (*Ado* 4.1.278–86)

It is again a speech act of declaration that opens the loving dialogue. Benedick protests, that is to say he formally and emphatically declares by invoking a third party – the Latin ancestor of the verb 'protest', *testor*, goes back to the etymon *tri, three (cf. Walde). It takes three to protest. Like Claudio's swearing his love before the friar, Benedick's protestation of love is not merely addressed to his beloved – his solemn words appeal to a higher (presumably male) authority that watches over the declaration's 'truth', and in this way provides the speech act with its contractual, binding power.[9] It is therefore not surprising that Beatrice's 'Beside-the-Point Answer' sets out with naming this authority: 'Why then, God forgive me.' As her asking for God's forgiveness implies, she will disappoint this third party; she will exclude it from the love that happens between the two of them. As a consequence, she will rid the famous three words of love of their performative, their contractual power. She again neutralises Benedick's declarative speech act and thus turns it into a loving gesture, a 'proffering' as Roland Barthes (*A Lover's Discourse* 149) choses to call it: '*I-love-you* has no "elsewhere" – it is the word of the (maternal, amorous) dyad' (*A Lover's Discourse* 148). When Benedick asks her to 'protest her love' 'with all her heart', he inadvertently provides Beatrice with all that is needed to exhibit the absurdity of this request: 'I love you with so much of my heart that none is left to protest.' The speech acts of protesting or declaring do not belong or contribute to making love.[10] On the contrary, they do something different and thus threaten to convert a relationship of love into a procedure of contract, of rights, of exchange and bargain.

Beatrice's witty sentence does to itself what her trenchant repartees used to do to Benedick's confessions. It is, initially, itself a declaration of love – a declaration of love, however, that performatively undermines its own possibility as an effective speech act. Her old motto still holds true: '[B]elieve me not – and yet I lie not. I confess nothing, nor I deny nothing.'

And yet, her verbal manoeuvre is an active, an affirmative move. Tongue-in-cheek, she 'frighten[s] the word' protest 'out of his right sense': put at the end of the sentence, it oscillates between its meaning in transitive and in intransitive use. Unlike Benedick, she does not protest her love – however, she does not protest against it, and that is to say against Benedick's advances, either. On the contrary, she obviously loves him with all her heart.

Beatrice deploys a consistent linguistic strategy. Her aim is to escape the seizure, the encroachment, the violent and lasting touch of contract and instead make room for a more fragile practice of words; a practice that does not use language as an instrument to reach predefined goals. Her words do not appropriate what they touch. Beatrice's gesture is always a double, a paradoxical one. It keeps at a distance what it approaches – and at the same time it approaches what it keeps at a distance. In Jacques Derrida's words, Beatrice 'touches without touching', her words 'caress':[11]

> That is why I am tempted to say [. . .] that there where I touch without touching, in caressing, the order of the promise itself is what finds itself thereupon exceeded or disqualified, and with it the order of what one quietly thinks and fits under the category of performatives, of an 'I can' that would have the power to produce an event through a legitimatized speech act, in a sure context, and following agreed-upon conventions. The event as such, if there is any, couldn't care less about the performative or the constative. (Derrida *On Touching* 78–9)

The fragile event that Beatrice's verbal caresses are producing is called love – love 'couldn't care less about the performative or the constative'. Caressing with words works differently.

This is best illustrated by the 'scene' that Don Pedro – and probably the whole audience – would so eagerly see: Benedick's and Beatrice's being confronted with the 'truth' of their having been played upon, which happens during their marriage ritual. Not surprisingly, their marriage does not quite celebrate the 'perfect ceremony of love's right':

BEATRICE
[*Unmasks.*]:
[. . .] What is your will?
BENEDICK
Do not you love me?
BEATRICE
                        Why no, no more than reason.
BENEDICK
Why then your uncle and the prince and Claudio
Have been deceived – they swore you did.
BEATRICE
Do not you love me?
BENEDICK
                        Troth no, no more than reason.
BEATRICE
Why then my cousin, Margaret and Ursula
Are much deceived, for they did swear you did.
BENEDICK
They swore that you were almost sick for me.
BEATRICE
They swore that you were well-nigh dead for me.
BENEDICK
'Tis no such matter. Then you do not love me?
BEATRICE
No truly, but in friendly recompense. (*Ado* 5.4.73–83)

Viewed from the perspective of Don Pedro, Claudio and Leonato – that is to say from the perspective of those who embody and thus expect conventional 'true' love talk – Benedick and Beatrice indeed perform a 'dumb-show'.

No declaration, no confession, not even the slightest expression of their love passes the two fools' lips. The 'performative' as well as the 'constative' (cf. Austin) remain the affair of others: they are 'deceived' – and it is them that 'swear'. The three little words – *I-love-you* – are not pronounced. Both Beatrice and Benedick evade love's quasi magical formula and thus distort the declarative procedure of the ceremony. They confess nothing. However, don't they explicitly deny their love this time?

If we listen with Don Pedro's, Claudio's or Leonato's ears, we would have to conclude that, yes, this is what happens in the scene. However, we have learned from Beatrice that constative truth is not what her love talk is about: '[B]elieve me not – and yet I lie not.' Even if the three little words are not pronounced – what Benedick and Beatrice do with words in this scene is exactly what speaking the *I-love-you*-formula does according to Roland Barthes: Benedick's and Beatrice's speaking 'is not a symptom, it is an action' (*A Lover's Discourse* 152; transl. altered). They make love with words. '[One] speak[s] so that [the other] may answer, and the scrupulous form (the letter) of the answer will assume an effective value, in the manner of a formula' (Barthes *A Lover's Discourse* 152). It is indeed the 'scrupulous form (the letter) of the answer' that this loving dialogue is all about. Benedick and Beatrice faithfully and meticulously repeat the characteristic formulas issued from the other's lips. They take, as Benedick once puts it, 'pleasure [. . .] in the message' (*Ado* 2.3.244).

Their verbal behaviour is inspired by one of the great lovers of world literature: Ovid's nymph Echo (cf. Ovidius liber tertius, ll. 339–510). There is, however one decisive difference: their story is not of a desperate, unreciprocated love, but one of shared, mutual and thus paradoxically intertwined action. They are both the other's echo. Beatrice echoes Benedick's question: 'Do not you love me?'; Benedick resounds Beatrice's answer: 'no more than reason.' In fact, almost every syllable of their conversation turns out to have a correlate in the other's, in the lover's discourse. The few words that stand on their own are charged with metalingual meaning. Their acted-out love is not a question of 'matter' – but of 'friendly recompense'. They do not delight in what is said: 'Everything is in the *speaking* of it' (Barthes *A Lover's Discourse* 149). 'Jouissance is not spoken, but it speaks' (Barthes *A Lover's Discourse* 149; transl. altered). The scene exhibits

> the necessity, for the amorous subject, not only to be loved in return, to know it, to be sure of it, etc. (all operations which do not exceed the level of the signified), but to hear it said in the form which is as affirmative, as complete, as articulated as his own. (Barthes *A Lover's Discourse* 152)

Benedick and Beatrice completely leave out, they escape, they negate and abandon the message's signified content – they thereby reduce their *I-love-you* to its effective operation: 'what matters is the physical, bodily, labial proffering of the word: open your lips and let it out (be obscene)' (Barthes *A Lover's Discourse* 152).

The event of love cannot be enquired after with a question: 'Then you do not love me?' Love is 'no such matter'; it is no thing whose absence or presence could be confirmed with 'true' words. Love has to be *made* as a linguistic, a labial caress.[12] This is not an operation of 'truth'. It is not done 'truly', 'but in friendly recompense'. Paradoxically enough, 'to be truly touched with love' asks for a suspension of 'truth'. That is why Benedick and Beatrice, the two with 'no true drop of blood' in them, turn out to be so talented for it. Only when the contractual, the patriarchal frame has lost its seizing grip can love start to affect as an event between two beings. Not as a weak word of consent answering the male dictate of contractual conditions, but 'in friendly recompense': as an active, a reciprocal gesture, of unheard-of mutuality between intimate friends – this is 'to be truly touched with love'.

And Yet: 'Kill Claudio' – The Gendered Trouble of Walking the Talking

And yet: the neat distinction between Beatrice and Benedick's loving contacts and Claudio and Hero's binding contracts is undermined once in the play. This happens at a crucial moment, and, to make matters worse, in the very middle of Beatrice and Benedick's linguistic caresses. It is the scene of their 'protesting' their love, analysed above, that is framed by circumstances that are not at all compatible with the notion of 'caressing' in the way we have developed it. Benedick's famous 'I do love nothing in the world so well as you', with which we began our reading of their linguistic caresses, is preceded by the two characters talking about the wrongs that Hero, Beatrice's close friend, has suffered. In the course of their small dialogue, Beatrice lays out a cue that Benedick will later pick up for his purposes: 'Ah, how much might the man deserve of me that would right her!' (*Ado* 4.1.261-2). Of course, Benedick – not without reason, one might say – feels himself to be this man. The chivalric quest to avenge Hero in order to win the love of Beatrice is latently present throughout the scene as an option for substituting the game of verbal wit for something 'more material', less playful and untrustworthy. It is Benedick who eventually chooses this option; however, the unmistakable statement of a chivalric deed remains closely tied to the power of words. In fact, the deed Beatrice asks of Benedick forms a supplement for the confession of love that they both appear to be unable to perform linguistically.

Here is a longer passage, parts of which we already analysed above. This time, attention shall be paid to the shift caused by Benedick picking up Beatrice's earlier cue and resorting to the classical means of proving one's love by deed:

BENEDICK
By my sword, Beatrice, thou lovest me.
BEATRICE
Do not swear and eat it.

BENEDICK
I will swear by it that you love me, and I will make him eat that says I love not you.
BEATRICE
Will you not eat your word?
BENEDICK
With no sauce that can be devised to it. I protest I love thee.
BEATRICE
Why then, God forgive me.
BENEDICK
What offence, sweet Beatrice?
BEATRICE
You have stayed me in a happy hour; I was about to protest that I loved you.
BENEDICK
And do it, with all thy heart.
BEATRICE
I love you with so much of my heart that none is left to protest.
BENEDICK
Come, bid me do anything for thee.
BEATRICE
Kill Claudio.
BENEDICK
Ha, not for the wide world.
BEATRICE
You kill me to deny it. Farewell. (*Ado* 4.1.273–90)

The complicated play between 'sword' and 'word' (which probably sounded very similar in early modern English) is initiated by what appears to be a conventional formula of swearing used by Benedick: 'By my sword, Beatrice, [. . .]'. However, as Beatrice notices right away, Benedick 'eat[s]' his pledge, that is, forswears it, even before confessing or promising anything: instead of protesting his own love, he paradoxically 'pledges' – or rather postulates – Beatrice's love. Beatrice knows that Benedick is a notorious word-eater; a sword, however, does not pass one's lips as harmlessly as a foreswearing word. It is this implication that Beatrice hints at by making use of the oscillating reference of 'eat *it*'. Viewed closely, the option of walking the talking, that is, shifting from word to sword, has been activated already in Benedick's initial 'pledge'. Read as a statement instead of a confession or pledge, his words are confirmed as true by the following, famous imperative: it is with regard to or even because of his sword that Beatrice supposedly loves him. However, as long as the fencing between the two stays on the level of an exchange of witty words, Benedick proves able to parry Beatrice's verbal attacks. She may have succeeded in urging him to extend his initial paradoxical pledge, which now contains a promise in his own name. However, Benedick's 'and I will make him eat that says I love not you' uses the same equivocation Beatrice had employed in order to neutralise the consequences of his speech act: with his promise he grants himself the option of eating his words when saying 'I love not you'. Beatrice's answer indicates that she again sees through Benedick's escape and the two start into the second round of their witty game, consisting of the mutual 'protestations' analysed above.

As this second round ends with the same result, Benedick draws the joker: he invites Beatrice to perform the speech act that builds the bridge from word to sword, from language to deed. Shakespeare seems to have choreographed this central passage even into the very names of his protagonists: Benedick's alludes to his talent for eloquence – *bene dictum*, 'well said' – and it is Benedick himself who makes the audience aware of an imperative inscribed in Beatrice's name that echoes her central challenge of the scene: when Benedick repeatedly calls her name in an attempt to stop her leaving, Beatrice cuts him short, resulting in 'Beat–' (*Ado* 4.1.312). It is not accidental that this unintended 'imperative' answers Beatrice's bemoaning Hero, who is 'wronged, [. . .] slandered, [. . .] undone' (*Ado* 4.1.310–1). This time, it is not up to

Beatrice to live up to her name, but to Benedick, who is supposed to make her happy instead (*Beatrice* = 'she who makes happy'). However, would he have ultimately succeeded in making her happy (*beata*) by having 'beaten' (*Ado* 5.4.108) ('killed') – Benedick's own word – Claudio in a duel?

In other words – how seriously can Beatrice's imperative be taken? Does Benedick's prompt, spontaneous reply help in finding an answer to this question? Although Benedick has been waiting to be asked to perform some kind of revenge for Hero's wrongs, Beatrice's imperative clearly surprises him, catches him on the wrong foot. It is not about 'devising impossible slanders' (*Ado* 2.1.126), not about 'ill word[s that] may empoison liking' (*Ado* 3.1.86); caressing is to turn into stabbing, the loving touch into a lethal one, into one that ultimately transgresses the mutual suspension of touch and annihilates the other (instead of being open to its touch in return). Benedick is forced to leave his comfort zone of verbal wit and the power of words. In fact, Beatrice's imperative puts Benedick in a place which resembles the one in which Don Pedro, Claudio and Hero had placed her and Benedick: she knows that killing Claudio is not Benedick's 'office' (*Ado* 4.1.266); his cowardice is an open secret. According to Don Pedro – who toys with Benedick, whom he knows to be eavesdropping – Benedick 'avoids [quarrels] with great discretion, or undertakes them with a most Christian-like fear' (*Ado* 2.3.186–7). Beatrice even suspects him of not having killed a single enemy at war: 'But how many hath he killed? For indeed I promised to eat all of his killing' (*Ado* 1.1.40–1). It is not despite him suiting the task poorly but exactly because of the apparent mismatch, I would argue, that Beatrice chooses this particular knight for her quest. In this regard, the sub-subplot of Benedick's violent revenge mirrors the subplot of him being set up with Beatrice. We may be witnessing a Chinese-box structure of plays-within-plays: it looks as if Beatrice's imperative introduces the potential for tragedy into the comedy. However, by casting Benedick in the role of the chivalric revenger, the tragedy turns out another comedy, a comedy-within-the-comedy plotted by Beatrice.

This comedy is primarily a comedy of the sexes. Beatrice herself introduces the gender bias of her plans of revenge: 'It is a man's office', she states, 'but not yours [Benedick's]' (*Ado* 4.1.266). According to the logic of the formulation, Benedick is a man – but not quite. Unavoidably, the question arises: why? What is it that separates him from 'his own' gender, and does he have any chance at all of standing the trial of manliness to which Beatrice has challenged him?

Benedick may be merely a type, perhaps even the epitome of the man of his time, just one of the '[s]cambling, outfacing, fashion-monging boys', as Antonio calls them, '[t]hat lie, and cog, and flout, deprave, and slander, / [. . .] And speak off half a dozen dangerous words, / How they might hurt their enemies, if they durst, / And this is all' (*Ado* 5.1.94–9). Beatrice takes the same line when provocatively complaining to Benedick that 'manhood is melted into courtesies, valour into compliment, and men are only turned into tongue, and trim ones, too' (*Ado* 4.1.317–19). The question remains as to why exactly Benedick, who may be said to be 'all tongue', and whose cowardice is legendary, should be chosen to redeem manhood – if not for the sake of comedy. There can be no doubt: Benedick's turning from word to sword promises to produce another 'dumb-show' (*Ado* 2.3.211).

'By my sword': the sword plays a major role in the quest set up by Beatrice. However, it does not merely symbolically represent the discourse of chivalric heroics and manliness that is associated with justice, bringing death and letting live. Shakespeare's play makes use of the sword with regard to its phallic involvement in the dynamics of the sexes, as psychoanalysis would put it. Benedick is a man, in so far as he, unlike the female figures, bears a sword. The phallic

Caressing with Words: *Much Ado About Nothing* [171]

implication is exposed by Margaret in an exchange of witty remarks with Benedick, who, tired of talking to her (instead of Beatrice), acknowledges his verbal defeat:

BENEDICK
A most manly wit, Margaret, it will not hurt a woman. And so, I pray thee, call Beatrice. I give thee the bucklers.
MARGARET
Give us the swords; we have bucklers of our own.
BENEDICK
If you use them, Margaret, you must put in the pikes with a vice, and they are dangerous weapons for maids.
(*Ado* 5.2.15–22)

Margaret twists the conventional phrase used by Benedick into a formulation of the phallic dynamics of heterosexuality: she associates the bucklers, a passive means of defence, usually curved in form, with the female vulva, which she takes, in the typical heterosexual logic, to be in need of the 'sword', meaning the penis. Benedick refuses to be drawn into this dynamic of giving and taking – despite the fact that, as a man, his possession of what is needed raises him to a powerful position. Instead, he points Margaret to an alternative use of the female bucklers, one which promises to satisfy the needs without resorting to swords: a spike in the centre forms part of the buckler (no sword needed); putting it in 'with a vice' combines the sense of 'screwing' (cf. *OED*, 'vice, *n.2*'), that is, having sexual intercourse, and the corruption of morals (cf. *OED*, 'vice, *n.1*'): no matter whether 'putting in the pikes with a vice' signifies masturbation or homoerotic practices, Benedick advocates a deviant solution to the problem, one that does not involve swords and therefore does not comply to the heterosexual norm.

Apart from its obvious sexual innuendos, Margaret's 'Give us the swords' repeats and renews Beatrice's imperative. Benedick's second answer, less characterised by surprise and more by his typical use of wit, may not so much disclose his stance towards the initial imperative, but the possible sexual implications of the latter. 'Kill Claudio' may also be read as a test of sexual orientation; Benedick bears a sword – is he, however, able and willing to use it 'appropriately'?

Claudio is not any 'victim' to be killed by Benedick's hand; he is his current 'sworn brother' (*Ado* 1.1.68), as Beatrice puts it. With regard to the plan of revenge, Benedick may thus be the odd one out in a very personal way. It is again Beatrice who raises suspicions about the nature of Claudio and Benedick's close relation. Even before finding out about Claudio, made to appear as her rival to Benedick by Beatrice's questioning, she enquires after – and jokes about – Benedick's stance towards men:

> MESSENGER
> And a good soldier too, lady.
> BEATRICE
> And a good soldier to a lady; but what is he to a lord?
> MESSENGER
> A lord to a lord, a man to a man, stuffed with all honourable virtues.
> BEATRICE
> It is so, indeed, he is no less than a stuffed man; but for the stuffing – well, we are all mortal. (*Ado* 1.1.50–6)

There can be little doubt about the sexual nature of Beatrice's punning with 'stuffed', as Margaret two acts later cracks the same joke, this time at Beatrice's expense:

> BEATRICE
> I am stuffed, cousin. I cannot smell.
> MARGARET
> A maid, and stuffed! There's goodly catching of cold.
> (*Ado* 3.4.58–60)

Once the suspicion of a 'dubious' sexual orientation is raised, not only Beatrice's talking about the 'sworn brother[s']' 'voyage to the devil' (*Ado* 1.1.77–8) but also certain formulations by Benedick himself are heard with different ears. He himself raising the question of his being 'converted' (*Ado* 2.3.21) is a case in point:

BENEDICK
[. . .] I have railed so long against marriage. But doth not the appetite alter? A man loves the meat in his youth that he cannot endure in his age. [. . .] [T]he world must be peopled. (*Ado* 2.3.228–33)

Benedick's food imagery somehow transgresses his merely quarrelling with his attitude towards marriage. The word 'meat' opens up a huge spectrum of meanings, referring mainly to different aspects of the sexualised human body. Benedick is not asking himself whether some kind of (sexual) appetite has begun to arise in him, but wonders whether his appetite 'alter[s]'. The proverb he associates, significantly, does not refer to his new 'matrimonial' appetite but to the old, the one that is to be replaced. The semantic oscillations of 'meat' even capture this sexual conversion: 'meat' being used as a slang word for 'penis' (cf. *OED*, 'meat, *n.*' 6.b.) may be implied by 'the meat in his youth';[13] 'meat' can, however, also signify '[t]he human body (esp. a woman's body) regarded as an instrument of sexual pleasure' (*OED*, 'meat, *n.*' 6.a.). At the very beginning of the play Leonato rather prophetically alludes to this new, apparently heterosexual appetite that could be acted out between Benedick and Beatrice, introducing an alternative to Beatrice's toying with Benedicks supposed homoerotic tendencies that dominate the scene:

LEONATO
Faith, niece, you tax Signor Benedick too much. But he'll be meet [meat!] with you, I doubt it not. (*Ado* 1.1.43–4)

To cut a long story short: is it Benedick's sexuality, his proving to be a prickly thistle (*Carduus benedictus*, cf. *Ado* 3.4.67–70) instead of handling a useful sword, that Beatrice's quest brings to the light? The assassination of his 'sworn brother' proves, obviously, not to be his office – what about his love for Beatrice?

Things seem to be simple: Benedick fails the trial of manliness, therefore the knight shall not win the princess. However, the princess, Beatrice, has a hand in Benedick's failure. It is for her that Benedick gives up an outward sign of manliness, his beard. Don Pedro and his comrades joyfully read Benedick's 'loss of a beard' (*Ado* 3.2.45) as an infallible sign of his having 'ta'en th'infection' (*Ado* 2.3.122) of their plotting. Her distaste for beards, which she voices in the presence of Leonato and Antonio, must have either been common knowledge or somehow passed on to Benedick:

> BEATRICE
> Just, if [God] send me no husband. For the which blessing I am at him upon my knees every morning and evening. Lord, I could not endure a husband with a beard on his face! I had rather lie in the woollen.
> LEONATO
> You may light on a husband that hath no beard.
> BEATRICE
> What should I do with him – dress him in my apparel and make him my waiting gentlewoman? He that hath a beard is more than a youth, and he that hath no beard is less than a man: and he that is more than a youth is not for me, and he that is less than a man, I am not for him.
> (*Ado* 2.1.25–32)

However, Benedick does not meet Beatrice's severe criteria just by having seen a barber. In fact, the riddle of someone beardless, 'not more than youth' but not 'less than a man' appears to be unsolvable. It would be if the hegemonic rules and assumptions of patriarchal, heteronormative society were applied. In fact, the figure that speaks these very words on stage embodies one possible solution to the riddle: a beardless youth who is not less than a man (merely a young 'man') but more: a woman! Beatrice's suggestion of dressing the beardless husband up and making him her waiting woman works as a metatheatrical joke about her part being played by a boy. Beatrice's paradoxical sexual preferences, however, transport the gender troubles implied in the practices of early modern theatre into the drama's fictional world: she does not look for or even help to bring about (in Benedick) the 'golden mean' of ideal manliness (cf. Crichton 623); Beatrice's desire is queer – it troubles the order of the sexes and longs for something different.

It is in this difference, this deviance, that Benedick and Beatrice meet. Rumours similar to the ones that Beatrice spreads about Benedick could be constructed about her as well: does her confession of having been Hero's 'bedfellow' 'this twelvemonth' (*Ado* 4.1.149), despite the convention of sharing beds in early modernity (cf. Classen 4), imply a certain homoerotic openness? Significantly, Benedick, the possible rival, explicitly asks her whether she spent last night with Hero. It is commonly agreed upon that Beatrice, at least with regard to language, is more 'phallic' than befits a woman: 'She speaks poniards,' Benedick says of her, 'and every word stabs' (*Ado* 2.1.226–7). 'O that I were a man' (*Ado* 4.1.302), Beatrice exclaims – her prickly tongue might be said to have led her halfway to realising this wish. However, instead of speculating about her gender or sexuality, we should turn to Benedick's answering Beatrice's desperate, gender-troubling wishes:

BEATRICE
[. . .] O that I were a man for his sake! Or that I had any friend would be a man for my sake! [. . .] He is now as valiant as Hercules that only tells a lie and swears it. I cannot be a man with wishing, therefore I will die a woman with grieving.
BENEDICK
Tarry, good Beatrice. By this hand, I love thee.

> BEATRICE
> Use it for my love some other way than swearing by it.
> (*Ado* 4.1.315–24)

Beatrice's moaning does not remain without effect: it moves Benedick to do what he had refrained from doing until now: he voices a direct, unparadoxical confession of love – or does he? His initial 'By my sword, Beatrice, thou lovest me' has, towards the end of the scene, turned into 'By this hand, I love thee', a remarkable shift. Beatrice, however, does not like this turn towards the contractual mode of love. She still advocates passing on from words to deeds. However, Benedick, I would argue, is less stuck in the verbal, contractual mode than Beatrice thinks. In fact, he cunningly prepares a way out of the fencing with the illocutive forces of speech acts – towards a caressing touch. The differences between his earlier and his later confession may shed light on his strategy. In her answer, Beatrice emphasises the fact that 'By this hand' can, like 'By my sword', also be understood in an instrumental way: hand or sword not as (material or gestural) support for swearing, but as the medium or means (cf. *OED*, 'by, *prep.* and *adv.*' V.) by which the love is realised or enacted. It is probably the violent, the lethal touch of killing Claudio that Beatrice has in mind by insisting on this transition from words to hand. However, other uses are possible, as Claudio shows to Leonato with regard to the use of his 'sword': 'Nay, never lay thy hand upon thy sword' (*Ado* 5.1.54), Leonato warns Claudio in a scene that parallels the comedy of Benedick challenging Claudio to a duel (here, it is another man 'unfit' for the office of chivalric satisfaction, the old Leonato). 'In faith, my hand meant nothing to my sword' (*Ado* 5.1.57), Claudio replies, jokingly turning (the provocative threat of a violent touch into (obscene talk about) lustful, masturbatory touch.

Benedick's strategy follows a similar path; however, it is not merely concerned with words, but obeys Beatrice's

Caressing with Words: *Much Ado About Nothing* [177

prompt to walk the talking. His decisive move takes place in the following lines:

BENEDICK
Enough, I am engaged, I will challenge him, I will kiss your hand, and so I leave you. By this hand, Claudio shall render me a dear account. (*Ado* 4.1.328–30)

The significance of these lines, I would argue, does not lie in what is talked about or what is promised. We could and we should condone the fact that there will not be a duel between Benedick and Claudio, and that the kind of 'account' that Claudio will eventually render Benedick remains the subject of the audience's punning fantasy ('a tale' or 'a count', . . .). The words spoken by Benedick refer to what happens in this short scene: a caressing touch. This caressing touch can only happen because Benedick has abandoned the sword along the way from his first confession ('By my sword' (*Ado* 4.1.273)) to his second ('By this hand' (*Ado* 4.1.329)). The transition from sword to hand has one decisive effect: what happens '[b]y this hand' does not obey the sword's active–passive difference of penetrating and thereby rendering penetrated. Unlike the touch of the sword, the touch of hands does not follow the logic of the phallus, does not trigger an asymmetrical dynamic of having and taking/needing. In other words, Benedick's touch of lips seals off another touch: his taking Beatrice's hands. Viewed closely, this double gestural touch is accompanied by a verbal touch. Walking does here not follow, does not 'realise', put into act the talking, but talking and walking converge. In her annotations, the Arden3 editor Claire McEachern rightly wonders whose hand 'this hand' refers to: is it Benedick's or Beatrice's? For swearing, this would be important – swearing by Beatrice's hand again neutralises the illocutionary force of Benedick's speech act. For a caressing touch, it is essential that both hands touch, undecidably, mutually – and thus let Beatrice and Benedick 'be truly touched with love'.

Philology and Theatre – The Friar's Double Touch

'[B]elieve me not – and yet I lie not. I confess nothing, nor I deny nothing.' Does this linguistic situation not appear somehow familiar to us? Are we not all experts of language use that has a – let's call it – loose or rather playful relation to reference, and that is somehow systematically deprived of its conventional performative forces? Like Benedick and Beatrice's love speech, the linguistic practices that I have in mind are 'in a peculiar way hollow or void'. These are the very words of an uncontested authority on the field:

> [A] performative utterance will, for example, be in a peculiar way hollow or void if said by an actor on the stage, or if introduced in a poem, or spoken in soliloquy. [. . .] All this we are excluding from consideration. (Austin 22)

In contrast to John Langshaw Austin, I suppose that we, as philologists, are somehow professionally attracted to this essential trait of literature. We are seduced by it; we may, hopefully, even love it.

Much Ado acquaints us with a representative of this affirmative attitude towards what I have called 'caressing touches': the friar. Although he may be regarded as the most unmanly of all the male figures in the play – Constantina Michalos calls him the 'Feminized Friar' (cf. Michalos) – it is he who settles all the ado in the end. He does not bear a sword, and yet he may be said to be not less but 'more than a man': 'quiet, patient, modest, obedient, nurturing and compassionate' as Michalos writes (1), he does not only embody a 'different' gender but, in a specific way, troubles the genders of others.

He intervenes by introducing a break: 'Hear me a little' (*Ado* 4.1.155), he exclaims, and later, even more explicitly,

'Pause awhile' (*Ado* 4.1.200), when Leonato passionately decides to seek his daughter's life. In a way, Leonato's 'Nay, never lay thy hand upon thy sword' (*Ado* 5.1.54) echoes the friar's earlier intervention: the latter suspends the violent touches that Leonato envisions – 'These hands shall tear her' (*Ado* 4.1.191) – and instead attempts to 'contaminate' him with his own 'female' patience. The male 'office' of defending one's honour by sword or even bare hands is the friar's main adversary. He reintroduces the distance that separates him (as a friar) from worldly affairs into the ado in which he finds himself involved. The distance does not only defer the violence of laying hands on Hero; it also creates the tension that establishes a state of suspension. This suspension is, I would argue, the suspension constitutive for touch. With the state of suspension, the friar does not only introduce a time-out, a short break, after which things will go on as before, but interrupts 'this course of fortune' (*Ado* 4.1.157) in order to change it. The suspension of touch is to be productive; it is to make change possible. However, the productivity of touch works in a very specific way: in a way that is not subjected to the intentional action of the individual. On the contrary, for the productivity of touch to take effect, individual agency – that is, in the early modern patriarchal society, mostly male agency – has to be suspended. As a consequence, an openness ensues which creates the opportunity for things to happen, for contingency to get into touch with the 'course of fortune'.

The friar twice introduces a suspending distance, twice promotes touch: the first instance could be called philological, the second theatrical. We have already encountered the first: he interrupts the heat of the dramatic action, that is, Leonato's thirst for an honour killing, in order to discuss a reading. In fact, the practice of reading Hero's corporal signs itself implies a sort of suspension, a way of not taking part in the action, of 'be[ing] silent' and 'giving way unto this course of fortune' (*Ado* 4.1.156–7), as the friar says. Significantly, he does not present his reading as uncovering the 'truth', but nevertheless aims at and succeeds in persuading the others of what he thinks he has observed:

> FRIAR
> [. . .]
> Trust not my reading nor my observations,
> Which with experimental seal doth warrant
> The tenor of my book; trust not my age,
> My reverence, calling nor divinity,
> If this sweet lady lie not guiltless here
> Under some biting error.
>   (*Ado* 4.1.165–70)

The logical construction that the friar resorts to is complicated – and voices a paradox: the condition that decides whether the reading is to be trusted or not contains the reading itself. 'If Hero is guilty, then the friar's reading (finding her not guilty) should not be trusted' formulates a tautology, as does its negation. In other words, the friar openly admits that his reading cannot claim truth, that there is no transition from mere 'reading' to 'fact'. With his 'age', 'reference', 'calling' or 'divinity', he negates all the contextual evidence that could lend his reading authority. One might say that he himself presents his appeal for trust as 'in a peculiar way hollow or void', and this is exactly why he ultimately succeeds in touching his listeners, contaminating them with his touch, drawing them into a state of suspension that he has initiated. The friar performs the same verbal touch that will take place a little later between Benedick and Beatrice with the latter's: '[B]elieve me not – and yet I lie not.'

In its very void, in its open dispensation with ultimate, 'factual' truth, the friar's reading does not provide Leonato, Benedick and Beatrice with a justification for revenge; Beatrice's 'Kill Claudio' does not follow on from the friar's reading. On the contrary, it is not lethal touches that the friar advocates but theatrical ones: touches that refrain from direct fatality, but carry in themselves the distance of an 'as if' instead. Playing theatre, staging a ceremony of mourning that includes in its cast Claudio, the 'perpetrator', further prolongs the state of suspension and hopes to contribute to a happy ending.

However, does the friar's plan really 'Change slander to remorse' (*Ado* 4.1.211)? Is it his intervention that brings forth the final reconciliatory outcome? Without doubt, it prevents the play from turning into a tragedy and so leaves the plot of love, revenge and honour killing to *Othello* or *The Duchess of Malfi*. However, this is not achieved in the way the friar had planned it: the theatrical intermezzos rather provide the time for the comic subplot of Dogberry and his colleagues to unfold, and thus to dismantle Don John's dark machinations. In other words, it gives contingency the opportunity to change the 'course of fortune'. By preventing tragedy and, as argued above, producing comedy instead, the friar's plan further spreads the state of suspension, spreads it beyond the fictional world: its comic tickles reach the audience in the theatre who probably know best about the strange powers of the 'as if' and its hollow speech acts.

As for Benedick and Beatrice, the absence of referential truth, the tickling precarity of the theatrical speech act, might be the reason the play touches us, might even be the reason for its emotional and critical efficacy. The fact that the play is not merely a true report of things past (or present) lends it forces that are not regulated and thus tamed by a pre-existing framing. As Jacques Derrida has shown (cf. *Limited Inc.*), these forces are not foreign to the world and our everyday (linguistic) lives. However, we are certainly not used to the intensity with which these unruly forces move us in the theatre. On the contrary, John Langshaw Austin's attempts to exclude this sort of speech act from linguistic analysis might expose the liminal and almost abject status they hold in contemporary society.

Exposing oneself to such sorts of disorderly speech expressions thus implies a challenge. As a consequence of their not following predefined or referentially stabilised contractual pathways, they challenge us to read, to feel and to find new, creative ways of answering them. If we are not to stifle these anarchic forces – as the traditional scholarly habitus of 'explaining' unfortunately suggests we do – we cannot but affirm the unexpectedness of their effects and let them interact with what we have come to accept as our reality (cf. Culler).[14] This precarious relation promises to be a much richer way of connecting these speech acts to our surroundings, to our societal, epistemological reality, than reducing them to distorted documents of historical truth, or actualisations of a conventional, contractual framework. It accounts for the fact that Shakespeare's theatre is more than a relic of early modern times; it accounts for the dramatic power of words that has left remarkable traces on the last centuries and continues to do so.

When abandoning the contractual, the conventional dimension of language, Shakespeare's *Much Ado* might thus speak about more than an unusual way of making love with words. It might speak about more than a linguistic strategy that two of its characters have discovered for themselves. '[H]ow to be truly touched with love' might be a question that touches upon us – the audience, the readers, the philologists – more than we might have thought. Is not this caressing with words what theatre, what literature – and what philology is all about?

Notes

1. Diana E. Henderson puts this more directly: 'Hero has always been upstaged by her cousin Beatrice' (193).
2. The role of language in *Much Ado* is quite well researched. As Claire McEachern's 'Introduction' to the Arden3 edition indicates, interest in the rhetorical tradition (sometimes in connection with a feminist agenda) is still the dominant approach to the play's linguistic characteristics. She adds an analysis of the rhetorical phenomenon of euphuism to the existing studies of

language for which she provides a helpful overview. Her list includes: Brian Vickers, *The Artistry of Shakespeare's Prose*; Anthony B. Dawson, 'Much Ado about Signifying'; John Drakakis, 'Trust and Transgression: The Discursive Practices of *Much Ado About Nothing*'; Stephen B. Dobranski, 'Children of the Mind: Miscarried Narratives in *Much Ado About Nothing*'; Marta Straznicky, 'Shakespeare and the Government of Cxomedy: *Much Ado About Nothing*'; Lynne Magnusson, 'The Pragmatics of Repair in *King Lear* and *Much Ado About Nothing*', and Maurice Hunt, 'The Reclamation of Language'.

3. Amy Crunelle-Vanrighe's and Jean E. Howard's articles follow a similar logic.

4. With the exception of Natalia Carbajosa's 'Beatrice y Benedick en *Much Ado About Nothing*: Análisis pragmatic', the pragmatic dimension of speech has not yet been explicitly analysed for *Much Ado*. It features latently in examinations of style, as in Brian Vickers's *The Artistry of Shakespeare's Prose*, but is severely limited in this framework.

5. Diana E. Henderson reflects on the cultural and patriarchal prejudices involved in evaluating Hero's silence: 'The received sense of Hero's passivity, it should be noted, depends on the cultural assumption that equates speech with activity' (194). Henderson suggests that staging the scene in a gender-sensitive way unleashes its potential: 'It is up to the director whether Hero's silence indicates complaisance in her given role or others' patronizing presumptuousness (or both)' (194). The same holds true for a philological reading of the scene.

6. For marriage in Shakespeare specifically, see Margaret Loftus Ranald, '"As Marriage Binds, and Blood Breaks": English Marriage and Shakespeare'. An analysis of the role of marriage in *Much Ado* can be found in Claire McEachern, 'Fathering Herself: A Source Study of Shakespeare's Feminism' (272–5).

7. Similarly, Bruce R. Smith speaks of a 'fit between the physical and the verbal' (*Phenomenal Shakespeare* 171).

8. The semantic spectrum of 'nothing' – from 'noting' to 'the female genitals' – has become a topos of the scholarly debates around *Much Ado*. For an early overview, see the chapter on

Much Ado in Paul A. Jorgensen, *Redeeming Shakespeare's Words*. In her famous feminist article on Ophelia, Elaine Showalter, rather in passing, introduces the name Luce Irigaray, and her way of thinking sexual difference, to the debate of 'nothing' (cf. 79). Although Showalter does not elaborate on this intellectual horizon, I am indebted to the connection she sketches.

9. It is this patriarchal instance of a third party watching over and mandating 'truth' that Jean E. Howard's reading focuses on: '[Shakespeare's play] can be read [...] as encoding the process by which the powerful determine truth' (179). She is, however, not aware that Benedick and Beatrice evade and undermine this authority.

10. Carla Mazzio suggests a deep affinity between the erotic and touch on an abstract, conceptual level: 'The realm of the erotic, with desire always in some sense linked to what is not there, is perhaps the most powerful vehicle for representing the infinite potential and the elusiveness of touch' ('Acting with Tact' 166).

11. Donald R. Wehrs was probably the first to employ a notion of touch inspired by contemporary thinking in an article on Shakespeare's comedies. The intellectual frame, however, differs significantly from the one chosen here: whereas Wehrs builds his argument on the humanist tradition, the two we resort to, Barthes and Derrida, cultivate an outspokenly non-humanist (or even anti-humanist) approach – which is not to be mistaken as unethical. Barthes and Derrida certainly belong to what Wehrs pejoratively labels 'postmodernism' (2). It is against this intellectual trend that Wehrs writes his article. As far as I can see, *Much Ado* has hardly been read with either Derrida or Barthes – Anthony B. Dawson's mentioning Barthes's *Sade, Fourier, Loyola* has to be called a rare exception.

12. Luce Irigaray has famously expanded on the notion of the labial that both implies a linguistic as well as a sexual dimension. It is no coincidence that the concept of touch is important for her argument as it is for our reading of the play: 'The value granted to the only definable form excludes the one that is in play in female autoeroticism. The one of form,

of the individual, of the (male) sexual organ, of the proper name, of the proper meaning [. . .] supplants, while separating and dividing, the contact of at least two (lips) which keeps woman in touch with herself, but without any possibility of distinguishing what is touching from what is touched' (*This Sex Which is Not One* 26).

13. Benedick's deliberations that 'the world must be peopled' are reminiscent of the fair youth section at the beginning of Shakespeare's *Sonnets*.
14. The 'hollow or void' theatrical speech acts thus join in alliance with what Jonathan Culler sees as the 'main effect of theory' (4), namely its critical force: 'the disputing of "common sense"' (4), the 'attempt to show that what we take for granted as "common sense" is in fact a historical construction' – or, in the words of our chapter, questioning what we take for granted as the 'true' reality of reference or as the 'true' frame of contract.

CHAPTER 4

TOUCHING FRACTIONS:
TROILUS AND CRESSIDA

After all this thou wilt say to thyself, 'How insecure is the ground upon which all our alliances and friendships rest, how liable to cold downpours and bad weather, how lonely is every creature!' (Nietzsche *Human All-Too-Human* 293)

The Problem – Fractions and Factions

The bonds of heaven are slipped, dissolved and loosed
And with another knot, five-finger-tied,
The fractions of her faith, orts of her love,
The fragments, scraps, the bits and greasy relics
Of her o'ereaten faith, are bound to Diomed. (*TC* 5.2.163–7)

These are the words that Troilus, the protagonist of William Shakespeare's *Troilus and Cressida*, speaks at the moment of his bitterest defeat: he has lost his beloved Cressida to Diomedes, a Greek enemy. All had begun the way love stories have since *Romeo and Juliet*: with a sleepless night spent together. Not even the setting of the Trojan War, with the Greeks besieging the town and their daily fighting, could prevent the two Trojan lovers being found together – although the services of a matchmaker, quite appropriately named Pandarus, were needed to facilitate their union. However, their luck proves to be short. In the morning, news arrives that the war parties have agreed on a deal: Cressida is to be delivered to the Grecian camp in order to release the Trojan warrior Antenor, who has been taken captive by the Greeks the day before. Troilus promises to visit her in the Greek camp, and they exchange vows to be true to one another, before Cressida is handed over to a Greek ambassador, Diomedes, who immediately brings her to his confederates. It is this self-same Diomedes whom Troilus finds Cressida flirting with when he delivers on his promise. With Troilus observing covertly from the bushes, the two even arrange an encounter that night. Troilus had thought Cressida 'his', 'tied with the bonds of heaven' (*TC* 5.2.161) – now '[t]he bonds of heaven' prove to be 'slipped, dissolved and loosed'. What he held to be 'true' – not only in the sense of 'faithful' and 'trustworthy' (*OED*, 'true, *adj.*'; 1.a.) but also signifying 'not liable to break or give way', 'firm', 'reliable', 'sound' (*OED*, 'true, *adj.*'; 1.†d.) – is shattered to pieces, lies in 'fractions', 'orts', 'fragments', 'scraps' and 'bits'. It is, however, not only (Troilus's) love and (Cressida's) faithfulness that Shakespeare's play shows to be broken and fragmented. The failure of their loving bond stands paradigmatically for other defective, corrupted bonds that become themes in *Troilus and Cressida*: social bonds holding together the fighting collectives in war.

The second, 'historical' storyline of the play, which narrates a short but decisive period of the Trojan War, turns out to be one of these fractions and factions as well. Rather than the unending battle of two proud armies, Shakespeare's play depicts two social collectives whose fight for inner cohesion superimposes the confrontation with the enemy. '[T]heir fraction is more our wish than their faction' (*TC* 2.3.96), Nestor says about the dispute between his fellow warriors Achilles and Ajax – an argument that exposes an alarming state of affairs in the Grecian army. Even Ulysses' sly strategic skills cannot restore the social cohesion of a powerful war party; it is not his intervention but a personal motive, Patroclus's death, that convinces Achilles to finally join the fights. The Trojan hero Hector is not killed by a heroic effort by the Greek army but brutally slaughtered in an ambush that Achilles has laid for him – he dies unarmed as a victim of violent personal revenge.

In other words, even the Greek triumph of having killed the greatest of the Trojans' heroes – a triumph that clearly prefigures the fall of Troy – cannot, in Shakespeare's play, undo the impression of their social coherence being in severe crisis, and remaining there. Despite his death equalling a heavy military defeat, Hector's description of the 'dull and factitious nobles of the Greeks' (*TC* 2.2.209) is not contradicted by the course of events shown on stage. Things are no better on the Trojan side. Their collective crumbles into factions as well. In Shakespeare's play, the Trojan heroes even discuss the controversial question of returning Helena without reaching an agreement – they question the very reasonability of the war they have already been fighting for several years. The same fractions open up again when Cassandra and Hecuba confront Hector with their prophetic visions of his impending death. Although some of his male comrades try to convince the great warrior not to go to the battlefield that day, he does not listen and gets killed. The Trojan repression of the crisis of social bonds proves fatal; it ends with the complete destruction of their collective.

Troilus's dictum that 'The bonds of heaven are slipped, dissolved and loosed' can thus indeed stand as a motto for *Troilus and Cressida* as a whole, for both the love story and the historical plot. It accounts for the dark, pessimistic atmosphere that emanates from the play. More than this, the phrase brings to words one main problem that this 'problem play' (cf. Tillyard) stages and explores. It is a problem of social cohesion, of social bonds, or rather of a (historical) transformation of social bonds, of what holds together social collectives.

We should not forget that, in his monologue, Troilus not only bemoans the failure/loss/corruption of a specific model of social bonds – he also introduces an alternative to the 'old', bygone ideal, an alternative that he despises because it is the way that his rival Diomedes has bonded with Cressida: the 'bonds of heaven' have been replaced by 'another knot, five-finger-tied'. An early modern emblem can help us understand how this special 'knot' works:

Figure 4.1 Taken from George Wither, *A Collection of Emblemes, Ancient and Moderne*, p. 99.

It is a knot of two times five fingers – a touch of hands that establishes a social relation. The interesting emblem, however, shows that there is more to the depicted bond than just hands. The emblem's composition is structured by the figure of a cross – the arms joined by the central touch of hands establish a horizontal line, whereas a vertical line is formed by the altar, the burning heart, the hands, the skull and the sun. The emblem thus illustrates both of the bonds we have just discussed, and connects them to each other. The horizontal line visualises the human 'knot, five-finger-tied', the vertical line between altar and sun is a remnant of the 'bond of heaven', which sacralises and stabilises the social relation established by the clasping hands. The setting clearly alludes to the marriage ritual: 'it re-presents the ritual act of hand-fasting, the touch between man and woman legally affirming their marriage' (Tribble '"O, she's warm"' 69). The 'hands and hand-fasting', which Farah Karim-Cooper finds 'at the centre of the ritual' of the *Book of Common Prayer* (*The Hand* 54–5), is a prime example of a human five-finger-human bond sanctified by that of heaven, as depicted in the emblem. However, the emblem's pictorial composition is deeply ambiguous. The skull clearly dominates the image and thus uncannily reverses the emblem's message. Instead of death being defeated by the bond that is instantiated by a touch of hands, the emblem associates the clasp of hands with death and corruption, with the frailness of time. The outright contradiction of the emblem's paratexts confirms this impression: one, the epigram, claims that true love outlives death; the other, written in a circle around the emblem, reading 'jusque à la mort' [till death], reintroduces death as the final limit.

The explanatory text following the emblem is surprisingly unequivocal. It is highly sceptical of the epigram that it sets out to comment upon. Rather than placing trust in the bond of 'Hands' that 'True-love hath tyde', it is steeped in anxiety: the 'paire of *Loving-hands*' only 'seeme to be' 'close, and fast-united' (Wither 99) – in fact, their connection proves loose enough to necessitate open warnings and threats: 'Thy secret fault, shall one day, be revealed' (Wither 99) and punished. The trust in 'true love' and in the bond of hands avouching this love has turned into severe doubt – instead of *truth*, it is *falsehood* that the emblem is concerned with. 'Thy *Falsehood*, till thy *dying*, thou shalt rue' (99): on this sentence, the didactic poem beneath the emblem ends.

In the world to which the emblem is addressed, the stabilising influence of 'the bonds of heaven', of the emblem's vertical axis, has obviously weakened significantly. As an effect, the responsibility for a lasting social relation has shifted onto the horizontal axis of worldly human affairs. It is only via the detour of the individual's conscience and its concern for salvation that religion secures a last remnant of access on the stability of the 'bond five-finger-tied'.

The emblem's world is that of *Troilus and Cressida*. It is a world in which the touch of hands ceases to be merely the symbol of social relations actually held together by a powerful system of transcendent values, by the 'bonds of heaven'. The touch of hands, or, more generally, a whole assemblage of human haptic encounters, begins to become itself the foundation of social relations. It is the human 'five fingers' that tie this new knot, and that account for the new collective's cohesion. *Troilus and Cressida* shares the emblem's anxiety that results from this ground-breaking transformation. However, instead of attempting to restore the old system with warnings and threats, it ruthlessly explores the workings of the new social dynamics.

As the play's title indicates, the love story of Troilus and Cressida serves as the model for Shakespeare's explorations of transforming social bonds. The links, however, that connect this exemplary social relation between two individuals to the historical events (the strife between two mythical war parties) are manifold. Hector probably explains the most obvious one before his Trojan comrades, when he claims that the abduction of Helena itself has to be counted as an offence against the 'moral laws / Of nature and of nations' (*TC* 2.2.184–5):

> HECTOR
> What nearer debt in all humanity
> Than wife is to the husband? If this law
> Of nature be corrupted through affection,
> [...]
> There is a law in each well-ordered nation
> To curb those raging appetites that are
> Most disobedient and refractory. (*TC* 2.2.175–82)

In order to analyse the assemblage of human haptic encounters that *Troilus and Cressida* exhibits as a new foundation of social bonds, I will therefore cross-fade between the two storylines. I will read the encounter of the two lovers as the key to a new regime of social cohesion which also regulates the foundation of larger collectives.

'What, billing again?' – Of Words and Touches, Constant Men and False Women

When the play begins, Troilus and Cressida are not yet a couple. Indeed, they have not even spoken a word to one another. Pandarus, Cressida's uncle, has accepted the task of facilitating the relationship on behalf of Troilus. He arranges a meeting and tries to bring the two shy lovers together. In order to bear witness to their mutual consent and thereby establish an acceptable relationship, Pandarus counts on the power of words: 'Swear the oaths now to her that you have sworn to me' (*TC* 3.2.39–40), he tells Troilus, and obviously intends to initiate an exchange of vows. However, it is not Troilus but Cressida who responds to Pandarus's request: she 'draw[s] backward' (*TC* 3.2.43). As her later behaviour confirms, she is repelled by the binding power of words. When Troilus does not follow Pandarus's second attempt to make him talk, the broker decides to resort to a more patient strategy: he unveils Cressida. However, the plan does not work out the way it was intended – Pandarus's words to Troilus imply that the two lovers still do not talk, but start to caress each other instead: 'So, so, rub on, and kiss the mistress' (*TC* 3.2.48). Is it again Cressida who responds to Pandarus's request, this time not withdrawing from but approaching Troilus and thereby preventing him from speaking to her? 'You have bereft me of all words, lady' (*TC* 3.2.53), he tells Cressida – and is immediately interrupted by Pandarus: 'Words pay no debts; give her deeds' (*TC* 3.2.54). The broker-between is obviously dissatisfied with Troilus's verbal intervention. Troilus does not swear oaths, he does not even speak in the first person. Cressida is the grammatical subject of the sentence he utters; it revolves around her completely: it is her with whom the sentence starts ('You'), and it is her with whom it ends ('lady'). Troilus misses the appropriate perlocutionary mode that is expected from him, because his words are incapable of executing the 'deeds' that Pandarus wants them to do. When the lovers exchange another kiss, Pandarus changes tactic. Instead of establishing the bargain with words, he switches to the lovers' non-verbal, their 'haptic' behaviour, which appears to be better suited to realise his plans. He reads the lovers' kiss as the utterance of mutual consent he has been waiting for: 'What, billing again? Here's "In witness whereof the parties interchangeably"' (*TC* 3.2.56–7). As in his later quasi-ritualistic marriage 'ceremony', Pandarus here blends the 'old' religious ritual[1] with the legal proceedings of trade and accounting. The ambiguous vocabulary 'billing' paradigmatically short-circuits the haptic gesture of touching, caressing (*OED*, 'bill, *v.*2'; 3.) with the mercantile notion of keeping the books (*OED*, 'bill, *v.*3'). It thereby embeds the social regime of touch in a specific sociohistorical context.

Despite his being involved in the haptic procedure of approaching Cressida, Troilus turns out to be a man of words. '[H]e values language', notes Sharon Harris, 'his own – and the illusions he can create thereby' (77).² He wants to be bound to Cressida in the traditional, verbal way, affirming the lovers' oaths, even though he knows their idealised messages are hard to match in real life. His beloved, on the contrary, does not believe in the binding power of words. As Sharon Harris again writes, 'Shakespeare uses Cressida to mock such rhetorical conventions' (78). This is best expressed by one of the most controversial speech acts of the play: when Troilus swears his faithfulness to her ('truth can speak truest not truer than Troilus' (*TC* 3.2.94)), she does not answer this vow with a vow by herself, but instead asks him to have sex with her ('Will you walk in, my lord?'), a baffling turn of events which Philip Edwards considers to be Cressida's 'finest moment' (48). For Cressida, social cohesion is not brought about by words.

As the scene exhibits several times, it is touch, the encounter of bodies, that she seeks and in which she trusts. It is therefore only logical that she prefers not to speak at all: 'Sweet, bid me hold my tongue' (*TC* 3.2.125), she asks Troilus, 'Stop my mouth' (*TC* 3.2.129).

When Cressida eventually breaks her silence and suddenly begins to talk about her love to Troilus, the audience gets an idea of her 'problem' with language. She confesses her love, only to qualify the confession as soon as it has left her lips:

CRESSIDA
Prince Troilus, I have loved you night and day
For many weary months.
[. . .]
I love you now, but till now not so much
But I might master it. In faith, I lie; (*TC* 3.2.109–17).

There is a constitutive problem with Cressida and speaking 'truly'. This problem is best exhibited by the paradoxical speech act she produces: 'In faith, I lie;' – language, in its constative and performative dimension, is hollowed out.[3]

What, though, is Cressida's constitutive problem with language all about? She herself tells Troilus that it is neither the awkward situation nor the matchmaking activities of her uncle Pandarus. It is, as Cressida puts it, 'mine own company' (*TC* 3.2.140) that gets in the way. She is not the 'thing inseparate' (*TC* 5.2.155) that Troilus takes her to be until the end of the play:

> CRESSIDA
> I have a kind of self resides with you,
> But an unkind self that itself will leave
> To be another's fool. Where is my wit?
> Would be gone. I speak I know not what. (*TC* 3.2.142–6)

Cressida is in herself plural, a collective of conflicted selves. Her mode of 'individuation' (rather 'dividuation')[4] differs significantly from Troilus's. He is individuated as a 'thing inseparate', as 'so eternal and so fixed a soul' (*TC* 5.2.172). 'I am as true as truth's simplicity' (*TC* 3.2.164), Troilus claims of himself, and it is the simplicity, the 'absence of compositeness' (cf. *OED*, 'simplicity, *n.*'; 1.a.), that substantiates his words: it is Troilus's archaic individuation that accounts for his words' constative 'truth', as well as for their perlocutionary, binding effect.

In contrast to the fixity and timelessness, to the 'eternity' of Troilus's soul, Cressida's mode of (in)dividuation is one of intrinsic motion, of metastable forces – of difference and time:[5] 'I love you *now*, but *till now* not so much.' The truth that guarantees the social power of binding words relies, by contrast, on stable and unchanging identity, on a concept that is highly allergic to the complex processes of time and becoming.

Cressida's answer to Troilus's vow of truth and simplicity thus can only be ambiguous: her 'In that I'll war with you' (*TC* 3.2.166) will turn out to come true in its dark, cruel, deeper meaning later in the play. Her composite (in)dividuation does not emulate, but it will 'war with', will attack and defeat, Troilus's eponymous true simplicity.

A comparable ambiguity haunts the quasi-ceremony that Pandarus officiates to celebrate the relationship between the two lovers:

> PANDARUS
> Go to, a bargain made. Seal it, seal it; I'll be the witness. Here I hold your hand, here my cousin's. If ever you prove false one to another, since I have taken such pains to bring you together, let all pitiful goers-between be called to the world's end after my name: call them all panders. Let all constant men be Troiluses, all false women Cressids, and all brokers-between panders! Say 'Amen'.
> TROILUS
> Amen.
> CRESSIDA
> Amen. (*TC* 3.2.192–9)

The 'bargain' is not sealed by words but with two gestures of touch: a handshake and a kiss. As Emily Ross has shown in her detailed analysis of this scene before the background of early modern customs and legal practice, there are elements in the ceremony that indicate that what takes place in the scene might be a legally binding (though clandestine) marriage. It is, however, not the words that serve as evidence for this reading. On the contrary, 'a canon court would have difficulty judging them to be legally (although clandestinely) married because their vows do not conform to *sponsalia per verba de praesenti*' (Ross 412). Furthermore, 'the commercial double-meanings that underlie Pandarus's words make his role as celebrant suspect and make questionable the sanctity of any union he presides over' (Ross 408).

> On the other hand, there does seem to be sufficient evidence to rule that the ceremony espoused the couple. Although the vows they swore do not conform to the anecdotal models and are not phrased as *sponsalia per verba de future*, they are formally solemnized by a patriarch of Cressida's family, who might legitimately take that role in the absence of Cressida's father. They are performed in a private home, which was the usual location for spousals, and are accompanied by an exchange of appropriate gifts. Should this case be legally disputed, it seems probable that a court would accept (with Pandarus' testimony as witness) that a spousal contract had been created between Troilus and Cressida. (Ross 412)

Emily Ross also points to the fact that there is documentary evidence that 'Shakespeare himself contracted a spousal between Stephen Belott and Mary Mountjoy, Mary being the daughter of the family he was staying with' (407); in other words, he acted out Pandarus's office at some time before 1604, when the official marriage took place. Since there was a court case years later, it is documented that 'They weare made suer by Mr Shakespeare by geuing there consent, and agreed to marrye, (geuing eache others hand to the hande *[deleted]* and did marrye' (G. E. Bentley 76–80). What the legally binding ceremony officiated by Shakespeare himself and the one under Pandarus's guidance have in common is the haptic gesture that confirms and perhaps even expresses their consent and agreement to marry. While in the 'real' Mr Shakespeare's case the role of the words spoken – the 'trouths', the marriage or spousal vows – remains unclear, words in Pandarus's ceremonial clearly undermine the official ritual, especially the fact that Pandarus interprets the 'affair' they are to 'seal' with a kiss as 'a bargain' is significant. It clashes with the quasi-religious framing of the ritual and underlines the worldly nature of the bond that is about to be established. More than this, the notion of 'bargain' bears associations that undermine the expectations of eternal fixity connected to a religious interpretation of the marital bond. The word 'bargain' is believed by some to go back to the notion of the barge:

> Old French *bargaigne-r* = Provençal *barganhar*, Italian *bargagnare* < late Latin *barcāneāre, barcāniāre* (in Capit. Charles the Bald), which Diez proposes to refer (through *barcāneus: see *bargain n.1*) to *barca* 'a bark or barge, which,' according to the definition of Isidore, 'carries goods to and fro'; thence might arise the sense either of 'go backwards and forwards, come and go as to a matter, be off and on' (compare modern French *barguigner* to hesitate, have difficulty in making up one's mind), or of 'trade, traffic, deal'. (*OED*, 'bargain, *v.*')

Mercantile vocabulary – with its imagery of circulation, of fluidity, of varying situations of property, of passing on from hands to hands, of 'coming and going', of a quick succession of contacts – together with the underlying affirmation of time and change, is a very important conceptual pool that Shakespeare uses repeatedly with regard to the new regime of touch and social cohesion.

Viewed closely, what the two lovers confirm with their 'Amen' has nothing to do with their relationship; all they verbally sign is the coinage of words in case of their future falsity. The early modern viewers in the London theatre know that the condition of Pandarus's perlocutionary speech act ('If you prove false') must have been met. As a result of the popularity of Chaucer's tales, Troilus and Cressida were already synonyms for constancy and falsehood in Shakespeare's time, and the word 'pander' had entered the English vocabulary, signifying a 'go-between' (or 'pimp').

However, the fact that the two lovers will be untrue does obviously not prevent the 'bargain'. Troilus and Cressida's relationship is founded not on true statements; it is founded on touch, which makes a crucial difference. It is this difference that shapes the tragedy of the couple's ill-fated love, which reaches its climax when Troilus watches Cressida flirt with Diomedes in the Greek camp. Troilus understood Pandarus's 'bargain' to establish a relation sanctified by 'the bonds of heaven'. In fact, his relationship with Cressida had been held together by the same 'knot, five-finger-tied' that now binds Cressida to Diomedes. He misread the gesture of touch to be the symbol of a holy, eternal bond, guaranteed by a powerful system of transcendent values. However, in the world of *Troilus and Cressida*, the touch of hands, or more generally, a whole regime of human haptic encounters, has itself become the foundation of social relations. It is the human 'five fingers' that tie this new knot and that account for the cohesion of the new collective. '[T]he ground upon which all our alliances [. . .] rest' has become 'more insecure', 'the traditional bonds that once defined human relations are replaced', and a '[p]roper relationship is destroyed', writes Gayle Greene ('Shakespeare's Cressida' 136). Social cohesion is still generated, but in a different, more complex way.

Cressida's liaison with Diomedes exposes what has already latently characterised her relationship to Troilus. Their 'five-finger-tied' knot is not based on truth, but on falsity: 'I will not keep my word' (*TC* 5.2.105), Cressida says to Diomedes, a notoriously 'false-hearted rogue' (*TC* 5.2.86) of whom Thersites claims that '[t]he sun borrows of the moon when [he] keeps his word' (*TC* 5.2.91–2). Their 'bond' does not suffer from this. On the contrary, as she had already confessed to Troilus, Cressida's self is divided, and it is this division that makes her flirting with Diomedes possible. Troilus is right to recognise two Cressidas when watching them flirting: 'This she? No, this is Diomed's Cressida' (*TC* 5.2.144). 'This is and is not Cressid' (*TC* 5.2.153). Both relationships are negotiated not by 'true' words but avouched by touch: 'Diomed's' Cressida 'strokes [Diomed's] cheek', and 'Troilus's' Cressida attempts to kiss the sleeve Troilus has given her as a token of their love. The knot between Cressida and Troilus is loosened when Diomed snatches the sleeve from her and thus prevents 'their' touching by kiss.

From the perspective of the 'constant man' Troilus, Cressida must appear a false woman, and that is to say morally corrupted, because she has not kept her word and is unfaithful. As Arlene Okerlund and Paul Gaudet emphasise, literary criticism has long followed Troilus's 'masculinist ideology [. . .] that persistently stabilizes textual meaning by reifying, fixing Cressida' (Gaudet 126) and thus obviously helps in dealing with this 'drama of incoherence' (Gaudet 128). Shakespeare's play complicates the apparently clear-cut 'moral' opposition of constant versus false, however: the two are coded as two different modes of individuation, two different structures constituting the human as a social being. Troilus, the man of binding words, 'truth's authentic author to be cited', is the remnant of a world whose social organisation and coherence followed simple principles: stabilised by the 'bond of heaven', the human being is 'so eternal and so fixed a soul', a self-identical 'thing inseparate', that its interaction in social structures can be regulated by a handful of speech acts that maintain and perpetuate the few pillars of community (marriage, hierarchy/degree, the enemy . . .). Stephen X. Mead is right to emphasise that 'the verb *to be* [. . .] speaks [. . .] eloquently of Troilus's world view' (254–5), the view of a world that is defined by stasis, by the complete absence of the dynamics of change and becoming.

Cressida, the woman of touch,[6] is of a much more complicated (in)dividuation, 'a desperately elusive character', as Holly A. Crocker notes (308): she is, in herself, false – not constant and simple, but a composite of conflicting selves, of competing forces. Cressida is sensitive to the shifts and developments in her (social) surrounding. The sets of warring forces of which she is composed closely interact with the field of forces that she is embedded in as a social being. She is individuated by coming into touch with her changing environment. As a result, the concrete actualisation of her own composition of selves is subject to change, is constituted as time-sensitive.

'The bonds of heaven are slipped, dissolved and loosed' – Troilus's statement does not so much describe a failed love as it provides a striking analysis of the world of *Troilus and Cressida*. Cressida's 'fractions', 'orts', her 'fragments', 'scraps' and 'bits' represent a world that has lost its wholeness; 'The unit and married calm of states' has long been 'divert[ed] and crack[ed], ren[t] and deracinate[d]', as Ulysses bemoans. The Greek and the Trojan war parties are split into conflicting fractions. Instead of planetary 'fixure', this world is characterised by '[c]ommotion' (*TC* 1.3.97–101). It is therefore Cressida's talent for establishing social cohesion under these new circumstances that might soothe the diehards, the old reactionary 'frights' and 'horrors' facing the dynamics of a world that is about to become modern.[7]

"*Twere better she were kissed in general*' – closing the ranks and the openness of contingent touch

Shakespeare's play uses Cressida's 'displacement', her sudden handover to the Grecian camp, to transfer her touching mode of social cohesion from the level of the individual to that of community. In the Greek camp, Cressida, all on her own, encounters the enemy – and immediately bonds with the Greek heroes – through the touch of lips.

'Our general doth salute you with a kiss' (*TC* 4.5.20), Nestor comments on Agamemnon's 'welcoming' Cressida with a gesture of touch; a gesture that Ulysses' suggestion "Twere better she were kissed in general' (*TC* 4.5.22) extends to a sort of welcome ritual that involves the whole group of Greek heroes.[8] Feminist readers are certainly right to recognise in this procedure of welcoming the violent integration by appropriation of a female body into patriarchal society. Cressida is, like Helena, 'a commodity within the circuit of exchange', writes Carol Cook ('Unbodied Figures' 38). However, Ulysses' plan fails. Cressida herself explains and performs why touch as touch is not to be misunderstood as appropriation.

Having 'welcomed' several heroes, she refuses to kiss Menelaus. By insisting on 'his' kiss, Menelaus gives Cressida the opportunity to take the floor and show her verbal prowess. Instead of 'touching' him with her lips, Cressida touches him with her tongue – in a linguistic way – by responding to his advances with rhyming replies that take control of the situation and outwit him in a spectacular fashion. Cressida is not as feeble and 'defenceless' (Langis 23) as many, even feminist, readings take her to be. She is not, 'like Helen', an 'innocent victim' (Okerlund 4). She is neither limited to 'only act the part of war trophy' (Crocker 325), nor reduced to 'the object by which men among other men judge their own value' (Vaughan 217). '[H]er sexual allure' is not 'the only power she has' (Vaughan 218) and, as the scene shows, she does not have to 'accept concubinage to avoid rape' (Helms 38). 'By denying a kiss to Menelaus, Cressida counters the group act of appropriation and intimidation by reasserting control of her own body' (Gaudet 138).

The main argument with which she confronts her rhetorical opponent exposes an important trait of the gesture of kissing touch that is performed in the scene. Menelaus's impatient request, 'Lady, by your leave', is countered by Cressida with 'In kissing, do you render or receive?' Menelaus's answer, 'Both take and give' (*TC* 4.5.36–8), at the same time disqualifies him from kissing (because he has, as a cuckold, proven not to give enough) and strengthens Cressida's role in the whole scene. By making Menelaus declare touch to be an ineluctably reciprocal gesture, Cressida emphasises her own contribution to all the kissing done before.

Cressida's verbal interventions performatively confirm the reciprocity of touch that she claims. Cressida even matches the smartest and wittiest of the Greeks, Ulysses, who joins the rhetorical battle of rhymes when Menelaus has arrived at his wits' ends. 'A woman of quick sense,' Nestor concludes (TC 4.5.55). Ulysses comes to a similar but less positive or admiring judgement:

> ULYSSES
> Fie, fie, upon her!
> There's language in her eye, her cheek, her lip,
> Nay, her foot speaks; her wanton spirits look out
> At every joint and motive of her body.
> O, these encounterers, so glib of tongue,
> That give accosting welcome ere it comes,
> And wide unclasp the tables of their thought
> To every tickling reader! Set them down
> For sluttish spoils of opportunity
> And daughters of the game. (TC 4.5.55–64)

Ulysses, who initiated the 'general' kissing, in the end has to fight hard to evade Cressida's kiss. The scene of touch has got out of hand. Apparently, the 'exchanged kiss on the mouth' fulfils neither its ritualistic function of welcome nor its contractual function as a '"kiss of [imposed!] peace", [which] often followed hand-holding as a way of sealing a contract' (Classen 5). Instead, Ulysses' long tirade identifies Cressida as a threat to the very system of community which he wanted her to become a subject (or rather, an object!) of. Paradoxically enough, it is exactly the gesture of touch, the gesture he attempted to use as a means of subjugation, that turns out to be a dangerous alternative to the 'conventional', 'traditional' – and patriarchal – way of organising social cohesion. This does not come as a surprise: as Constance Classen notes, it was a cultural topos that '[f]eminine touch could be seen as constituting a serious threat to masculine dominance – as the image of woman as a deadly spider indicated' (76).

Cressida is dangerous because she is an 'encounterer': she offers her whole body as a site for social con-*tact*; like a ship approaching sideways, moving parallel to the shore (cf. *OED*, 'accost, *v.*'; etym.), she maximises the contact surface. Language, as a means of social interaction, is thus suspended or hypertrophically subverted, because it no longer follows the conventions of truth, of binding speech acts regulated by (patriarchal) traditions (cf. the right to speak first that Cressida mentions). Cressida's (body) language is 'dangerous' because it defies (male) control.

It would be imprecise to call the social relations that Cressida establishes social 'bonds'. They are not brought about by encapsulating, by imposing, an outer boundary in a gesture of closure (binding, tying), they are not an effect of in- or exclusion. The social cohesion that Cressida impersonates is created through an opposing gesture. 'Ulysses is repelled by what he sees as the bodily *openness*, the speaking flesh' (Cook 'Unbodied Figures' 49). Instead of closure, it is opening up, exposing oneself, that causes a social connection: 'encounterers' like her 'wide *unclasp* the tables of their thought / To every tickling reader!': not bond but con-tact.

The significance of Cressida's gesture is heightened by the circumstances of the scene. Cressida arrives as a stranger and representative of the enemy; it is striking that she so quickly comes into rather intense touch with the Greek heroes. The con-tact she establishes undermines or opens up a system of community that the play shows as outlived and corrupted, but that Ulysses attempts to restore: the unity of Greeks that is constituted by their fighting against the Trojan enemy. Whereas Ulysses' idea of community follows the simple Schmittian logics of friend and enemy (cf. Schmitt),

Cressida is open to bond with '*every* tickling reader'. It is touch and 'opportunity' – that is to say con-tingency, not a pre-stabilised order of friend and enemy, that her modern notion of community is based upon. The mode of touch introduced to the audience by Cressida proves exemplary not only for the domain of love, but also for the field of war and the political or societal domain to which the play is also – and perhaps mainly – dedicated.

Call to Arms – War and Love

In Shakespeare's play, Thersites, the 'leering chorus' (Bevington *Shakespeare's Ideas* 135), repeatedly impersonates the dramaturgical function of the ancient choir. He summarises and comments on the events of the fictional world, addressing his words directly to the audience. The second scene of the fifth act may serve as an example of this. It ends with Thersites, alone on stage, summing up the gist of *Troilus and Cressida*: 'Lechery, lechery, still wars and lechery; nothing else holds fashion' (*TC* 5.2.201–2). '[W]ars and lechery', these two words obviously refer to the two main storylines, the 'interlocking plots of love and war' (Langis 4) that Shakespeare's play combines: the Trojan War with the ensuing inner conflicts on the one hand, the love affair of Troilus and Cressida on the other. However, the opening of Thersites' phrase, the pair of 'lechery, lechery' that corresponds to the ensuing pair of 'wars and lechery' somehow undermines the clear-cut distinction: 'war' is apparently embedded in lechery; the logic of correspondence between the two pairs rhythmically following each other, 'Lechery, lechery, still wars and lechery', implicitly associates 'war' with lechery. Is the play about war and lechery – or does 'war' simply turn out to be another variety of lechery?

Although the morally pejorative denotation dominates its meaning, the noun 'lechery' carries interesting connotations: it is etymologically derived from the French *lêcher*, 'to lick', and thus signifies the habit of social encounters that are performed by touches of the tongue. In other words, the practice of *lechery* forms part of the social regime of touch. War, however, does not obviously involve the practice of kissing and licking. Nevertheless, '[t]he sexual and martial are inextricably linked' (Vaughan 215), not only in a metaphorical way, as Virginia Mason Vaughan suggests, or indirectly, as in Lorraine Helms's argument, which puts forward that '[c]ombat *is* a form of intimacy, for it demands empathy to foresee and forestall the enemies' maneuvers' (34). In the ancient or early modern version that Shakespeare's play brings to the stage, war is still performed as an exchange of violent 'touches': of hits and blows, of strikes. By referring to Jean-Pierre Vernant, Unhae Langis points us to the fact that 'the ancient Greek word *meignumi* for sexual union also meant to join and meet in battle' (3). Things are not too dissimilar with regard to the English language. As their semantic potential indicates, many martial, violent touches quite easily shift to signifying touches of love or erotic touches. 'Striking' becomes 'stroking' (cf. 'strike, *v.*'; 3.) and 'hits' and 'blows' are common vocabulary for describing the sexual act, as Cressida herself demonstrates: 'If I cannot ward what I would not have hit, I can watch you for telling how I took the blow – unless it swell past hiding [. . .]' (*TC* 1.2.258–60).

When Hector announces the challenge for a duel, he intends to fight with one of the Greek heroes, and the transition from love to war becomes explicit:

HECTOR
[. . .] Kind, princes, lords,
If there be one among the fair'st of Greece
That holds his honour higher than his ease,
That seeks his praise more than he fears his peril,
[. . .]
That loves his mistress more than in confession

With truant vows to her own lips he loves,
And dare avow her beauty and her worth
In other arms than hers; to him this challenge:
   (*TC* 1.3.264–72)

At first, the theme of love merely appears to form part of Hector's attempt to challenge the Grecians' honour. Avowing and defending the beauty of one's mistress belongs to the chivalric ideal[9] that Hector contests and therefore appears to be suitable as a rhetorical gauntlet. However, the explicit analogy of making love and making war to which Hector gives voice somehow surpasses the theme of honour for which it was supposed to serve as an argument: loving 'more than in confession / With truant vows to her own lips' is not a statement of an ideal, a sacralised 'bond of heaven' – it signifies intimate body contact (which, as contact, is intrinsically 'truant', that is, fleeting, time-sensitive): the touch of lips. This bodily contact is transferred to an apparently 'higher', 'nobler' level: it is to be performed '[i]n other arms than hers'. On the one hand, this transference wittily replaces the human arms with the homonymous instruments of war; on the other, it substitutes the mistress's caressing touch with another – the combatant's violent strikes. This uncanny continuity of the bodily gesture of touch upstages the theme of 'honour' and 'praise' with which Hector's challenge had begun. Carol Cook calls this 'the eroticization of combat'. 'The "other arms"', she continues, 'are not only weapons but also the combatants' own arms as they grapple in violent embrace' ('Unbodied Figures' 43). '[H]onour' and 'praise' form the centre of a social regime, of a discursive system regulating social bonds and community that appears to be incompatible with the bodily notion of touch that continuously haunts Hector's challenge. Touch, the embrace between lovers and enemies, emerges as a rivalling foundation of social bonds.

How 'hollow' (*TC* 1.3.80) the regime of 'honour' has become, not only so far as the Greek army is concerned but even with regard to Hector's Trojan community, is shown an act later. The Trojan heroes discuss whether they should simply return Helena to the Greeks or continue the fighting and bloodshed. Troilus is the most outspoken of the pro-war fraction – and his (only) argument for re-establishing cohesion among the Trojan war party is 'honour'. His eponymous constancy comes to the fore in his appeal 'to stand firm by honour' (*TC* 2.2.68); Helena 'is a theme of honour and renown' (*TC* 2.2.199) that brings with it the 'advantage of a promised glory' (*TC* 2.2.204). Troilus directly dismisses objections that the peace faction (led by nobody less than Hector) lodge: according to Troilus, the new, humanist values of 'reason and respect' (*TC* 2.2.49–50) that Hector invokes cannot match the old, absolute values of '[m]anhood and honour' (*TC* 2.2.47). However, Troilus's 'argument' not only leans on the chivalric notion of individual honour and glory, but entails an important implication for social cohesion and community. This implication emerges when Troilus praises 'the goodness of a quarrel / Which hath our several honours all engaged' (*TC* 2.2.123–4). The 'quarrel' has a positive effect that renders it 'righteous': it 'engages', it 'binds' (cf. *OED*, 'engage, *v.*'; 4.a.) the several to form one – the end of the conflict threatens to dissolve the cohesion of the collective. Carl Schmitt famously declared this type of formation of unity, based on the conflicts of friends and enemies, to be the foundation of all political community: 'The distinction of friend and enemy denotes the utmost degree of intensity of a union or separation, of an association or dissociation' (26).

According to Schmitt, it is the confrontation of friend and enemy, of two collectivities of human beings that, at least potentially, fight and are willing to kill that constitutes the most intense degree of association.[10] Hector encounters the power and allure of this social mechanism. Even though he does not believe Troilus's argument of honour and discovers other, personal motives at play, he will finally agree to continue fighting. Hector's voice was likely to have been met with approval among the London early modern audience. He is the 'proponent of rational prudence in the debate' (Langis 13); his rational, stoic argument countering Troilus's is certainly the best in the rhetorical contest among the Trojan heroes:

HECTOR
The reasons you allege do more conduce
To the hot passion of distempered blood
Than to make up a free determination
'Twixt right and wrong; for pleasure and revenge
Have ears more deaf than adders to the voice
Of any true decision. [. . .] (*TC* 2.2.168–73)

However, in the end it is he himself who announces the decision to continue the war. The question of fighting the enemy is obviously not one of rational arguments. It follows different motives, as Carl Schmitt writes: 'There exists no rational purpose, no norm no matter how true, no program no matter how exemplary, no social ideal no matter how beautiful, no legitimacy nor legality which could justify men in killing each other for this reason' (49). The idea of war constitutes and defends an association of human beings. As Lorraine Helms has shown, Niccolò Machiavelli provided the early moderns with a precursor to Schmitt's idea: 'In the Proheme to *The Arte of Warre*, translated into English in 1560, Machiavelli argues that war is the foundation of public life and military structure society's best model' (Helms 31). Helms, however, also points us to another passage from Machiavelli's work that indicates why Machiavelli is not a good reference for the 'old' model of society and social cohesion for which Ulysses and Troilus stand: 'If one could change one's nature with time and circumstance, fortune would never change' (Machiavelli 25). Helms rightly associates this maxim with Cressida; it is an antidote, a strategy to cope with the 'infidelity of time' that characterises the 'modern' world of Shakespeare's *Troilus and Cressida*. It might be Hector's 'tragic fault' to remain 'constant' and not 'change [his] nature with time and circumstance' on this occasion – as we will see, he is in some respects close to Cressida's (in)dividuation – that seals his own and the Trojans' downfall.

Hector's decision does not seem to be so much based on care for his personal honour but on concern about the cohesion of the collective: 'For 'tis a cause that hath no mean dependence / Upon our joint and several dignities' (*TC* 2.2.192–3). The social bond that the fight against enemy ties is one of *closure*: it is about defining a collective identity against the enemy, against the foreign 'other'. The 'Schmittian' mechanism of cohesion works by drawing borders and, in this way, instantiating a logic of in- versus exclusion.

In Shakespeare's *Troilus and Cressida*, the foundation of this mechanism is shown to be collapsing, at the latest when Hector eventually fights his duel against Ajax. Their encounter stages a miniature of the war: two of the greatest heroes face each other, representing the hostile parties and fighting for their causes. However, the duel is somewhat displaced from the start: 'The combatants being kin / Half stints their strife before their strokes begin' (*TC* 4.5.93–4), as Agamemnon puts it. In other words, the 'real possibility of physical killing' that Schmitt (33) regards as the *conditio sine qua non* for the friend–enemy relation – and thus for the formation of a political community – is suspended.

The reason for this suspension is as interesting as it is significant: Ajax is related to Hector via an aunt who had been abducted by the Greeks – the Trojan abduction of Helena, the cause of the present strife and model, merely answered this seizure as an act of revenge. The two parties prove not as strange, as 'other', to one another as Schmitt would have enemies be. It is more than questionable whether a closure capable of constituting a community can work with the groups being not as homogenous and exclusive as a clear-cut distinction of friend and enemy asks for. Moreover, Hector's refusal to fight 'to the edge of all extremity' (*TC* 4.5.69) turns out not to be restricted to Ajax. Hector, 'This blended knight, half Trojan and half Greek' (*TC* 4.5.87), is known for sparing his enemies, as his 'courtesy' with regard to his arch-enemy Achilles – who will only moments later contract his killing – spectacularly emphasises (cf. *TC* 5.6.14–22).

The duel with Ajax therefore stands as a model for the conflict as such, a quarrel that is an important catalyst for social cohesion. Community is not generated by closure, by closing the ranks but, on the contrary, by opening arms for the enemy. Instead of defending boundaries and defeating the threatening foe by a fatal, final touch of arm, the duel ends with a friendly, almost explicitly homoerotic gesture:

HECTOR
[...]
Let me embrace thee, Ajax.
By him that thunders, thou hast lusty arms!
Hector would have them fall upon him thus.
Cousin, all honour to thee! [*They embrace.*] (*TC* 4.5.136–9)

'These homosocial relationships' are not simply 'all analogues to the military hierarchy' as Lorraine Helms (32) suggests. What Carol Cook has called 'Hom(m)o-sexuality' ('Unbodied Figures' 42) is, indeed, 'repeated at the level of the war' ('Unbodied Figures' 43), but it does not necessarily need 'the mediation of a woman to "come by" on another' ('Unbodied Figures' 43). As Hector had prefigured in his challenge to the duel, it is indeed '[i]n other arms' than those of the mistress that social bonds will be 'fought out'; the fact that the duel literally ends in Ajax's 'lusty arms' emphasises that the bond the two warriors tie does not essentially differ from the lovers' knot. It is not about the individual or collective honour that is gained in competition by defeating or annihilating the other; it is not about closing ranks against the enemy. It is about opening up to the other: admitting, allowing, suffering touch. War's use of arms obviously offers an ambiguous, bistable figure. It establishes, at the same time, the 'extreme case' (Schmitt 39), where the conflict between friend and enemy may find a lethal solution and a situation with the licence, the necessity to touch, to approach the other's body and thus 'bond' with him.

Hector's gesture of touch multiplies after it has ended the duel. It spreads among the Greek camp as if by contagion. It obviously has nothing to do with the Trojan blood that circulates in Ajax's veins and transgresses the boundary of friend and enemy. Hector embraces Ajax twice, and they shake hands before embracing both Menelaus and Nestor. Over the course of the scene, he also shakes Achilles' and Diomedes' hands (five-fingered-tied knots, so to speak) – only Ulysses somehow evades Hector's friendly touch.

Agamemnon is certainly right in claiming that 'The issue is embracement' (*TC* 4.5.149). Touch as a catalyst for social relations, social *con-tact*, is the whole scene's theme. The duel is not embedded by chance into two scenes of intense touching: not only by Hector's tour of embraces and shaking hands through the Greek camp which follows, but also in the scene of Cressida's arrival in the Greek camp, which 'preludes the ritual exchange of embraces among the men themselves' (Cook 'Unbodied Figures' 44).

The two scenes framing the duel clearly mirror each other. They are scenes of arrival and welcome, where representatives of the Greek and the Trojan war parties encounter each other on 'Greek ground', so to speak, and have to establish a social relation that suspends or even transgresses the enmity they fight out on the battlefield. This is achieved in a similar way in the two episodes: by touch.

Shakespeare's play presents its audience with two characters who defy this mode, two characters who are portrayed as phobic to touch: Troilus and Ulysses. It is no coincidence that the Trojan and the Greek watch the spectacle of Cressida's adulterous flirting with Diomedes side by side. Although 'officially' enemies in arms, they prove to be brothers in spirit, at least as far as their (reactionary) conception of social cohesion and organisation is concerned. In a prominent and much-discussed speech in the first act,[11] Ulysses explains his (outdated) vision of the 'sane', the well-ordered state of the world. It is a world governed by 'degree, priority and place' (*TC* 1.3.86) in which, in analogy to the perfect and stable organisation of planets, each singular element finds its constant, authentic place. Compared to this model, the world of *Troilus and Cressida* is, from the beginning, 'out-of-joint':

ULYSSES
What raging of the sea, shaking of earth,
Commotion in the winds, frights, changes, horrors,
Divert and crack, rend and deracinate
The unit and married calm of states
Quite from their fixure! (*TC* 1.3.97–101)

'[R]aging', 'shaking', 'changes' – it is '[c]ommotion', the dynamics of (violent) movement, that differentiates the present state of affairs from the planetary model characterised by eternal 'fixure'. The 'bonds of heaven' that Troilus notes to be slipped when Cressida binds her 'five-finger-tied knot' with Diomedes clearly belong to the (old) social regime sketched out by Ulysses. Troilus, 'truth's authentic author to be cited', must certainly be understood as the paradigmatic subject of this system. Given Troilus's emphasis on 'manhood', Cressida accepted her place relative to his authentic male position when bonding with him. In this patriarchal system, her affair with Diomedes is a typical instance of what Ulysses classes as a 'neglection of degree' (*TC* 1.3.127) which, in his opinion, characterises the corrupt, feverish state of the world.

'How could communities [...] / But by degree stand in authentic place?' (*TC* 1.3.103–8), Ulysses asks, and intends his apparently rhetorical question to campaign for the restoration of a bygone world. However, Cressida takes this question literally and gives an unexpected answer: the community she 'founds' might not be 'authentic', but the social regime of touch she embodies is nevertheless capable of initiating social relations and a certain social cohesion. Certainly, this cohesion works differently: touch does not tie eternal bonds – it carries the notion of time in its very concept, *as* touch. Touch is not to be understood as a desperate 'grasping'; it knows of a beginning and an end. It is, as Ulysses reproaches the 'encounterer' Cressida, dependent on 'opportunity', on con-tingency. The same holds true for the community of warriors that forms by embraces and handshakes when Hector is welcomed in the Trojan camp:

AGAMEMNON
What's past and what's to come is strewed with husks
And formless ruin of oblivion;
But in this extant moment, faith and troth,
[...]
From heart of very heart, great Hector, welcome.
  (*TC* 4.5.167–72)

Furthermore, the community of touch is all but 'authentic'. On the contrary: as Cressida's knot five-finger-tied with Diomedes exhibits, it is based on *falseness*, on being and not being Cressida. Again, Hector's performance of community confirms this model. When meeting the Greek heroes, Hector is at the same time deadly enemy and friend – both *hospes* and *hostis* – a paradoxical relation that subverts Carl Schmitt's clear-cut distinction.

The social regime of touch that *Troilus and Cressida* explores is based on a paradigm different from the one on which Carl Schmitt grounded his theory of community.

Whereas Schmitt posits the constellation of war, with its defining difference of friend and enemy in order to build a system of ex-/inclusion on this primary difference, Shakespeare decides for a primal scene of love:

PANDARUS
[...] Love, love, nothing but love, still love, still more!
For, O, love's bow
Shoots buck and doe.
The shaft confounds
Not that it wounds,
But tickles still the sore. (*TC* 3.1.109–14)

Although Pandarus's song speaks of 'love, love, nothing but love', it nevertheless embeds war into the lechery it sings about. Love's 'bow' and 'shaft' introduce the war material, the 'other arms', whose touch carries the potential for lethal harm. However, the punchline of the song shifts this apparently violent touch to a pleasingly erotic one: 'Yet that which seems the wound to kill' (*TC* 3.1.116) in fact receives sexual pleasure – the deaths that love's bows and shafts cause turn out to be only little, orgasmic deaths. In order to fabricate this shift with rhetorical means, the song resorts to the phallic concept of penetration. The shaft metaphorically transforms into the male member that tickles sexually. This male connotation is, however, suspended by the framing logic of the song as such. Love's arrows are shot from the middle, so to speak, they '[s]hoot[ ] buck and doe'. Moreover, the shaft does not 'wound[ ]', does not penetrate the flesh, but 'confounds'. Tickling creates social cohesion between the two lovers by way of 'confound[ing]', by 'pouring together' and creating a mix. The verb 'confound' carries strong negative connotations, denoting destruction and failure. However, Pandarus's song clearly contrasts the 'male' penetrative practice of wounding – unequivocally destructive and negative – with the ambiguous 'female' practice of tickling, a surface-phenomenon that confounds, 'neglects degree', that is certainly dangerous, but also proves to be a source of sexual pleasure and social cohesion.

Tickling and stroking, explicitly erotic touches, are a theme in the play, which guarantees that war is indeed embedded in 'lechery'. Cressida caressing Troilus and stroking Diomedes mirrors the 'touchy' nature of Helena. Shakespeare draws her as a coquette, a 'femme fatale' (Helms 36; Langis 2), an 'encounterer'. Pandarus might tell a lie when he boasts that she has 'tickled' Troilus's chin (*TC* 1.2.131); the audience however experiences her on stage, flirting with Pandarus and presumably even touching his 'fine forehead' (*TC* 3.1.102). Cressida and Helena are thus twin-figures: the male, armed and violent conflict is just interplay – war continues love, and only partially by other means. As Pandarus's theorisation and Hector's practice of war show, it need not only be about wounding and annihilating the other. The violent encounters can shift to become tickling encounters, germs for social relations initiated by contingent touch, for con-tacts.

The violent, defensive move of closing the ranks, of excluding the stranger, the other – the enemy – and killing him is based on the constitution of an absolute difference (friend versus enemy). This difference will eventually become an absolute, a final hierarchy, since in the essential 'extreme case', only one of the two parties will survive. By contrast, 'tickling', caressing and kissing are characterised by an inherent mutuality. In kissing (the same holds true for embracing) you 'take and give', Cressida explains; 'love's bow / Shoots buck and doe', Pandarus sings. However, as a paradigm for social cohesion, love generates much less stability than war, for several reasons: 1) There are no simple distinctions that structure the world of love (like enemy and friend); the conditions for successful relationships ('opportunity') are much more complex and thus unforeseeable (cf. contingency) – they cannot as easily be discursively produced as the friend–enemy distinction. 2) Touch is time-sensitive and does not generate a stable, irreversible result, like the death of the enemy for war; the social relation it creates thus remains inherently uncertain. 3) Loving touch is always in danger of shifting back to violence; as caressing requires opening up, exposing oneself as its vital/essential condition, it makes one vulnerable to becoming the victim of malicious violence. This is why Carl Schmitt confronts opponents of his theory, pacifists who attempt to develop a theory of community that dreams of a non-violent principle of social cohesion, with a simple argument: 'It would be ludicrous to believe that a defenseless people has nothing but friends, and it would be a deranged calculation to suppose that the enemy could perhaps be touched [gerührt] by the absence of resistance' (Schmitt 53). '[T]he unmoored vulnerability of Cressida's femininity' (Crocker 324) should not be misunderstood as merely a personal or structural weakness that is to be overcome. Feminists like Arlene Okerlund are certainly not wrong in emphasising 'her vulnerable position' (Okerlund 13) among the Greek warriors. Shakespeare's play, however, shows that Cressida is capable of exercising a certain power out of this very vulnerability. She creates 'an intensity of vulnerability that forcefully counters the empowering virtues of the warrior community' (Crocker 309). Vulnerability is thus not a personal weakness, or the weakness of her sex, but a key characteristic of the haptic mode of bonding, of establishing the social cohesion that Cressida advocates and embodies.[12]

Touch does not follow a calculable, mechanical logic. Exposing oneself, offering the conditions for social, caressing touch, does not guarantee a loving, touching answer. Touch cannot be enforced; it remains dependent on opportunity, on improbable mutual goodwill, on con-tingency. Exposing oneself to touch, trusting in touch, is therefore always dangerous.

Shakespeare's *Troilus and Cressida* exhibits the frailty of the regime of touch with a tragic example: Hector's death.

He is killed by Achilles' Myrmidons, in what has to be seen as a contract killing:

ACHILLES
Come here about me, you my Myrmidons;
[...]
And when I have the bloody Hector found,
Empale him with your weapons round about:
In fellest manner execute your arms.
[...]
It is decreed Hector the great must die. (*TC* 5.7.1–8)

Although Hector defeats Achilles on the battlefield (and spares him), Achilles does not back away from his cruel project of revenge for his intimate friend Patroclus. When he discovers Hector, who has already ceased fighting for this day and is unarmed, he calls on the Myrmidons to execute the plan: 'Strike, fellows, strike!' (*TC* 5.9.10) At this very moment, Hector encounters Achilles, as he had encountered him the day before: Achilles had invited 'the most valorous Hector to come unarmed to [his] tent' (*TC* 3.3.293). With this second encounter, Hector is again unarmed, 'he is caught off guard in a state of *gumnos*' as Unhae Langis writes (16), again resorting to a Greek concept which he takes from Jean-Pierre Vernant: '*gumnos* – a term which in this military context means "unarmed"', but can also carry the meaning 'exactly like a woman' (Langis 15). In other words, it is here Hector who falls victim to '[t]he dangers of being in a feminine, unarmed state' (Langis 15), to the 'unmoored vulnerability of [. . .] femininity'.

Hector's defencelessness – 'I am unarmed. Forgo this vantage, Greek' (*TC* 5.9.9) – does not 'touch' Achilles. It is not 'lusty arms' that Hector meets, but the violent, lethal material of war: they do not make him blush or encourage circulation – as loving touches do ('rub on!') – but are intended to 'empale' him, for ever. It is not love's life but war's death that is Hector's fate.

Although Pandarus's legendary formula ('[l]et all constant men be Troiluses, all false women Cressidas, and all brokers-between panders!') significantly divides up the two models of constancy and falseness along the lines of sex, the play undermines any reading that tries to extract a simple misogynistic message from it. *Hamlet*'s 'Frailty, thy name is woman' (*Ham.* 1.2.146) does not reverberate in *Troilus and Cressida* without a decisive complication:[13] the 'problem' associated with femininity, 'frailty', is, as Hector's fate shows, not a specifically female problem. On the contrary, frailty indicates a problem of the world that Shakespeare's plays explore and analyse. 'Frailty' derives from 'fragile', and is closely related to 'fragment', 'fraction', and therefore to the world of *Troilus and Cressida*, which consists of broken 'scraps', 'bits' and 'orts'. The opposite of 'male' simplicity and timeless fixity, Cressida's female falseness, frailty and her individuation's sensibility to time thus resonate with the 'modern' world: the early prototype of modern subjectivity that Shakespeare explores in *Troilus and Cressida* is decidedly 'female'. Its male, constant counterpart is an alien element, a remnant of an old order that has ceased to exist. The mourning for the loss of this simple male order may find expression as misogynistic aggression – it is nevertheless Cressida, Hector and their 'female' regime of touching fractions that the play is concerned with, and which brings the play into contact with early modern life.

Was Ulysses then right to shun touch? The gloomy end of *Troilus and Cressida* seems to support this standpoint. However, he is portrayed as a person 'out of touch'. Except for the cuckold Troilus, with whom he watches Cressida's falling for Diomede, Ulysses is isolated. Unlike Ulysses, Troilus at least looks towards some sort of future: he is spurred on by the motive of revenge. Ulysses' focus is exclusively on the past. Shakespeare makes him the representative of a bygone world, whose restoration is but a vain fantasy.

Troilus and Cressida stages a world 'divert[ed], 'crack[ed]' and 'deracinate[d]', a world of dynamic 'fractions', of 'raging' 'commotion'.[14] Nostalgically conjuring up the bygone 'unit and married calm of states', or the 'fixure' guaranteed by the 'bonds of heaven', does not help to establish social cohesion in this 'new world'. Although a dangerous and always imperfect solution, 'another knot', probably 'five-finger-tied', will have to create a new kind of social cohesion; social cohesion that does not know of eternal fixture or of transcendent stabilisation, that is not prefigured by a simple system of regulating principles ('degree, priority and place', family, etc.). A radically improbable foundation of social relations that is not based on a closed system but on the openness of con-tingent and ambiguous encounters – on con-tacts: a social regime of touch.

> 'Friends, there are no friends!' thus cried the dying sage;
> 'Foes, there is no foe!'— thus shout I, the living fool.
> (Nietzsche, *Human, All-Too-Human*, 294; transl. altered)

Of Brokers-between – Theatre

> Much rather will he make the confession to himself:—
> Yes, there are friends, but they were drawn towards thee by error and deception concerning thy character; and they must have learnt to be silent in order to remain thy friends; [. . .]. (Nietzsche *Human All-Too-Human* 293)

Ulysses is portrayed as the most perseverant opponent of the new regime of social cohesion. He carefully evades Hector's and Cressida's touch and voices his objections against the mode of social relations embodied by Cressida. Nevertheless, in a later scene, he too finds himself a part of one of the play's paradigmatic communities of touch.

The particular social bond I have in mind is produced by 'opportunity'; it transgresses, like Cressida's and Hector's contingent social encounters, the boundary of friend and enemy. Ulysses guards the Trojan Troilus through the Greek camp and leads him to Calchas's tent, where Troilus hopes to meet Cressida. It is by mere accident that Ulysses and Troilus end up as 'joint' witnesses of Cressida's flirting with Diomedes, watching the scene together, hidden from the two protagonists' views. Their contingent alliance is thus a product of chance; more than this, it is a most improbable alliance that Shakespeare uses to illustrate the inescapability and the power of the social regime of touch.

It is no coincidence that Troilus and Ulysses find themselves grouped together, probably using one of the pillars on the platform stage to remain unnoticed. As shown above, they form one faction in the constellation around the problem of social cohesion that *Troilus and Cressida* explores: Troilus, like Ulysses, is a representative of the old order; it is from their shared concealment that Troilus charges the dissolution of the 'bonds of heaven'. However, the particular constellation of the scene imposes conditions upon the Greek and the Trojan hero that suspend their accustomed, their characteristic behaviour. Above all, Ulysses and Troilus, the two men of words, have to bridle their tongues in order not to reveal their presence. 'List!' (*TC* 5.2.19), Ulysses tells Troilus and has to remind him repeatedly of either holding his peace or leaving. Although forced into an exceptional situation, Troilus readily accepts its uncomfortable conditions: 'I pray you, stay. By hell and all hell's torments, / I will not speak a word' (*TC* 5.2.45–6). He is strangely riveted by the spectacle that unexpectedly unfolds before his eyes, a spectacle that he knows to deliver an unpleasant message to him. As analysed above, the spectacle that Troilus and Ulysses watch – Diomedes flirting with Cressida – is a spectacle of touch; Troilus and Ulysses witness the formation of a five-finger-tied knot, the formation of a 'haptic' community.

This is what Thersites' choric commentary appears to expose. Thersites is another secret witness of the scene, speaking aside to the audience: 'How the devil Luxury, with his fat rump and potato finger, tickles these together! Fry, lechery, fry' (*TC* 5.2.57–9). He is not just a second audience, watching the same scene as the first audience (Troilus and Ulysses) do. He has followed the two heroes and thus knows of their presence. He is, in Luhmannian terms, a 'second-order observer' (cf. Luhmann *Social Systems* xxxix): besides the actual spectacle, he also observes the observers' observing.[15] Furthermore, his aside does not interrupt, is not triggered by, Cressida's and Diomed's dialogue, but follows, and in a way answers, words exchanged by Troilus and Ulysses. The referent of Thersites' statement thus remains ambiguous: who is it that 'the devil Luxury' 'tickles together'? Diomedes and Cressida? Or Troilus and Ulysses? Who is it that forms a community of touch, as Thersites' choice of words – 'tickl[ing] together' – so aptly indicates?

As discussed above, the touching bond between Cressida and Diomedes is, literally, a given – he strokes her cheek. Furthermore, Cressida herself is aware that her relationship with Diomedes is an act of lechery, because it entails becoming unfaithful to Troilus. However, Thersites' malediction, 'Fry, lechery, fry', appears to concern/affect Troilus as well. 'By hell and all hell's torments, / I will not speak a word,' he tells Ulysses, and thereby uncannily associates himself with the 'frying' torments that Thersites connects to the act of lechery. Although he himself is not responsible for and does not personally take part in the act of lechery – an act of lustful touching – he is nevertheless affected, touched by it. Ulysses and the theatre audience testify to his suffering. In other words, the scene stages two different acts of 'social' touch taking place at the same time: a direct one between Diomedes and Cressida, and an indirect, a mediated one that affects the watchers of the spectacle, Troilus and Ulysses (and perhaps also Thersites). Ulysses' dictum that Cressida, as an 'encounterer', 'wide unclasp[s] the tables of [her] thought / To every tickling reader!' resonates with the double touch taking place in this scene. Cressida's touches do not only affect their direct addressees – like a text, a postcard (cf. Derrida *The Post Card*), they spread their influence beyond intentional address, bridging a certain distance, reaching not only Diomedes, but 'every tickling reader', here Troilus, Ulysses, Thersites and the theatre audience. This second, mediated touch is a paradoxical touch: it touches without touching. It touches at a distance and under the condition of prohibited immediate touch. In other words: it is deeply theatrical.

The conditions governing this paradoxical touch are the conditions imposed upon the audience in the constellation of theatre. The eavesdropping scene we are analysing is obviously metatheatrical:

> Eavesdropping is no doubt an extremely complex aspect of drama and performance, drawing attention to spectatorship in the theatre itself, with the spectators, in most cases, 'secretly' watching the events on the stage, reinforcing the meta-theatrical dimensions of the situation. (Rokem 114)

The eavesdroppers, Ulysses and Troilus, watch the same 'scene' that the 'real' audience is watching; Shakespeare exploits this set-up to explicate the conventions of the theatrical situation. As the scene exhibits, the theatrical situation is constituted by a fundamental prohibition of touch. The audience witnesses an event, takes part in a spectacle – under one condition: it agrees not to intervene. This is what Ulysses repeatedly ensures when he and Troilus watch Diomedes's flirt with Cressida. If Troilus's 'displeasure should enlarge itself / To wrathful terms' (*TC* 5.2.38–9), if he should decide to leave his concealment and intervene, the (meta)theatrical setting will collapse and Troilus, as an unruly Trojan in the

Greek camp at night-time, will be in lethal danger. Instead of leaving, Troilus agrees to subject himself to a regime of rules that are well known to the regular theatre visitor but that still had to be habitualised for the early modern audience of the rather new mass-medium public theatre (cf. Gurr *Playgoing in Shakespeare's London*; Hobgood *Passionate Playgoing in Early Modern England*). Troilus takes on a particularly passive role; he will not touch the two people he is watching in any way – he 'will not speak a word' (*TC* 5.2.46; 54), but follow Ulysses' imperative and merely '[l]ist[en]'. He will expose himself to the spectacle, will let his 'displeasure [. . .] enlarge' without proceeding to 'wrathful' action. Understandably, Ulysses remains sceptical as to whether Troilus, confronted with a spectacle that concerns him in a most intimate sense, will be able to stay in this role: 'You have not patience' (*TC* 5.2.44), he tells Troilus and calls the particular 'attitude' of the theatrical audience by an interesting name. When, some lines later, Troilus answers Ulysses' doubts/concerns, he picks up his companion's trenchant term:

> TROILUS [*to Ulysses, aside*]
> Fear me not, sweet lord.
> I will not be myself, nor have cognition
> Of what I feel. I am all patience. (*TC* 5.2.64–6)

The fact that Troilus promises 'not to be himself' should not be understood as a promise of indifference. It rather suspends the stimulus–response mechanism that, in real life, usually translates the experience of displeasure into (wrathful!) action in order to evade/escape/stop the harmful stimulus. Unlike *Hamlet*'s Claudio, who is trapped by collapsing a theatrical situation, breaking his 'character' or rather his theatrical role as a viewer, Troilus will perform the theatrical contract. He will not filter his feelings according to personal motives and interests, intervening accordingly. The constitutive distance that the theatre audience entertain to the fictive events they are confronted with in a theatre performance has to be 'artificially' produced for Troilus, who faces 'reality' and is forced to distance the events, thereby turning them into theatre. By motivating a metatheatrical scene in the guise of an eavesdropping scene, Shakespeare ingeniously stages the conventions of the theatrical situation, of the theatrical setting.

'I am all patience' can be read as a catchphrase for the role of the ideal theatre spectator: it does not express indifference, but the absence of resistance. The ideal spectator exposes him- or herself to the spectacle's emotions without restraint, suspending control, giving in to the feelings that are evoked by what he or she sees and hears. The etymology of *patience* suggests this metatheatrical reading: *patience* goes back to the Latin *patior*, denoting 'suffering', and is thus related to the Greek πάθος, *páthos*, one of the prominent technical terms of theatre theory. Deciding not to 'go off' (*TC* 5.2.42) but stay and watch, Troilus willingly subjects himself to suffering; he exposes himself to an experience of 'displeasure' that, nevertheless, appears to exercise a strong attraction on him. We encounter the typical paradox of theatre that, according to Aristotle, somehow generates pleasure from suffering (cf. Aristotle 75).

Troilus does suffer. 'You are moved, Prince' (*TC* 5.2.38), Ulysses notices, and this information appears redundant in the face of the situation that Troilus finds himself in. However, it is not. Against the background of how Shakespeare has drawn the figure of Troilus in the preceding scenes, his behaviour as a spectator is remarkable. Troilus is shown to be the very opposite of a sensitive character: 'His night with Cressida has made him insensitive and uncouth,' writes René Girard (128). There are indications that 'the all-important indifference of Troilus' is not 'only a brief phase', as Girard suggests (128). More than once he proves to be not only self-controlled but rather self-absorbed, stubborn even – the opposite of open to his surroundings. Cassandra's bursting in on an assemblage of the Trojan heroes and her interrupting their discussions with a disturbing 'performance' of her prophetic visions may serve as a case in point: 'Now, youthful Troilus, do not these high strains / Of divination in our sister work / Some touches of remorse?' (*TC* 2.2.113–15), Hector asks. 'I am no more touched than all Priam's sons' (*TC* 2.2.126), Troilus answers. Instead of being emotionally affected by Cassandra's 'clamour' (*TC* 2.2.106), by her energetic and theatrical crying out of her prophecies, he simply judges her to be 'mad' (*TC* 2.2.108; 122). In this instance, Troilus obviously has 'cognition / Of what [he] feel[s]', substituting a feeling with a 'rational' judgement and thus taking control of the situation. Hector's very question implies that Troilus's answer is more wishful thinking than grounded in careful observation. In contrast to Troilus, Hector appears to be touched by Cassandra's intervention. With regard to sensitivity, Hector is drawn as Troilus's counter-image: it is no coincidence that Troilus chides his older brother for his sparing the enemy in the battle ('Brother, you have a vice of mercy in you' (*TC* 5.3.37)). Troilus is obviously not as easily touched by pity as his brother. Troilus's reaction to the decision that his mistress Cressida has to leave Troy thus fits the mould. His rather unemotional and pragmatic dealing with the situation has irritated many critics. Does his 'cold', composed reaction indicate a lack of love for Cressida? I would suggest reading it as a dramaturgic choice. Troilus is characterised as self-controlled only to increase the effect of the scene when even he is finally 'moved'. It is the constellation of theatre that manages to integrate the touchophobic Troilus into the community of touch.

The same holds true for Ulysses. As shown above, he is at least as touchophobic as Troilus and, moreover, an outspoken enemy of the theatre. As a 'remedy' (*TC* 1.3.142) for the sickness of the state, its disturbing 'fever' that he diagnoses, he recommends fighting Achilles' and Patroclus's 'scurril jests' (*TC* 1.3.148). Ulysses charges Patroclus that, 'with ridiculous and awkward action – / Which, slanderer, he imitation calls – / He pageants us' (*TC* 1.3.149–51). The use of the Aristotelian technical term 'imitation' – the English translation of *mimesis* – indicates that what Achilles and Patroclus do is to be understood as theatre. The Greek heroes and their individual particularities provide the 'stuff for these two to make paradoxes' (*TC* 1.3.184) – that is to say, to create political resistance, speaking out against the hegemonic *doxa*. Ulysses represents the position of anti-theatricalism on stage, which brought forth a prominent debate that accompanied Shakespeare's career. Although this position is often associated with Puritanism, Ulysses does not meet the expectations linked with the typical stage Puritan. One might argue that he shows Puritan traits, as Janet Dawson does with reference to Ulysses' role as stage audience watching Cressida flirt with Diomedes:

> Ulysses, seen as a voyeur, might remind the audience of the Puritan censors in the City 'keeping an eye' on theatres located outside the city walls, perhaps more than strictly necessary, in order to find (and maybe surreptitiously enjoy) those scenes of moral turpitude they disapproved so much. (172)

With regard to his attitude towards theatre, one might discover in Ulysses the hypocrisy characteristic for the stage Puritan. However, he certainly does not embody the 'type of the proud ignorant puritan' (Hornback 138), 'the contemporary clownish, radical puritan stereotype' which Robert Hornback (125) has worked out as characteristic for the early modern stage. On the contrary, Ulysses is renowned for his smartness. Shakespeare depicts him as a strategic manipulator who secretly pulls the strings in the background. Furthermore, Ulysses' arguing for degree and hierarchy is at odds with the carnivalesque, anti-hierarchical impulse that Hornback and

Grace Tiffany expose as a trait of 'Puritan' positions in contemporary political-religious debates and, satirically exaggerated, as a characteristic of many Elizabethan stage Puritans. In contrast to Malvolio's anti-festivity, Ulysses' anti-theatricalism is not ridiculed. In *Troilus and Cressida*, Shakespeare has found a different way of dealing with a 'Puritan', a theatre-critical position. Ulysses is reintegrated into the community – and, paradoxically enough, it is a theatrical community, the community of the audience, that he becomes a part of.

It is com-passion[16] that holds, that 'tickles' this theatrical community together. The plurality of watchers is an important characteristic of the scene. Troilus does not only decide for himself not to 'go off'. Ulysses speaks of himself and Troilus in the plural: 'Let *us* depart, I pray you' (*TC* 5.2.38; my emph.), he tells Troilus, who, some lines later, replies: 'Nay, stay' (*TC* 5.2.54). Why does Troilus not send Ulysses away? He has long fulfilled his task as a guide. And why does Ulysses not simply leave the scene? Why does he care about Troilus, whom we should not forget to be a Trojan enemy?

In other words, the scene is about the constitution of community.[17] It reflects upon theatre's power to found a social bond. The theatrical situation produces a community, irrespective of degree, origin, sex and even of shared values. It is based on one sole principle – on the condition of being sensitive to touch – it is 'tickled together' by com-passion. In other plays, Shakespeare sounds the limits of this community. It not only brings together Greek and Trojan, theatre enthusiast and theatre enemy,[18] princes and prostitutes, but also touches the paradigmatic outsider figure, 'the Jew':[19]

> SHYLOCK
> Hath not a Jew hands, organs, dimensions, senses, affections, passions? Fed with the same food, hurt with the same weapons, subject to the same diseases, healed by the same means, warmed and cooled by the same winter and summer as a

Christian is? If you prick us do we not bleed? If you tickle us
do we not laugh? (*MV*, 3.1.53–9)[20]

The inclusion of Ariel, who is 'but air', a spirit, into the community of touch – he shows 'a touch of feeling' (*Tmp.* 5.1.20) when watching Prospero tormenting the court party in *The Tempest* – indicates that the argument is not a purely anthropological or humanist one. It is theatrical in that it transgresses any value-based, humanist standpoint. The community of touch, of shared 'patience' or com-passion, cannot be retranslated into a rational logic.

The theatricality of the 'indirect' touch taking place in the scene affects the 'direct' touch – the one between Diomedes and Cressida – that is performed simultaneously. In his discussion with Ulysses, Troilus's observations inadvertently locate the interaction between Cressida and Diomedes within the theatrical constellation. In the theatre analogy that the scene creates, the two represent the fictional spectacle, the actors performing on stage. The characteristics of touch worked out above begin to resonate intensely with the theatrical stage situation:

TROILUS
[. . .]
But if I tell how these two did co-act,
Shall I not lie in publishing a truth? (*TC* 5.2.124–5)

The '[b]ifold authority' (*TC* 5.2.151) that Troilus recognises, the fact that what he sees 'is and is not Cressid' (*TC* 5.2.153), turns out to be a precise, an apt description of the stage situation. What he sees is in fact an actor playing Cressida. The ambiguity, the lack of authenticity and truth forms the basis of theatre's fictionality.

TROILUS
[. . .]
Was Cressid here?

ULYSSES
                I cannot conjure, Trojan.
TROILUS
She was not, sure.
ULYSSES
                Most sure she was.
TROILUS
Why, my negation hath no taste of madness.
ULYSSES
Nor mine, my lord. Cressid was here but now. (*TC* 5.2.131–4)

In *The Tempest*, Shakespeare extensively argues that what theatre does can indeed be regarded as a form of conjuration. With his punning on the verb 'conjure' in *Troilus and Cressida* some years earlier, he explicates one decisive condition for theatre's conjurations: the community of the audience and their willingness to expose themselves to the ambiguous touch of the spectacle. Theatre *con-sures*, it does not *as-sure* or *en-sure*, it does not grant fixity by anchoring in truth; it brings together (cf. lat. *cum*), it merges, it 'confounds' (*TC* 3.1.112) incompatible sureties. Like the five-finger-tied knot between Diomedes and Cressida, this community is not based on authenticity and truth. Despite the irrationality that Troilus and Ulysses diagnose in their discrepant sureties, there is no 'taste of madness' in this paradoxical (remember the theatre's 'paradoxes'!) moment. The (theatrical) community of touch suspends the law of the excluded middle and thus undermines the stable distinction of rational versus mad that Troilus had so readily applied to ward off Cassandra's prophecies. This community is based on falseness: 'O Cressid! O false Cressid! False, false, false!' (*TC* 5.2.185), Troilus cries. However, theatre creates a situation in which this falseness is not univocally condemned as moral corruption, but affirmed. The audience agrees to expose themselves to two or three hours of 'falseness', being 'all patience' and somehow even generating pleasure from the suffering that joins them, from their co-experienced com-passion.

However, *Troilus and Cressida* does not merely portray the theatrical setting or describe a heterotopos where community and social bonds would work in a different way to the 'real world' which surrounds this special place. On the contrary, it uses the theatrical setting to explore a social regime of touch that resonates with the theatrical setting, but that transgresses/transcends the theatre's boundaries:

> Falseness with a good conscience; the delight in pretence erupting as a power that pushes aside, floods, and at times extinguishes one's so-called 'character'; the inner longing for a role and mask, for an *appearance* (*Schein*); an excess of capacities for all kinds of adaptation that can no longer be satisfied in the service of the nearest, most narrowly construed utility – perhaps all of this is distinctive not *only* of the actor? (Nietzsche *The Gay Science* 225–6)

Cressida's mode of individuation – her capacity to affect 'every tickling reader', her legendary falseness – is that of an actress. However, this is the way that she interacts, she does not need the theatrical situation with stage and audience to be an 'encounterer'. For her, '[a]ll the world's a stage' (*AYL* 2.7.140), but not in a medieval, theological-allegorical way. Shakespeare displaces, he inverts and distorts the old *theatrum mundi* topos, which in his rethinking takes on a specifically 'modern' meaning. Cressida does not act out a part assigned to her by a transcendent authority, with this authority also watching the play as its intended audience. In *Troilus and Cressida* – like *Hamlet*, steeped in metatheatrical allusions – all the world's not only a stage but has also become a theatre: the viewer(s) no longer watch(es) from somewhere beyond; they are co-present in the sphere of immanence. It is the theatrical act itself, taking place in-between actors and audience, in-between playing and applause, that assumes an important function in the social organisation of the world. In what has to be called a striking proto-Goffmanian moment (cf. Goffman), Ulysses gives voice to this theatrical social mechanism:

> ULYSSES
> [. . .] no man is the lord of anything,
> Though in and of him there be much consisting,
> Till he communicate his parts to others;
> Nor doth he of himself know them for aught
> Till he behold them formed in th'applause (*TC* 3.3.116–20).

The fact that 'no man is the lord of anything' is well known from the 'old' *theatrum mundi* concepts. It is not a higher authority, however, scripting the parts that guarantees the 'truth' of the world as a whole, but the interaction between players and audience that negotiates honour and worth. In this radically immanent conception of the world, the anchoring truth granted by the transcendent order, the divine 'playwright' and 'stage manager', has ceased to exist. What man is, his honours, virtues, his ideals and goals, and so on, has to be negotiated in the complex social processes of human interaction; divine providence and determination begin to be replaced by human responsibility and immanent social processes. 'Truth' is not a given, but the effect of 'communication'. Falsity, unavoidable and constitutive polyvalence/ambiguity provide the ground for a modern world, because they are the very condition of possibility for 'actual' decisions to be taken (cf. Luhmann *Social Systems*). In a univocal, perfectly ordered world there is no room (and no need) for human decisions or responsibility (its univocity has pre-decided everything, so to speak); the 'human' problem merely consisted of knowing this world, of finding a way to its truth – doing the right thing follows on directly from having gained access to truth (cf. Plato *Symposium*).

With the social processes of communication and interaction transforming into the core of a system of the world, the urgent need arises to establish, stabilise and further these processes. Shakespeare's *Troilus and Cressida* presents us with an impersonation of this important social task: Pandarus. He calls himself a 'broker[ ]-between' (*TC* 3.2.198), or 'goer[ ]-between' (*TC* 3.2.195–6) – what he does is mediating, bringing into con-tact, facilitating (improbable) touches. '[H]e tends to function almost allegorically in the play's action as "medium" and the problems it creates,' writes Richard D. Fly (153). With regard to his setting up Cressida with Troilus, Pandarus solves a social problem for which, according to Niklas Luhmann, a medium of communication ('love as passion') will emerge some hundred years later; the code of this 'generalised communication medium' slowly begins to develop in (the literature of) Shakespeare's time (cf. Luhmann *Love as Passion*). Pandarus, however, also contributes his mediating capacities to the establishment of another medium: he holds, he 'tickles together' the theatrical medium, bringing stage and audience into contact.

It is no coincidence that Pandarus delivers the play's epilogue; the position in-between character and the actor's 'real person', in-between fiction and the factual, the actual performance situation, obviously appeals to his competences as a 'goer-between': 'he actually serves as an intermediary between the play-world and the contemporary audience, extending the issue of mediation from the internal workings of the actual theatrical experience' (Fly 153).

Pandarus has already established contact with the audience in an earlier scene. Directly after his conducting the quasi-betrothal-ceremony and showing Troilus and Cressida 'a chamber with a bed' (*TC* 3.2.202–3), he addresses the viewers:

PANDARUS
[. . .]
And Cupid grant all tongue-tied maidens here
Bed, chamber, pander to provide this gear! (*TC* 3.2.205–6)

Pandarus constructs and exposes a parallel between his services as a matchmaker and theatre: the maidens he addresses are tongue-tied (and thus resemble Cressida in her problematic relation to language) because they are present as viewers in a theatre. As a consequence, the contact Pandarus establishes between stage and audience, though initiated and explained with words, will have to be 'executed', 'performed' in the same way as Troilus and Cressida have tied their knot only seconds before – by touch.

In the epilogue, Pandarus examines the success of the touching connection between stage and audience:

> PANDARUS
> Good traders in the flesh, set this in your painted cloths:
> As many as be here of Panders' hall,
> Your eyes, half out, weep out at Pandar's fall;
> Or if you cannot weep, yet give some groans,
> Though not for me, yet for your aching bones.
> Brethren and sisters of the hold-door trade,
> Some two months hence my will shall here be made,
> It should be now, but that my fear is this:
> Some galled goose of Winchester would hiss.
> Till then I'll sweat and seek about for eases,
> And at that time bequeath you my diseases. (*TC* 5.11.45–56)

As is typical for Shakespeare, the epilogue asks for the viewers' signs of approval, wrapping them in some sort of metaphorical guise that resonates with a prominent theme of the play. The weeping and groaning that Pandarus calls for follows an uncanny double coding: they are either symptoms of theatrical success (of having moved the spectators, whose bones would ache after at least two hours of standing in the pits or sitting on wooden benches in the galleries) or of (venereal) disease. In an earlier scene, Pandarus describes his own suffering from the same ambiguous symptoms: 'I have rheum in mine eyes too, and [. . .] ache in my bones'

(*TC* 5.3.104–5). The 'foolish fortune of this girl [i.e. Cressida]' troubles him, as does the 'whoreson rascally phtisic' (*TC* 5.3.101–3) that will, sooner or later, kill him. Against the background of the rather cynical analogy of the effect of theatre and venereal disease, Pandarus should not be surprised that his 'endeavour' as a 'pitiful goer-between' 'be so desired and the performance so loathed' (*TC* 5.11.38–9). However, despite the gloomy connotations of venereal disease – a hot topic in early modern London (cf. Boehrer; G. W. Bentley) – the epilogue that Pandarus delivers affirms the cultural practice theatre that it forms part of. Why then does it short-circuit performing plays and 'bequeath[ing] [. . .] diseases'?

As Pandarus himself alludes to in the epilogue, the cultural institution of the 'public theatre' and the business of organised prostitution, with all its health issues, were not to be separated in early modern London (cf. Lenz). They were located in the same district, Southwark, for the same reason: the district did not fall under the jurisdiction of the City, but the authority of the Bishop of Winchester. Brothels and theatres were frequented by the same people – customers and prostitutes – and the huge public 'success' of Southwark's brothels and theatres justifies Pandarus's claim that his 'endeavour is so desired'. His use of the word 'performance' hints at the theatricality of the two 'trades'. However, the 'performances' of theatre and prostitution are 'loathed' for the same reason: clerical authorities regard these 'seedy', 'shady' businesses as corruptive. The association of theatre with spreading diseases or causing fevers is a topos in anti-theatrical writing, as Daryll Chalk and others have shown (cf. Lenz; Sanders; Votava):

> it can be demonstrated that in antitheatrical literature the minds and bodies of the players and spectators were not merely poisoned or altered by the potential narcotic efficacy of theatre, they were *infected* and, crucially, imbued

with a powerful capability to infect others, to spread the disease of theatricality with an efficiency as dangerous as any plague epidemic. (Chalk 8)

Chalk finds the semantic field of contagion in the main proponents and pamphleteers of anti-theatricalism in early modern England: Edmund Grindal complained that 'there is no one thing of late [that] is more like to have renewed this contagion, than the practice of an idle sort off people, [...] I mean *these histriones*, common players' (269); John Rainolds bemoaned 'how the maners of all spectators commonlie are hazarded by the contagion of theatricall sights' (162–3); William Prynne claimed that 'the gracelesse wicked ones who daily visit [stage-plays], are many in number, contagious in quality, more apt to poyson, to infect all those who dare approach them, than one who is full of running Plague-sores' (152); 'they that came honest to a play, may depart infected,' wrote Stephen Gosson (G4r).

Shakespeare thus does not invent or construct an analogy for theatre and venereal disease, he merely seizes the argument of his enemies and uses it for his own purposes. It is obviously neither moral corruption nor the 'disease' itself that he is interested in, but the power, the capacity of spreading the disease, which the theatre's enemies readily ascribe to this loathed institution. It is a theatrical power of touch that Shakespeare affirms with *Troilus and Cressida*, a power of *con-tagion*,[21] of 'tickling together' (lat. *cum-tangere*).

Theatre's 'contagion' is present throughout the play. It surfaces repeatedly and becomes thematic, for example when Ulysses charges Achilles' and Patroclus's theatrical activities and accuses them of being responsible for the neglect of degree, for the corruption of the Greek camp: 'And in the imitation of these twain, / [...] many are infect' (*TC* 1.3.185–7), Ulysses states. The 'envious fever / Of pale and bloodless emulation' (*TC* 1.3.133–4) spreads to the theatre audience at the latest when they become witnesses to Patroclus's 'imitations' in the play-within-a-play scene called 'the pageant of Ajax' (*TC* 3.3.280–300). The spectators in the pits or the galleries are most likely – and dramaturgically asked – to enjoy the comedy of the scene as much as Achilles does, who applauds the short performance when it is finished.

The audience becomes again thematically involved in theatre's contagions in one of Thersites' choric monologues that is directly addressed at the audience:

THERSITES
[. . .] All the argument is a whore and a cuckold; a good quarrel to draw emulous factions and bleed to death upon. Now the dry serpigo on the subject, and war and lechery confound all! (*TC* 2.3.69–72)

Thersites obviously speaks about the Trojan War – 'All the argument is a whore and a cuckold' – his words, however, also quite aptly 'summarise' the 'argument' of the play which the viewers he addresses are watching. Thersites' cursing 'the subject' with 'the dry serpigo' – 'A general term [. . .] for creeping or spreading skin diseases' (*OED*, 'serpigo, *n.*') often associated with syphilis (cf. Traub 74) – thus threatens to affect the audience, who are about to be *touched* by the tragic fate of Troilus and Cressida. Keeping in mind that Thersites probably delivers his curse from the forestage, making contact with the audience, the 'all' in his 'war and lechery confound all!' certainly transgresses the fictional, internal communicative system and includes the spectators viewing the play. '[W]ar and lechery' – Hector's fall and Troilus's loss of Cressida – are indeed what 'moves' the theatre attendants and what merges them together to form a plural mass called 'the audience': a community of patience, a community constituted by com-passion, by sharing the position of being exposed to con-tagion. In short, they are held together by con-'suffering' touch, by being 'tickled together'. The verb 'confound' thus, again, has to be read literally – from the Latin *con-* (*cum-*) *fundere*, 'pouring together' – implying the production of a mix that is characterised by con-sisting of different ingredients that have been brought into con-tact.

'Thersites is nearest to the audience in his level of awareness, and perhaps physically on stage,' writes Paul Gaudet (142). According to Arlene N. Okerlund, 'he is one of us – perhaps *is* us' (16). Like Pandarus, Thersites acts, here and on other occasions, as a go-between. Both bridge the constitutive gap between stage and audience and thus impersonate (and thereby expose) the 'miraculous' capacity of theatre: of touching at a distance, of touching without touching.

Like Pandarus, theatre functions as a multiplier of contacts. It has the power to con-taminate: to bring into touch, to con-stitute (temporal) communities – to spread its touch to provide a whole network that potentially affects 'every tickling reader'. It is a mass *medium*: theatre's 'magic', 'contact-free' touch that touches at a distance proves to be highly contagious; its touches multiply (in the audience) and permeate the social body. Its 'endeavour' of facilitating con-tact is highly 'desired' because the modern world, whose stability is (exclusively) generated by human interaction (trade, negotiations, etc.), is in need of intensification, multiplication and acceleration of social contacts. However, it is also loathed, and for understandable reasons.

Troilus and Cressida makes palpable the anxiety that the loss of the old transcendent order, with its stable 'bonds of heavens', and the emergence of a new social regime of touch evoke. The world has lost its wholeness, the fractions and fragments, bits and pieces hover in-between heaven and hell, without receiving order or stability from either of them. Instead, stability is expected to emerge from the in-between, just from the fact that contacts are established, that touch is facilitated, from con-tingency. The anxiety *Troilus and Cressida* exposes is the anxiety of mediality. The shift in paradigm is immense. However, the play indicates the awareness that there is no point of return, that this 'new way of the world' is unavoidable. More than this, it knows of theatre's important role in this 'new' world. Although it bemoans the bygone 'healthy' ages, and boastfully charges the spreading corruption, theatre is not an enemy, but an accomplice to the challenges of social complexity. It takes the chance to contribute to a world that does not receive its truth from a transcendent beyond, but that holds together by touch, by com-passion, by contingent contagion. This is why Pandarus, as long as he is still part of this world, affirms his morally corrupted activities and will continue his loathed 'performances':

> Till then I'll sweat and seek about for eases,
> And at that time bequeath you my diseases. (TC 5.11.55–6)

Notes

1. As the Arden3 editors, following Oxford1, write, 'The phrasing also imperfectly recalls the betrothal ceremony in the *Book of Common Prayer*' (Shakespeare *Troilus and Cressida* 256).
2. Shanon Harris's critique of Troilus's verbosity resonates with Gayle Greene's impression that 'Troilus shows more interest in the style and idea of love than in Cressida herself, and it is this which accounts for his failure to know her' ('Language and Value' 278).
3. Gayle Greene and Stephen X. Mead have read *Troilus and Cressida* in the context of the notion of value that was about to change from an intrinsic quality to a relational quantity, which deeply affected the reliability of language: '*Troilus and Cressida* is about money as language and language as money' (Mead 239); 'Vows do not guide actions; right and wrong, among other things, lose their names' (Greene 'Language and Value' 274).
4. 'Dividuation' is a concept sketched out by the French philosopher Gilles Deleuze. On the basis of this concept, Michaela

Ott has recently developed a 'Theory of Participation', which affirms 'dividuation' and holds it up against the notion of 'the individual'. I would like to support this theoretical move with my (affirmative) reading of Cressida.

5. 'The play is a commentary on [...] the infidelity of time,' writes Unhae Langis (26). With this exploration of a (modern) world completely governed by this uncanny and ineluctable 'infidelity', Shakespeare dares to advance on territory that Friedrich Nietzsche and Gilles Deleuze only begin to examine in greater detail centuries later.

6. As Constance Classen has established, associating tactility with femininity is an established topos of the early modern period: 'Touch, taste and smell were generally held to be the lower senses and thus were readily linked to the lower sex – women', which 'reinforced the cultural link between femininity and the body, for these senses were closely tied to intimate bodily experience' (75). The fact that 'touch is very often personified as a woman' (Karim-Cooper *The Hand* 168) chimes with this observation.

7. 'The society from which Cressida's nature takes its shape is thus modern and familiar,' notes Gayle Greene ('Shakespeare's Cressida' 137). In *Shakespeare: The Dark Comedies to the Last Plays*, R. A. Foakes describes how twentieth-century critics, beginning with George Bernard Shaw, discover 'how "modern" the play is' (44).

8. Joseph Papp has argued that this 'welcome ritual' has to be read as a gang rape, cynically choreographed by Ulysses (cf. 60). Against the historical/cultural background of touch and kiss, of which Constance Classen is an expert, a welcome kiss between strangers might have been habitual. This is what Erasmus of Rotterdam observed in late fifteenth-century England, to his astonishment: 'the first act of hospitality is a kiss, and when guests depart, the same entertainment is repeated' (203; cf. Classen 4). The kisses in the scene analysed ambiguously oscillate between these two extremes of rape and hospitality.

9. *Troilus and Cressida* has been read as primarily concerned with the notion of the chivalric ideal: 'It is the very conven-

tion of the chivalric ideal itself that Shakespeare is questioning, and Cressida's function in that aspect of the play must not be ignored' (Harris 78).
10. 'An enemy exists only when, at least potentially, one *fighting collectivity of people confronts a similar collectivity* [*Feind ist nur eine wenigstens eventuell, d.h. der realen Möglichkeit nach* kämpfende *Gesamtheit von Menschen, die einer ebensolchen Gesamtheit gegenübersteht*]' (Schmitt 28).
11. I do not quite agree with Gayle Greene, who regards it as 'the quintessential expression of the Elizabethan idea of order' ('Language and Value' 271).
12. The idea of a community based on vulnerability resonates with Judith Butler's recent thinking about what she calls 'precariousness'.
13. 'Cressida is the clearest representative of woman's "frailty" in his plays, the "frailty" that Hamlet says is woman's "name"' (Greene 'Shakespeare's Cressida' 133).
14. Stephen X. Mead's '"Thou art chang'd": Public Values and Personal Identity in *Troilus and Cressida*' shows that Shakespeare clearly thinks of this 'new world' as one governed by capitalist principles.
15. Diana E. Henderson, referring to *Much Ado*, describes Thersites' position as homologous to that of the theatre audience: 'the theatrical audience is privileged in being positioned as the most voyeuristic Watch of all' (196).
16. Compassion is here understood in the way that Jean-Luc Nancy interprets the term, emphasising the aspect of 'suffering together', that is, of a productive interaction that presupposes vulnerability (cf. Chapter 1,'Theatre's Offence: *Hamlet* and *The Tempest*', p. 69–70).
17. Along the lines that Judith Butler in *Notes toward a Performative Theory of Assembly* and Jacques Rancière in *The Emancipated Spectator* have drawn, I understand this (theatrical) community both as situative/performative and fragile; a problem or a challenge rather than a prestabilised given. The theatrical situation does not sublate the heterogeneity of the actants involved. On the contrary, it brings heterogeneous

actants into touch – aiming for a critical, but unforeseeable, *mutual* response.

18. Astonishingly enough, the affirmation or even overestimation of the (potentially dangerous) power of theatre united the opponents of the so-called anti-theatrical debate: '[a] chorus of voices – from both attackers and defenders of the theatre, as well as from playwrights themselves – saw the theatre not only as a vehicle for representing drugs and poisons, but as a kind of drug or poison itself,' writes Tanya Pollard (*Drugs and Theater in Early Modern England* 9). Eve Rachele Sanders supports this claim: 'both sides in the debate shared concerns about the dangerousness of theater' (393). By suggesting that 'performance does indeed alter the actor, as well as the spectator', Shakespeare 'acknowledges an argument found in antitheatrical tracts' (Sanders 410).

19. Michael Witmore points out 'the symmetry of male and female affect and sensation' (422) expressed in a passage of *Othello*, which resonates with the passage in *The Merchant of Venice*: 'Let husbands know,' says Emilia. 'Their wives have sense like them: they see and smell, / And have their palates for both sweet and sour, / As husbands have' (*Oth.* 4.3.92–5).

20. I am indebted to Tobias Döring's indication to an audience at a conference in Munich that Shylock's two categories of touches – pricking and tickling – might encode the two main genres of theatre, tragedy ('If you prick us do we not bleed?') and comedy ('If you tickle us do we not laugh?').

21. Cf. Diomedes' speaking of Helena's 'contaminated carrion weight' (*TC* 4.1.73).

CODA: A PHILOLOGY OF TOUCH

Shakespeare's plays touch their audience – and they do so at a distance. In the preceding chapters, we have encountered many instances of this distance. All took their start from theatre's basic conditions: with the separation of stage and audience, a boundary between the fictional world of the characters and the real world of the theatre 'assembly'. Over the course of this study, we have reconstructed how Shakespeare plays with this boundary, his doubling it onstage in play-within-a-play scenes which expose its characteristics. The onstage theatre chimes with the experience of attending a play, one that we all share. This boundary does not hermetically seal off what it separates. Horatio and Hamlet show unmistakable, bodily signs (their paleness, their trembling) of having been 'touched' – although they have encountered a ghost (which everyone knows cannot be touched). The same holds true for Troilus when he observes Cressida and Diomedes flirting with each other. He watches from a distance; what he sees and hears is not addressed to him, and yet it causes him great suffering.

We might therefore be tempted to call theatre's boundary 'porous' or even 'permeable'. However, things are more complicated: emotions do not simply travel from stage to audience, transgressing the boundary that separates the two.

Affects are generated through the contact between the play and its recipients. The difference between permeating the boundary and establishing contact appears minimal, but it is decisive. Unlike transgressing an obstacle, establishing contact does not remove the boundary. A certain distance, though perhaps minimal, remains. This distance, which contains the tension between the movements of approximation and a final degree of repulsion, is the defining characteristic of touch. Touch establishes the encounter of at least two, bringing the partners of touch into a productive nearness. However, they do not merge into one, but remain separate. Hamlet does not become a ghost, or the ghost a living human. Troilus does not leave his hideout, nor does he (immediately) go for Diomedes' throat. Nevertheless, it would be wrong to say that nothing happens.

What looks less radical than an act of transgression has its own power. The relationship that touch brings forward is unique. Whereas transgression implies a one-directional movement of a certain active entity which breaks into and subverts a regime thought to be static and passive, touch does not know of a passive or an active part. It is characterised by an ineluctable mutuality. Touching and being touched cannot be distinguished; they take place at the same time. As a consequence, all the partners involved in a touching encounter are affected, are changed by their entering into touch. Touch therefore embraces anarchic qualities. It suspends social hierarchies and imbalances of power because it drags everyone and everything that participates in a touching encounter into a process of becoming, irrespective of their status or authority.

As we have seen, on the level of plot, touch is associated with femininity or outsider status. Beatrice and Cressida may be the epitome of characters versed in touch. However, a particular capacity for touch (culturally associated with femininity in the early modern period) is not tied to gender.

Hamlet, Richard, Benedick, Hector – they all operate (also) in the 'minoritarian'[1] mode of touch. Like Beatrice and Cressida, they create what could be called circumstances of suspension. They introduce a certain distance which suspends habitual proceedings, regulated by an established order of things, and makes relationships of touch possible. This is not a simple thing to do. On the contrary, artistry is required to bring about relationships of touch. Beatrice masterfully suspends the referential and contractual power of speech, smoothing the way for linguistic caresses. Hamlet's theatrical madness works in a similar fashion, facilitating the distribution of contaminating touches. Richard's attitude towards truth and reliable speech acts is well known. Handing over his sword to Lady Anne exposes his successful strategy of suspending the (gendered) social order and working his way up to the throne in a minoritarian fashion, using the anarchic powers of touch. Hector sparing Ajax incurs his combatants' disapproval, making him an outsider. He suspends the killing of the defeated enemy and thereby makes an encounter 'in other arms' possible. However, as Hector's case illustrates, encounters in the mode of touch are fragile. Touching requires exposing oneself to the other, 'unfolding oneself', as the beginning of *Hamlet* puts it. The vulnerability implied always involves a certain risk – the risk of the state of suspension coming to an end and the fragile (caressing) mutuality shifting to violence. When the distance constitutive for touch is bridged, the boundaries break and a different relationship comes to the fore: the (mortal) combat of one against the other, which aims for the annihilation of the other, for the dissolution of all tension – eat or be eaten.

It is no coincidence that touch in Shakespeare's theatre is not only associated with femininity and minoritarian status, but also with the art of theatre itself. Richard, the 'deepe dissimuler', is a 'deep tragedian'; Beatrice's and Benedick's 'empty' speech acts mirror the theatrical use of language;

Pandarus's matchmaking brings not only the intra-fictional couple, but also play and audience into (potentially infectious) contact. There are structural reasons for theatre's astonishing capacity for touch, which, paradoxically, is made possible by establishing unbridgeable distance. The divide of stage and audience – or rather, since the spatial boundary can well be crossed, the impossibility of penetrating the boundary of fiction – create a remarkably stable, paradigmatic state of suspension. As elaborated upon in the introduction, the particularities of early modern theatre (its natural light, its being architecturally less optimised for visual illusion than for bodily proximity) intensify the power of its state of suspension and the structural mutuality it entails.

Shakespeare's plays produce and reflect upon (at least) two significant theatrical experiences. First, although all the 'substantial' sources of bodily and legally binding impact and personal emotional attachment thought to be responsible and necessary for any kind of change in the real word are suspended, theatre proves itself able to touch, to move its audience. 'What' is it that has this capacity to move? As we have seen in *Hamlet*, *The Tempest* and *Richard III*, Shakespeare's theatre revolves around this very question. The 'insubstantial', the 'bottomless', the 'shallow', the 'superficial' (that is, ontologically minor instances) are discovered to be influential actants that contribute significantly to the way of the world. With this observation, theatre not only affirms its own power, but also questions the hegemonic, the *major* ontological intuitions that prevail outside theatre's *minor* heterotopos. This is not an abstract, philosophical argument (which would probably be of little use to the theatregoer), but has social effects that can be experienced in the theatre. Second, in *Troilus and Cressida*, *Much Ado* and *The Tempest*, Shakespeare exposes the social effect arising from the insubstantial, from processes of touch that are not ontologically or epistemologically grounded. Communities emerge out of con-tact, out of com-passion, out of suffering together, without any framing criterion of sameness or a common enemy that would hold the community together. Troilus and Ulysses watching Cressida flirt with Diomedes epitomise this theatrical community of touch. Touch brings together heterogeneous partners (they are enemies, fighting each other on the battlefield), and they stay enemies. There is no reason for them to form a community, and yet they do. It is a temporal, a fragile one, but sufficiently stabilised by the theatrical spectacle they witness. Beatrice and Benedick's relationship also comes about as a community of touch. It is 'based' on lies, set up as a theatrical spectacle, formed by non-contractual, void speech acts – and yet it is not fake. Something loving, an unmistakable linguistic caress, happens in their approximation that always maintains the (productive and lively) tension of repulsion.

As the onstage theatre-watchers Troilus and Ulysses show, these theatrical experiences do not simply come to the audience without their assistance. Their discussion leads to an agreement that shows the basic traits of a theatrical contract which also spells out the constitutive characteristics of touch. They agree to be 'all patience', meaning two things: 1) to respect the boundary between the spectacle they are watching and their hideout, that is, not to interfere with what they experience (aspect of distance!); 2) to expose themselves to the spectacle, to 'unfold' themselves to what they experience, not to be shy of contact and run away (aspect of nearness, of being an 'encounterer').

What are *we* to make of this 'touchophile' attitude, we scholars, whose job it is to come into touch with theatre, with performance and with texts? Can we agree on a 'contract of contact' that, as Shakespeare's audiences do, further unleashes the forces of the insubstantial and helps distribute and amplify the capacities of Shakespearean theatre? I think it a difficult but all the more important challenge for academic writing to join the community of touch and compassion, extending its reach beyond the walls of the theatre into the realm of intellectual production and university teaching. The aim must be to not lose touch and thereby deprive Shakespeare's theatre of its power to move and affect the way of the world.

Inspired by Shakespeare's theatre and its affinity to touch, my study has attempted to perform what can be called a 'philology of touch', whose main objective is to be sensitive to and distribute the (affective, conceptual, social) capacities of the works of art to which it is dedicated. In order to do so, it has to find a position in touch with the text or artistic production, instead of writing *about* a piece of art from the 'objective' but untouchable position of a god-observer. Paradoxically, this 'inside' position is a minoritarian one: it can neither claim a more direct, immediate grasp of things nor the security of the stable, reliable contextualising framing, which always presupposes the idea of an objective, majoritarian standpoint. This does not mean to bracket all historical, epistemological or cultural knowledge, but asks for patience. A philology of touch does not undertake a journey of expedition which starts in well-known territory, setting out into the unknown in order to complete the map of the world until no white spots are left. Instead, it starts from the middle. It begins with an encounter and attempts to make this encounter a fruitful one, from which intellectual, political and social impulses issue. That is all.

There cannot be a guarantee of success, but there are certain conditions to be met in order to make a touching encounter possible. We have come across and have found models for these conditions in the preceding chapters. The productive nearness of touch demands respect for and care of distance. This is much easier said than done, because of the basic operation of the humanities: understanding something, always entails comprehending it, *grasping* it, making it one's one. *Grasping* as appropriation annihilates the distance constitutive for touch, and thereby brings an end to any touching encounter. Creating the situation of suspension that we have encountered in Shakespeare's theatre is therefore a central task for a philology of touch. Similarly to theatre and its basic structure, philology, in its love for texts, resorts to structural help in stabilising the productive distance needed for a situation of suspension. Texts are never quite present. Reading Shakespeare intensifies this initial situation: the centuries separating us historically, culturally and epistemologically from Shakespeare's theatre present an obstacle for a thorough understanding of it – however, they facilitate productive, touching encounters. The tension between historicising and making Shakespeare 'present' has proven to be enormously productive in Shakespeare Studies, perhaps the most proliferating intellectual 'problem' of recent decades. A philology of touch affirms this tension. Not as a conflict or a 'problem' to be solved, but as a situation of suspension which provides the perfect conditions for a touching intellectual encounter.

My study has taken this in-between as its starting point. All that is needed to proceed in the mode of a philology of touch can be learned from Troilus, Horatio, Hamlet or any open-minded theatregoer: the readiness to expose oneself to the forces and affects of theatre and texts, to cease control, to unfold oneself, to become an 'encounterer'. The aim is not to tame anything that is about to happen by immediately translating it into the realm of the well-known, but to give it room for development according to its own, probably different rules and to become sensitive to its effects and functioning. It is therefore necessary to *initially* suspend any framing or knowledge and to hold back intuition and rapid understanding. The intellectual distance established in this way asks to be supplemented by entering into a nearness to the 'textual surface' which we encounter. Getting in touch with text and the performance of text means reading it as closely as possible, following the minutest textual detail in order to let this overly complex net of significations take maximum effect. Then: listen to the resonances issued by the reading. It is here that all the knowledge, context and framing come into play. Whatever chimes with the reading (that is, whatever amplifies its effect) can now be brought to it. This may be historicising context, epistemological background, anachronistic theory or problems of the twenty-first century – the only criterion (and this is a very harsh, selective criterion!) is that the result has the capacity to touch *with* the text, and thus to make a difference.

What might sound like an academic 'anything goes' proves to be the very contrary in practice: a textual encounter that does not merely talk about a text, contextualise it, or force it to support some preformed idea, but instead engenders an unforeseeable intellectual, political or critical stimulus *together with it* is highly improbable. Doing justice or living up to a text may be a question of touch – of 'give and take', as Cressida would say, of a mutuality that cannot be academically enforced or stabilised, but has to be desired. Shakespeare's theatre might contaminate us with this desire – which could be called philo-logy.

Note

1. The notion of 'minoritarian' versus majoritarian is borrowed from Gilles Deleuze and Félix Guattari's *A Thousand Plateaus*, esp. 351–423 and *Kafka: Toward a Minor Literature*.

BIBLIOGRAPHY

Adair, Vance. 'Back to the Future: Subjectivity and Anamorphosis in *Richard III*', *Critical Survey* 9.1 (1997): 32–58.

Agamben, Giorgio. *Sovereign Power and Bare Life*, trans. Daniel Heller-Roazen. Homo Sacer. Stanford, CA: Stanford University Press, 1998.

Ahmed, Sara. *The Cultural Politics of Emotion*. Edinburgh: Edinburgh University Press, 2004.

Anderson, Thomas Page. *Performing Early Modern Trauma from Shakespeare to Milton*. Burlington, VT: Ashgate, 2006.

Aristotle. *Poetics*, trans. Stephen Halliwell et al. Loeb Classical Library. Cambridge, MA: Harvard University Press, 1995.

Austin, John Langshaw. *How to Do Things with Words: The William James Lectures Delivered at Harvard University in 1955*. Oxford: Clarendon Press, 1962.

Barthes, Roland. *A Lover's Discourse. Fragments*, trans. Richard Howard. London: Penguin, 1990.

—. *The Neutral: Lecture Course at the College de France (1977–1978)*, trans. Rosalind Kraus and Denis Hollier. New York: Columbia University Press, 2007.

Bentley, Gerald Eades. *Shakespeare: A Biographical Handbook*. New Haven: Yale University Press, 1961.

Bentley, Greg W. *Shakespeare and the New Disease*. Bern: Peter Lang, 2012.

Berger, Harry. 'Against the Sink-a-Pace: Sexual and Family Politics in *Much Ado About Nothing*', *Shakespeare Quarterly* 33.3 (1982): 302–13.

—. *Imaginary Audition: Shakespeare on Stage and Page*. Berkeley, CA: University of California Press, 1989.
Bevington, David. *Shakespeare's Ideas: More Things in Heaven and Earth*. Oxford: Wiley-Blackwell, 2008.
—. 'The Tempest and the Jacobean Court Masque', in *The Politics of the Stuart Court Masque*, ed. David Bevington, Peter Holbrook and Leah S. Marcus. Cambridge: Cambridge University Press, 1998. 218–43.
Blanchot, Maurice. *The Space of Literature*, trans. Ann Smock. Lincoln, NE: University of Nebraska Press, 1982.
Blumenberg, Hans. *Beschreibung des Menschen*. Frankfurt am Main: Suhrkamp, 2006.
—. *Paradigms for a Metaphorology*, trans. Robert Savage. Ithaca, NY: Cornell University Press, 2016.
—. *Shipwreck with Spectator: Paradigm of a Metaphor for Existence*, trans. Steven Rendall. Studies in Contemporary German Social Thought. Cambridge, MA: MIT Press, 1997.
Boehrer, Bruce. 'Early Modern Syphilis', *Journal of the History of Sexuality* 1.2 (1990): 197–214.
Burton, Robert. *The Anatomy of Melancholy*. Oxford: Printed by Iohn Lichfield and Iames Short, 1621.
Butler, Judith. *Notes Toward a Performative Theory of Assembly*. Cambridge, MA: Harvard University Press, 2015.
Cahill, Patricia. 'Take Five: Renaissance Literature and the Study of the Senses', *Literature Compass* 6.5 (2009): 1014–30.
Calderwood, James. *Metadrama in Shakespeare's Henriad, Richard II to Henry V*. Berkeley, CA: University of California Press, 1979.
—. *Shakespearean Metadrama: The Argument of the Play in Titus Andronicus, Love's Labour's Lost, Romeo and Juliet, A Midsummer Night's Dream and Richard II*. Minneapolis, MN: University of Minnesota Press, 1971.
—. *To Be and Not To Be: Negation and Metadrama in Hamlet*. New York: Columbia University Press, 1983.
Campana, Joseph. 'Killing Shakespeare's Children: The Case of Richard III and King John', *Shakespeare* 3.1 (2007): 18–39.
Carlson, Marvin. *The Haunted Stage: The Theatre as Memory Machine*. Ann Arbor. MI: University of Michigan Press, 2001.

Cavell, Stanley. *Disowning Knowledge: In Six Plays of Shakespeare*. Cambridge: Cambridge University Press, 1987.
Chalk, Darryl. '"A Nature But Infected": Plague and Embodied Transformation in *Timon of Athens*', *Early Modern Literary Studies* 19 (2009): 1–28.
Charnes, Linda. *Notorious Identity: Materializing the Subject in Shakespeare*. Cambridge, MA: Harvard University Press, 1993.
—. 'We Were Never Early Modern', *Philosophical Shakespeares*, ed. John J. Joughin. London: Routledge, 2000. 53–68.
Classen, Constance. *The Deepest Sense: A Cultural History of Touch*. Urbana, IL: University of Illinois Press, 2012.
Clough, Patricia Ticineto, ed. *The Affective Turn: Theorizing the Social*. Durham, NC: Duke University Press, 2007.
Cook, Carol. '"The Sign and Semblance of Her Honor": Reading Gender Difference in *Much Ado About Nothing*', *PMLA* 101.2 (1986): 186–202.
—. 'Unbodied Figures of Desire', *Theatre Journal* 38.1 (1986): 34–52.
Craik, Katharine A., and Tanya Pollard. 'Introduction: Imagining Audiences', *Shakespearean Sensations: Experiencing Literature in Early Modern England*, ed. Katharine A. Craik and Tanya Pollard. Cambridge: Cambridge University Press, 2013. 1–28.
Crichton, Andrew B. 'Hercules Shaven: A Centering Mythic Metaphor in *Much Ado About Nothing*', *Texas Studies in Literature and Language* 16.4 (1975): 619–26.
Crocker, Holly A. '"As false as Cressid": Virtue Trouble from Chaucer to Shakespeare', *Journal of Medieval and Early Modern Studies* 43.2 (2013): 303–34.
Crunelle-Vanrighe, Amy. '"Imitari is Nothing": L'Amour dans *Much Ado About Nothing*', *Études Anglaises: Grande-Bretagne, États-Unis* 47.3 (1994): 257–66.
Culler, Jonathan. *Literary Theory: A Very Short Introduction*. Oxford: Oxford University Press, 1997.
Curran, Kevin. 'Phenomenology and Law: Feeling Criminal in *Macbeth*', *Criticism* 54.3 (2012): 391–401.
Curran, Kevin, and James Kearney. 'Introduction', *Criticism* 54.3 (2012): 353–64.

Dawson, Anthony B. 'Much Ado about Signifying', *SEL* 22.2 (1982): 211–21.
Dawson, Janet. 'Order and Disorder in Two Versions of *Troilus and Cressida*: The Case of Ulysses', *Sederi* 11 (2002): 169–77.
Day, Gillian M. '"Determinèd to prove a villain": Theatricality in *Richard III*', *Critical Survey* 3.2 (1991): 149–56.
Deleuze, Gilles. *Cinema 2: The Time-Image*, trans. Hugh Tomlinson and Robert Galeta. Minneapolis, MN: University of Minnesota Press, 1997.
—. 'Plato and the Simulacrum', trans. Mark Lester and Charles Stivale, in *The Logic of Sense*. London: The Athlone Press, 1990. 253–66.
—. 'Un manifeste de moins', in *Superpositions*. Paris: Éditions de Minuit, 1979. 85–131.
Deleuze, Gilles, and Félix Guattari. *Kafka: Toward a Minor Literature*, trans. Dana Polan. Minneapolis: University of Minnesota Press, 1986.
—. *A Thousand Plateaus: Capitalism and Schizophrenia*. Minneapolis, MN: University of Minnesota Press, 1987.
—. *What is Philosophy?*, trans. Hugh Tomlinson and Graham Burchel. European Perspectives. New York: Columbia University Press, 1994.
Derrida, Jacques. *La Dissémination*. Paris: Seuil, 1972.
—. *Limited Inc*, trans. Jeffrey Mehlman and Samuel Weber. Evanston, IL: Northwestern University Press, 1988.
—. *On Touching, Jean-Luc Nancy*, trans. Christine Irizarry. Stanford, CA: Stanford University Press, 2005.
—. *The Post Card: From Socrates to Freud and Beyond*, trans. Alan Bass. Chicago: University of Chicago Press, 1987.
—. *Specters of Marx*, trans. Peggy Kamuf. London: Routledge, 1994.
—. *Spurs. Nietzsche's Styles. Éperons. Les Styles de Nietzsche*, trans. Barbara Harlow. Chicago: University of Chicago Press, 1979.
DiPietro, Cary, and Hugh Grady. 'Presentism, Anachronism and the Case of *Titus Andronicus*', *Shakespeare* 8.1 (2012): 44–73.
—. *Shakespeare and the Urgency of Now*. London: Palgrave Macmillan, 2013.

Döring, Tobias. *Performances of Mourning in Shakespearean Theatre and Early Modern Culture*. Early Modern Literature in History. Basingstoke: Palgrave Macmillan, 2006.

Edwards, Philip. 'The Declaration of Love', in *Shakespeare's Style: Essays in Honor of Kenneth Mui*, ed. Philip, Edwards, Inga-Stina Ewband and G. K. Hunter. New York: Cambridge University Press, 1980. 39–50.

Egan, Gabriel. 'Reconstructions of the Globe: A Retrospective', *Shakespeare Survey* 52 (1999): 1–16.

Egan, Robert. *Drama within Drama: Shakespeare's Sense of His Art in* King Lear, The Winter's Tale, *and* The Tempest. New York: Columbia University Press, 1975.

Erasmus, Desiderius. *The Epistles of Erasmus from His Earliest Letters to His Fiftieth Year*, trans. Francis Morgan Nichols, vol. I. New York: Russell & Russell, 1962.

Escolme, Bridget. *Talking to the Audience*. Abingdon: Routledge, 2005.

Fernie, Ewan. 'Shakespeare and the Prospect of Presentism', *Shakespeare Survey* 58 (2005): 169–84.

Fischer-Lichte, Erika. *The Transformative Power of Performance: A New Aesthetics*. New York: Routledge, 2008.

Flagstad, Karen. '"Making This Place Paradise". Prospero and the Problem of Caliban in *The Tempest*', *Shakespeare Studies* 18 (1986): 205–33.

Fly, Richard D. '"I cannot come to Cressid but by Pandar": Mediation in the Theme and Structure of *Troilus and Cressida*', *Studies in Renaissance Drama* 3.1 (1973): 145–65.

Foakes, R. A. *Shakespeare: The Dark Comedies to the Last Plays. From Satire to Celebration*. London: Routledge, 2005.

Foucault, Michel. *Fearless Speech*. Los Angeles: Semiotext(e), 2001.

—. *The Order of Things: An Archaeology of the Human Sciences*, trans. R. D. Laing. New York: Pantheon, 1970.

Freud, Sigmund. 'Drei Abhandlungen zur Sexualtheorie', *Gesammelte Werke V*, ed. Anna Freud. Fischer: Frankfurt am Main, 1942. 27–145.

—. 'Über Deckerinnerungen', *Gesammelte Werke I*, ed. Anna Freud. London: Imago, 1952. 531–54.

—. 'Zur Einführung des Narzißmus', *Gesammelte Werke X*, ed. Anna Freud. London: Imago, 1946. 136–70.

Gallagher, Lowell, and Shankar Raman. 'Introduction', in *Knowing Shakespeare: Senses, Embodiment and Cognition*, ed. Lowell Gallagher and Shankar Raman. London: Palgrave Macmillan, 2010. 1–29.

—, eds. *Knowing Shakespeare: Senses, Embodiment and Cognition*. London: Palgrave Macmillan, 2010.

Garber, Marjorie. 'Descanting on Deformity: *Richard III* and the Shape of History', in *The Historical Renaissance: New Essays in Tudor and Stuart Literature and Culture*, ed. Heather Dubrow and Richard Strier. Chicago: Chicago University Press, 1987. 79–103.

Gaudet, Paul. '"As True as Troilus," "As False as Cressid": Tradition, Text, and the Implicated Reader', *English Studies in Canada* 16.2 (1990): 125–48.

Gillies, John. 'Shakespeare's Virginian Masque', *ELH* 53.4 (1986): 673–707.

Gilman, Ernest B. '"All Eyes". Prospero's Inverted Masque', *Renaissance Quarterly* 33.2 (1980): 214–30.

Girard, Renée. '"A Woeful Cressid' 'mongst the Merry Greeks": The Love Affair in *Troilus and Cressida*', in *A Theatre of Envy*. Oxford: Oxford University Press, 1991. 121–34.

Goffman, Erving. *The Presentation of Self in Everyday Life*. New York: Anchor, 1959.

Gosson, Stephen. *Playes Confuted in Fiue Actions*. London: Imprinted for Thomas Gosson, 1582.

Greenblatt, Stephen. 'Fiction and Friction', *Shakespearean Negotiations: The Circulation of Social Energy in Renaissance England*. Berkeley, CA: University of California Press, 1988. 66–93.

—. *Hamlet in Purgatory*. Princeton, NJ: Princeton University Press, 2001.

Greene, Gayle. 'Language and Value in Shakespeare's *Troilus and Cressida*', *SEL* 21.2 (1981): 271–85.

—. 'Shakespeare's Cressida: "A kind of self"', in *The Woman's Part: Feminist Criticism of Shakespeare*, ed. Carolyn Ruth

Swift Lenz, Gayle Greene and Carol Thomas Neely. Urbana, IL: University of Illinois Press, 1980. 133–49.

Grindal, Edmund. 'Letter XXVII. To Sir W. Cecil', in *The Remains of Edmund Grindal*. Cambridge: Cambridge University Press, 1843 [1563]. 268–9.

Gurr, Andrew. *Playgoing in Shakespeare's London*. Cambridge: Cambridge University Press, 1987.

—. 'The Shakespearean Stage', *The Norton Shakespeare*, ed. Stephen Greenblatt et al. New York: Norton, 2008. 79–99.

Harris, Sharon. 'Feminism and Shakespeare's Cressida: "If I be false . . ."', *Women's Studies* 18.1 (1990): 65–82.

Harvey, Elizabeth D. 'Introduction', *Sensible Flesh: On Touch in Early Modern Culture*, ed. Elizabeth D. Harvey. Philadelphia, PA: University of Pennsylvania Press, 2003. 1–21.

—, ed. *Sensible Flesh: On Touch in Early Modern Culture*. Philadelphia, PA: University of Pennsylvania Press, 2003.

Hawkes, Terence. 'Conclusion: Speaking to You in English', in *Shakespeare in the Present*. London: Routledge, 2002. 127–43.

—. *Shakespeare in the Present*. London: Routledge, 2002.

Hays, Janice. 'Those "soft and delicate desires": *Much Ado* and the Distrust of Women', in *The Woman's Part: Feminist Criticism of Shakespeare*, ed. Carolyn Ruth Swift Lenz, Gayle Greene and Carol Thomas Neely. Urbana, IL: University of Illinois Press, 1980. 79–99.

Healy, Margaret. 'Anxious and Fatal Contacts: Taming the Contagious Touch', in *Sensible Flesh: On Touch in Early Modern Culture*, ed. Elizabeth D. Harvey. Philadelphia, PA: University of Pennsylvania Press, 2003. 22–38.

Heidegger, Martin. *Sein und Zeit*. Tübingen: Niemeyer, 2006.

—. *What is Called Thinking?*, trans. Fred D. Wieck and J. Glenn Gray. Religious Perspectives. New York: Harper & Row, 1968.

Heller-Roazen, Daniel. *The Inner Touch*. New York: Zone Books, 2007.

Helms, Lorraine. '"Still Wars and Lechery": Shakespeare and the Lost Trojan Woman', in *Arms and the Women: War, Gender, and Literary Representation*, ed. Helen M. Cooper, Adrienne

Auslander Munich and Susan Merrill Squier. Chapel Hill, NC: University of North Carolina Press, 1989. 25–42.

Henderson, Diana E. 'Mind the Gaps: The Ear, the Eye, and the Senses of a Woman in *Much Ado About Nothing*', in *Knowing Shakespeare: Senses. Embodiment, and Cognition*, ed. Lowell Gallagher and Shankar Raman. London: Palgrave Macmillan, 2010. 192–215.

Heywood, Thomas. *The Dramatic Works*, vol. 2. 6 vols. New York: Russell & Russell, 1964.

Hobgood, Allison P. 'Feeling Fear in *Macbeth*', in *Shakespearean Sensations: Experiencing Literature in Early Modern England*, ed. Katharine A. Craik and Tanya Pollard. Cambridge: Cambridge University Press, 2013. 29–46.

—. *Passionate Playgoing in Early Modern England*. Cambridge: Cambridge University Press, 2014.

Holland, Peter. 'Openings', in *Shakespeare and the Making of Theatre*, ed. Stuart Hampton-Reeves and Bridget Escolme. Basingstoke: Palgrave Macmillan, 2012. 14–31.

Hornback, Robert. '"Very devout asses": Ignorant Puritan Clowns', in *The English Clown Tradition from the Middle Ages to Shakespeare*. Woodbridge: Boydell & Brewer, 2009. 102–42.

Howard, Jean E. 'Renaissance Antitheatricality and the Politics of Gender and Rank in *Much Ado About Nothing*', in *Shakespeare Reproduced: The Text in History and Ideology*, ed. Jean E. Howard, Marion F. O'Connor and Margaret Ferguson. New York: Methuen, 1987. 163–87.

Howard, Jean E., and Phyllis Rackin. 'Richard III', in *Engendering a Nation: A Feminist Account of Shakespeare's English Histories*. Feminist Readings of Shakespeare. London: Routledge, 1997. 100–18.

Hunt, Maurice. 'The Reclamation of Language in *Much Ado About Nothing*', *Studies in Philology* 97.2 (2000): 165–91.

Irigaray, Luce. *An Ethics of Sexual Difference*, trans. Carolyn Burke and Gillian C. Gill. London: Continuum, 2004.

—. *Speculum of the Other Woman*, trans. Gillian C. Gill. Ithaca, NY: Cornell University Press, 1985.

—. *This Sex Which is Not One*, trans. Catherine Porter and Carolyn Burke. Ithaca, NY: Cornell University Press, 1985.

Jackson, Ken. 'Phenomenology and God: All is True – Unless You Decide in Advance What Is Not', *Criticism* 54.3 (2012): 469–77.

Jones, Robert C. *Engagement with Knavery: Point of View in* Richard III, The Jew of Malta, Volpone, *and* The Revenger's Tragedy. Durham, NC: Duke University Press, 1986.

Kant, Immanuel. *Critique of Pure Reason*, trans. Paul Guyer and Allen W. Wood. The Cambridge Edition of the Works of Immanuel Kant. Cambridge: Cambridge University Press, 1998.

—. *Kritik der reinen Vernunft*, ed. Wilhelm Weischedel. Frankfurt am Main: Suhrkamp, 1974.

Karim-Cooper, Farah. *The Hand on the Shakespearean Stage: Gesture, Touch and the Spectacle of Dismemberment*. London: Bloomsbury, 2016.

—. 'Touch and Taste in Shakespeare's Theatres', in *Shakespeare's Theatres and the Effects of Performance*, ed. Farah Karim-Cooper and Tiffany Stern. London: Bloomsbury, 2013. 214–36.

Karim-Cooper, Farah, and Tiffany Stern. 'Introduction', in *Shakespeare's Theatres and the Effects of Performance*, ed. Farah Karim-Cooper and Tiffany Stern. London: Bloomsbury, 2013. 1–10.

—, eds. *Shakespeare's Theatres and the Effects of Performance*. London: Bloomsbury, 2013.

Kearney, James. 'Phenomenology and Ethics: "This is above all strangeness": *King Lear*, Ethics and the Phenomenology of Recognition', *Criticism* 54.3 (2012): 455–67.

Kehler, Dorothea. 'Shakespeare's *Richard III*', *The Explicator* 56.3 (1998): 118–21.

Kirby, Vicky. *Telling Flesh: The Substance of the Corporeal*. New York: Routledge, 1997.

Knapp, James. 'Phenomenology and Images: Static and Transformative Images in Shakespeare's Dramatic Art', *Criticism* 54.3 (2012): 377–89.

Knowles, James. 'Insubstantial Pageants. *The Tempest* and Masquing Culture', *Shakespeare's Late Plays: New Readings*, ed. Jennifer Richards and James Knowles. Edinburgh: Edinburgh University Press, 1999. 108–25.

Kott, Jan. *Shakespeare Our Contemporary*, trans. Boreslaw Taborski. London: Methuen, 1967.

Kristeva, Julia. 'Women's Time', *Signs* 7.1 (1981): 13–35.
Kyd, Thomas. 'The First Part of Ieronimo', *The Works of Thomas Kyd*. Oxford: Clarendon Press, 1955. 296–337.
Lacan, Jacques. 'The Signification of the Phallus', trans. Bruce Fink, in *Écrits: The First Complete Edition in English*. New York: Norton, 2006. 575–84.
Langis, Unhae. '"Desire is Death" in Shakespeare's *Troilus and Cressida*', *Early Modern Literary Studies* 24.1 (2015): 1–31.
Lenz, Joseph. 'Base Trade: Theater as Prostitution', *ELH* 60.4 (1993): 833–55.
Liebler, Naomi C., and Lisa Scancella Shea. 'Shakespeare's Queen Margaret: Unruly or Unruled?' *Henry VI: Critical Essays*, ed. Thomas A. Pendleton. New York: Routledge, 2001. 79–96.
Loraux, Nicole. *Mothers in Mourning*, trans. Corinne Pache. Ithaca, NY: Cornell University Press, 1998.
Loxley, James, and Mark Robson. *Shakespeare, Jonson, and the Claims of the Performative*. New York: Routledge, 2013.
Luhmann, Niklas. *Love as Passion: The Codification of Intimacy*, trans. Jeremy Gaines and Doris L. Jones. Cambridge, MA: Harvard University Press, 1986.
—. *Social Systems*, trans. John Bednarz Jr. and Dirk Baecker. Stanford, CA: Stanford University Press, 1996.
Machiavelli, Niccolò. *The Prince*, trans. Mark Musa. New York: St. Martin's Press, 1964.
Machon, Josephine. *Immersive Theatres: Intimacy and Immediacy in Contemporary Performance*. London: Palgrave Macmillan, 2013.
Mack, Maynard. 'The World of Hamlet', *Yale Review* 41 (1951/52): 502–23.
Magnusson, Lynne. 'The Pragmatics of Repair in *King Lear* and *Much Ado About Nothing*', in *Shakespeare and Social Dialogue: Dramatic Language and Elizabethan Letters*, ed. Lynne Magnusson. Cambridge: Cambridge University Press, 1999. 141–62.
Marchitello, Howard. 'Artifactual Knowledge in *Hamlet*', *Knowing Shakespeare: Senses, Embodiment and Cognition*, ed. Lowell Gallagher and Shankar Raman. London: Palgrave Macmillan, 2010. 137–53.

Massumi, Brian. *Parables for the Virtual*. Durham, NC: Duke University Press, 2002.

Mazzio, Carla. 'Acting with Tact: Touch and Theater in the Renaissance', in *Sensible Flesh: On Touch in Early Modern Culture*, ed. Elizabeth D. Harvey. Philadelphia, PA: University of Pennsylvania Press, 2003. 159–86.

—. 'The Senses Divided: Organs, Objects, and Media in Early Modern England', in *Empire of the Senses: The Sensual Culture Reader*, ed. David Howes. Oxford: Berg, 2004. 85–105.

McEachern, Claire. 'Introduction', in *Much Ado About Nothing*. The Arden Shakespeare, Third Series. London: Bloomsbury, 2006. 1–144.

McNamara, Kevin R. 'Golden Worlds at Court: *The Tempest* and Its Masque', *Shakespeare Studies* 19 (1987): 183–202.

McNeir, Waldo F. 'The Masks of Richard the Third', *SEL* 11.2 (1971): 167–86.

Mead, Stephen X. '"Thou art chang'd": Public Values and Personal Identity in *Troilus and Cressida*', *Journal of Medieval and Renaissance Studies* 22.2 (1992): 237–59.

Michalos, Constantina. 'Shakespeare's Feminized Friar', *Discoveries* 22.1 (2005): 1–15.

More, Thomas. 'The History of King Richard the Thirde', *The vvorkes of Sir Thomas More Knyght*. London: Printed by Iohn Cawod, Iohn VValy, and Richarde Tottell, 1557. 35–71.

Nancy, Jean-Luc. *Being Singular Plural*, trans. Robert D. Richardson and Anne E. O'Byrne. Meridian, Crossing Aesthetics. Stanford, CA: Stanford University Press, 2000.

—. *Corpus*, trans. Richard Rand. New York: Fordham University Press, 2008.

—. 'The Image: Mimesis and Methexis', trans. Adrienne Janus, in *Nancy and Visual Culture*, ed. Carrie Giunta and Adrienne Janus. Critical Connections. Edinburgh: Edinburgh University Press, 2016. 74–92.

—. 'Rühren, Berühren, Aufruhr', *SubStance* 40.3 (2011): 10–7.

Nietzsche, Friedrich. *Beyond Good and Evil: Prelude to a Philosophy of the Future*, trans. Marion Faber. Oxford World's Classics. Oxford: Oxford University Press, 2008.

—. *The Gay Science. With a Prelude in German Rhymes and an Appendix of Songs*, trans. Josefine Nauckhoff and Adrian Del Caro. Cambridge Texts in the History of Philosophy. Cambridge: Cambridge University Press, 2001.

—. *The Genealogy of Morals*, trans. Horace B. Samuel. New York: Boni and Liveright, 1918.

—. *Human All-Too-Human*, trans. Helen Zimmern. Edinburgh: T. N. Foulis, 1910.

—. *Nachlaß 1869–1874*. Kritische Studienausgabe, ed. Giorgio Colli and Mazzino Montinari. Berlin: de Gruyter, 1999.

—. *Nachlaß 1880–1882*. Kritische Studienausgabe, ed. Giorgio Colli and Mazzino Montinari. Berlin: de Gruyter, 1999.

—. 'Twilight of the Idols', trans. Judith Norman, in *The Anti-Christ, Ecce Homo, Twilight of the Idols, and Other Writings*. Cambridge: Cambridge University Press, 2005. 153–230.

OED. Oxford English Dictionary Online. Oxford University Press, 2021, www.oed.com, 9 September 2021.

O'Rourke Boyle, Marjorie. *Senses of Touch: Human Dignity and Deformity from Michelangelo to Calvin*. Leiden: Brill, 1998.

Okerlund, Arlene N. 'In Defense of Cressida: Character as Metaphor', *Women's Studies* 7.3 (1980): 1–17.

Olk, Claudia. 'Performing Conscience in *Richard III*', *Anglia* 130.1 (2012): 1–18.

Outterson-Murphy, Sarah. '"Remember Me": The Ghost and Its Spectators in *Hamlet*', *Shakespeare Bulletin* 34.2 (2016): 253–75.

Ovidius. *Metamorphoses*, ed. William S. Anderson. Stuttgart: Teubner, 1985.

Papp, Joseph. 'Directing *Troilus and Cressida*', in *Troilus and Cressida*, ed. Bernard Beckerman and Joseph Papp. The Festival Shakespeare. New York: Macmillan, 1967. 23–72.

Le Petit Robert de la langue française, online database, ed. Alain Rey. Paris: Dictionnaires Le Robert, 2008, 9 September 2021.

Paster, Gail Kern. *The Body Embarrassed: Drama and the Disciplines of Shame in Early Modern England*. Ithaca, NY: Cornell University Press, 1993.

—. *Humoring the Body: Emotions and the Shakespearean Stage*. Chicago: University of Chicago Press, 2004.

—. *Reading the Early Modern Passions: Essays in the Cultural History of Emotion*. Philadelphia, PA: University of Pennsylvania Press, 2004.

Plato. *The Republic. Books 6–10*, trans. Christopher Emlyn-Jones and William Preddy. Loeb Classical Library. Cambridge, MA: Harvard University Press, 2014.

—. *Symposium*, trans. W. R. M. Lamb. Loeb Classical Library. Cambridge, MA: Harvard University Press, 1925.

Pollard, Tanya. 'Conceiving Tragedy', in *Shakespearean Sensations: Experiencing Literature in Early Modern England*, ed. Katharine A. Craik and Tanya Pollard. Cambridge: Cambridge University Press, 2013. 85–100.

—. *Drugs and Theater in Early Modern England*. Oxford: Oxford University Press, 2005.

Prynne, William. *Histrio-Mastix: The Players Scourge, or, Actors Tragaedie*. London: Printed by E. A. and W. I. for Michael Sparke, 1633.

Rackin, Phyllis. 'Women's Roles in the Elizabethan History Plays', in *The Cambridge Companion to Shakespeare's History Plays*, ed. Michael Hattaway. Cambridge: Cambridge University Press, 2002. 71–86.

Rainolds, John. *Th'Overthrow of Stage-Playes, by the Way of Controversie betwixt D. Gager and D. Rainoldes*. Middelburg: Printed by Richard Schilders, 1599.

Raman, Shankar. 'Hamlet in Motion', in *Knowing Shakespeare: Senses, Embodiment and Cognition*, ed. Lowel Gallagher and Shankar Raman. London: Palgrave Macmillan, 2010. 116–36.

Rancière, Jacques. *The Emancipated Spectator*, trans. Gregory Elliott. London: Verso, 2011.

Richardson, Catherine. *Shakespeare and Material Culture*. Oxford: Oxford University Press, 2011.

Rist, Thomas. 'Catharsis as "Purgation" in Shakespearean Drama', in *Shakespearean Sensations: Experiencing Literature in Early Modern England*, ed. Katharine A. Craik and Tanya Pollard. Cambridge: Cambridge University Press, 2013. 138–54.

Roach, Joseph R. *The Player's Passion: Studies in the Science of Acting*. Newark, DE: University of Delaware Press, 1985.

Rokem, Freddie. 'The Processes of Eavesdropping: Where Tragedy, Comedy and Philosophy Converge', *Performance Philosophy* 1.1 (2015): 109–18.

Rose, Steven. 'Love and Self-Love in *Much Ado About Nothing*', *Essays in Criticism: A Quarterly Journal of Literary Criticism* 20 (1970): 143–50.

Ross, Emily. '"Words, vows, gifts, tears and love's full sacrifice": An Assessment of the Status of Troilus and Cressida's Relationship According to Customary Elizabethan Marriage Procedure', *Shakespeare* 4.4 (2008): 397–421.

Röttger-Rössler, Birgitt, and Jan Slaby, eds. *Affect in Relation*. London: Routledge, 2018.

Rowe, Katherine. *Dead Hands: Fictions of Agency, Renaissance to Modern*. Stanford, CA: Stanford University Press, 1999.

Rubin, Gayle. 'The Traffic in Women: Notes on the "Political Economy" of Sex', *Towards an Anthropology of Women*, ed. Rayna R. Reiter. New York: Monthly Review Press, 1975. 157–210.

Ryan, Kiernan. *Shakespeare*. 3rd edn. Houndmills: Palgrave, 2001.

Rzepka, Adam. '"Rich eyes and poor hands": Theaters of Early Modern Experience', in *Knowing Shakespeare: Senses, Embodiment and Cognition*, ed. Lowell Gallagher and Shankar Raman. London: Palgrave Macmillan, 2010. 154–71.

Sanders, Eve Rachele. 'The Body of the Actor in *Coriolanus*', *Shakespeare Quarterly* 57.4 (2006): 387–412.

Schmitt, Carl. *The Concept of the Political*, trans. George Schwab. Chicago: University of Chicago Press, 2007.

Sedgwick, Eve Kosofsky. *Touching Feeling: Affect, Pedagogy, Performativity*. Durham, NC: Duke University Press, 2003.

Shakespeare, William. *As You Like It*, ed. Juliet Dusinberre. The Arden Shakespeare, Third Series. London: Bloomsbury, 2004.

—. *Hamlet*. ed. Ann Thompson and Neil Taylor. The Arden Shakespeare, Third Series. London: Bloomsbury, 2006.

—. *King Henry VI, Part 3*, ed. Eric Rasmussen and John D. Cox. The Arden Shakespeare, Third Series. London: Arden Shakespeare, 2001.

—. *King Lear*, ed. R. A. Foakes. The Arden Shakespeare, Third Series. London: Bloomsbury, 1997.
—. *Macbeth*, ed. Sandra Clark and Pamela Mason. The Arden Shakespeare, Third Series. London: Bloomsbury, 2015.
—. *The Merchant of Venice*, ed. John Drakakis. The Arden Shakespeare, Third Series. London: Bloomsbury, 2011.
—. *A Midsummer Night's Dream*, ed. Sukanta Chaudhuri. The Arden Shakespeare, Third Series. London: Bloomsbury, 2017.
—. *Much Ado About Nothing*, ed. Claire McEachern. The Arden Shakespeare, Third Series. London: Bloomsbury, 2006.
—. *Othello*, ed. E. A. J. Honigmann. The Arden Shakespeare, Third Series. London: Bloomsbury, 2016.
—. *Richard III*, ed. James R. Siemon. The Arden Shakespeare, Third Series. London: Bloomsbury, 2009.
—. *Shakespeare's Sonnets*, ed. Katherine Duncan-Jones. The Arden Shakespeare, Third Series. London: Bloomsbury, 2010.
—. *The Tempest*, ed. Virginia Mason Vaughan and Alden T. Vaughan. The Arden Shakespeare, Third Series. London: Bloomsbury, 1999.
—. *Troilus and Cressida*, ed. David Bevington. The Arden Shakespeare, Third Series. London: Bloomsbury, 1998.
—. *The Two Gentlemen of Verona*, ed. William C. Caroll. The Arden Shakespeare, Third Series. London: Bloomsbury, 2004.
Shoaf, R. Allen. *Shakespeare's Theater of Likeness*. Washington, DC: New Academia, 2006.
Shortslef, Emily. '"A thousand several tongues": The Drama of Conscience and the Complaint of the Other in Shakespeare's *Richard III*', *Exemplaria* 29.2 (2017): 118–35.
Showalter, Elaine. 'Representing Ophelia: Women, Madness and the Responsibilities of Feminist Criticism', in *Shakespeare and the Question of Theory*, ed. Geoffrey Hartmann and Patricia Parker. London: Routledge, 1990. 77–94.
Sidney, Philip. *The Defence of Poesie*. London: Printed for William Ponsonby, 1595.
Siemon, James R. 'Sign, Cause or General Habit? Towards an "Historicist Ontology" of Character on the Early Modern Stage', in *Nominalism and Literary Discourse. New Perspectives*, ed.

Hugo Keiper, Christoph Bode and Richard J. Utz. Amsterdam: Rodopi, 1997. 237–50.

Slotkin, Joel Elliot. 'Honeyed Toads: Sinister Aesthetics in Shakespeare's *Richard III*', *Journal for Early Modern Cultural Studies* 7.1 (2007): 5–32.

Smith, Bruce R. 'Afterword: Phenomophobia, or Who's Afraid of Merleau-Ponty?' *Criticism* 54.3 (2012): 479–83.

—. *Phenomenal Shakespeare*. Hoboken, NJ: Wiley-Blackwell, 2009.

—. 'Premodern Sexualities', *PMLA* 115 (2000): 318–29.

—. 'Within, Without, Withinwards', in *Shakespeare's Theatres and the Effects of Performance*, ed. Farah Karim-Cooper and Tiffany Stern. London: Bloomsbury, 2013. 171–94.

Smith, Irwin. 'Ariel and the Masque in *The Tempest*', *Shakespeare Quarterly* 21.3 (1970): 213–22.

Smith, Kristin M. 'Martial Maids and Murdering Mothers: Women, Witchcraft and Motherly Transgression in *Henry VI* and *Richard III*', *Shakespeare* 3.2 (2007): 143–60.

Straznicky, Marta. 'Shakespeare and the Government of Comedy: *Much Ado About Nothing*', *Shakespeare Studies* 22 (1994): 141–71.

Taylor, Diana. *The Archive and the Repertoire: Performing Cultural Memory in the Americas*. Durham, NC: Duke University Press, 2003.

Tillyard, E. M. W. *Shakespeare's Problem Plays*. London: Chatto & Windus, 1949.

Traub, Valerie. *Desire and Anxiety: Circulations of Sexuality in Shakespearean Drama*. London: Routledge, 1992.

Tribble, Evelyn. '"O, she's warm": Touch in *The Winter's Tale*', in *Knowing Shakespeare: Senses, Embodiment and Cognition*, ed. Lowell Gallagher and Shankar Raman. London: Palgrave Macmillan, 2010. 65–81.

—. 'Sight and Spectacle', in *Shakespeare's Theatres and the Effects of Performance*, ed. Farah Karim-Cooper and Tiffany Stern. London: Bloomsbury, 2013. 237–52.

Ungelenk, Johannes. *Literature and Weather. Shakespeare – Goethe – Zola*. Berlin: De Gruyter, 2018.

Van Laan, Thomas F. *Role-Playing in Shakespeare*. Toronto: University of Toronto Press, 1978.
Vaughan, Virginia Mason. 'Daughters of the Game: *Troilus and Cressida* and the Sexual Discourse of 16th-Century England', *Women's Studies International Forum* 13.3 (1990): 209–20.
Vickers, Brian. *The Artistry of Shakespeare's Prose*. London: Methuen, 1968.
Votava, Jenny. 'Comedy, the Sense, and Social Contagion in *Plays Confuted in Five Actions* and *The Comedy of Errors*', in *Contagion and the Shakespearean Stage*, ed. Darryl Chalk and Mary Floyd-Wilson. Basingstoke: Palgrave Macmillan, 2019. 25–46.
Walde, Alois. 'testor', *Lateinisches Etymologisches Wörterbuch*. Heidelberg: Winter, 1910. 777.
Waldron, Jennifer. 'Phenomenology and Theater: "The eye of man hath not heard": Shakespeare, Synaesthesia, and Post-Reformation Phenomenology', *Criticism* 54.3 (2012): 403–17.
Wehrs, Donald R. 'Touching Words: Embodying Ethics in Erasmus, Shakespearean Comedy, and Contemporary Theory', *Modern Philology: Critical and Historical Studies in Literature, Medieval Through Contemporary* 104.1 (2006): 1–33.
Wilson, Richard. *Shakespeare in French Theory*. London: Routledge, 2007.
Wither, George. *A Collection of Emblemes, Ancient and Moderne*. London: Printed by A. M. for Henry Taunton, 1635.
Witmore, Michael. 'Phenomenology and Sensation: Shakespeare, Sensation, and Renaissance Existentialism', *Criticism* 54.3 (2012): 419–26.
Worthen, William B. *Shakespeare and the Force of Modern Performance*. Cambridge: Cambridge University Press, 2003.
Wright, Thomas. *The Passions of the Minde in Generall. Corrected, enlarged, and with sundry new discourses augmented*. London: Printed by Valentine Simmes for Walter Burre, 1604.

INDEX

accountability, 65
action at a distance, 27–8, 116–17
Adair, Vance, 95–6, 142n
Affect Studies, 26–9
Ahmed, Sarah, 26
anamorphic stain, 96
anti-theatricalism, 7, 11, 226–8, 242n
  pamphlets, 12–13, 35n
  writing, 235–6
Aristotle, 3, 58, 62, 79n, 225–7
  Poetics, 7, 47, 62, 74, 225
assembly, 11–12, 241–2n, 243
asymmetry, 44–5, 66
  of modern theatre, 13–14
audience
  blurring of social distinctions, 12–13
  community of the audience, 228–31, 237
  contaminated with theatrical emotions, 2, 83, 237
  co-presence of actors and audience, 3, 86
  divide between stage and, 3, 246

  future, 8–9
  groundlings, 40–1
  second audience 222–5
  sound of the, 15
  stage and, 8, 231–4, 238, 243–6
  touch, 243
  see also spectators
Austin, John Langshaw, 33, 149, 164, 178, 181
authenticity, 4, 57–8, 89–91, 101–2, 110, 229–30

bareness of the stage, 15, 66
bargain, 154, 161, 192–9
Barish, Jonas A., *The Antitheatrical Prejudice*, 35n
Barthes, Roland, 144n, 157, 159, 184n
  A Lover's Discourse, 161, 164–5
beards, 174–5
belief and disbelief, 43–8, 110
Belott, Stephen, 197
Berger, Harry, 30, 152, 154
'Beside-the-Point Answers', 157, 161

Blanchot, Maurice, 33, 113, 115,
  The Space of Literature, 80,
    96–8, 103, 105, 108, 112,
    142n, 144n
Blumenberg, Hans, 33, 71
  Beschreibung des Menschen,
    35n, 52–3, 64–7
body, 11, 13, 18, 67–8, 79n, 84,
  94, 99, 145n, 173, 202–7,
  240n
bond of heaven, 186–91, 199–201,
  207, 213, 220–1, 238
bonds, 23–4, 96, 187–92, 204–7,
  211, 213–14, 231
Book of Common Prayer, 190
brokers-between, 219–39
brutal contiguity, 69–71, 76
Burton, Robert, *Anatomy of
  Melancholy*, 46–7
Butler, Judith, 241n
  *Notes toward a Performative
    Theory of Assembly*, 241–2n

Cahill, Patricia, 18, 36n
Campana, Joseph, 136
Carbajosa, Natalia, 183n
caressing, 193, 216–17, 245
  touch, 92, 175–8, 207
  with words, 148–84, 244
Carroll, William C., 142n
castration's effect, 120, 123–5
Cavell, Stanley, 18, 33, 110
Chalk, Daryll, 235–6
Charnes, Linda, 8, 142n
Chaucer, Geoffrey, 198
chivalric ideal, 166, 170–1, 176,
  207, 240–1n
Classen, Constance, 17, 76n, 175,
  203–4, 240n

closing the ranks, 201–5, 211, 216
collective response, 79n
communication, 37n, 41, 53, 112,
  134, 232–3
  as contamination, 18
com-munity, 70–1
community, 70, 72, 76, 200–39,
  241n, 247–8
  of touch, 91, 214, 222, 226–30,
    247
com-passion, 69–70, 228–9, 231,
  237, 239, 247
compassion, 62–3, 69, 72, 76,
  79n, 241n, 248
conceptual effects, 18–19
concerned, 42, 44–5, 56, 61, 65
confrontation of friend and
  enemy as intense degree of
  association, 187, 208–12
constant men and false women,
  192–201, 219
contact, 26–33, 59, 69–70, 116,
  184–5n, 204, 207
contaminating, 60, 63, 74, 79n
  contract of, 154, 159, 166, 198,
    247–8
  theatrical, 9–10, 15, 29–30,
    72–73, 76, 141, 233–4,
    237–8, 244–8
contact-free touch, 238
contagion, 12–13, 25–6, 29–30,
  33–4, 35–6n, 46–7, 59,
  69–72, 79n, 235–9
  theatrical, 1–37
  of 'touching this vision here',
    50–7
contamination, 46, 54, 72–4, 76,
  146n, 151
  communication as, 18

contingent touch, 201–5
contract, 89–91, 153–66, 175–6, 182, 185n, 197, 203, 245–7
  of contact, 247–8
  theatrical, 224
Cook, Carol, 150, 158–9, 202, 204, 207, 211, 212
Craik, Katherine A., 11, 17, 25
Critical Presentism, 31–2
Crocker, Holly A., 200, 202, 217
crossing of senses, 78n
crowding, 11–16, 69–70
Culler, Jonathan, 182, 185n
Curran, Kevin, 16, 78n

Dawson, Anthony B., 149, 183n, 184n
Dawson, Janet, 227
Day, Gillian M., 80, 133
death, 64, 71–3, 91, 95, 100, 103–9, 115, 122–30, 142n, 143n, 144n, 170, 188, 190, 215–18
declaration, 151–4, 156–63
deconstruction, 27–9
deep dissembler, 100–15
Deleuze, Gilles, 28–9, 87, 139, 239n, 240n
  A Thousand Plateaus, 35–6n, 79n, 147n, 250n
  Cinema 2, 35n
  Kafka: Toward a Minor Literature, 250n
  What is Philosophy?, 35n
depth, 80–147, 144n
Derrida, Jacques, 4–5, 27–8, 37n, 52, 157, 184n
  La Dissémination, 144n
  Limited Inc, 181

  On Touching, 4, 28, 52, 162
  Specters of Marx, 45n, 77n
  Spurs. Nietzsche's Styles, 113–41
  The Postcard, 223
desacralisation, 142n
DiPietro, Cary, 31–2
dissembling, 22, 84–6, 89–115, 125–6, 130, 138–9, 145n, 146n
dissemination, 144n
dissimulation, 94–9, 108–18, 121, 125–6, 131–5, 138–41
distemper, 63–5, 68, 209
dividuation, 195–6, 200, 210, 239–40n
Döring, Tobias, 242n
dumb-show, 155–6, 163, 170

ears, 41, 54–5, 58, 91, 78n, 151, 209
eavesdropping, 10, 169, 223–5
Edwards, Philip, 194
emotional disturbance, 62–4, 69–70, 76
emotional trouble, 44–6, 64, 87–8
emotions, theatrical, 2–3
Erasmus, Desiderius, 240n
erotic and touch, 184n, 206, 211, 215–16
eroticization of combat, 207–16
Escolme, Bridget, 30
essential solitude, 80–8, 96–8, 106

fabric, 21–2, 33, 83
fascination, 30, 83, 91, 105, 112, 142n
fear, 7, 47, 88, 94, 127, 137, 169
feigned, 50, 55, 57, 89–91
flattery, 91–3, 99–100, 129, 146n

Fly, Richard D., 233
Foakes, R. A., 240n
Foucault, Michel, 37n
   Fearless Speech, 93, 140
   The Order of Things, 93
fractions and factions, 186–92
frailty, 217, 219, 241n
frailty of regime of touch, 216–18
free soul, 56–61, 70–1
Freud, Sigmund, 96, 99, 124, 142n
friction between boundaries, 3, 9, 21, 73

Gallagher, Lowell, 16–17, 32
Garber, Marjorie, 142n, 143n
Gaudet, Paul, 200, 202, 238
gender, and vulnerability, 77n
gendered, trouble of walking the talking, 166–78
Gillies, John, 'Shakespeare's Virginian Masque', 78–9n
Girard, Renée, 225
The Globe, 11–15, 69–70
   Lord's Rooms, 13, 15
Goffman, Erving, 232
Gosson, Stephen, 12, 236
Grady, Hugh, 32
grasping, 19, 214, 248–9
Greenblatt, Stephen, 3, 21, 73, 158
   Hamlet in Purgatory, 71, 77n, 117, 140, 145n
Greene, Gayle, 199, 239n, 240n, 241n
Grindal, Edmund, 236
ground, 18, 33, 45, 107–114, 136, 144n, 144–5n, 145n, 186, 199, 232, 246
groundless world, 110–11

Guattari, Félix
   A Thousand Plateaus, 35–6n, 79n, 147n, 250n
   Kafka: Toward a Minor Literature, 250n
   What is Philosophy?, 35n

halberd, 117–20
Hamlet, 38–79
   Barnardo (character), 42–3, 46
   Claudius (character), 55–61, 65, 72–3, 78n
   deep, 101
   ghost, 42–59, 67, 71, 73–4, 77n, 78n, 79n, 145n, 243–4
   Hamlet (character), 48–59, 70–6, 79n, 110–11, 241n, 243–5
   heroics, 143n
   Horatio (character), 42–51, 75, 77n, 243, 249
   Laertes (character), 71–3
   Marcellus (character), 42–5, 49, 50–1, 53
   The Mousetrap, 56–9, 65
haptic, 26, 43–4, 51–3, 142n, 217
   behaviour, 193–4
   community, 221
   encounters, 191–2, 199
   gesture, 159, 193, 197
   logic, 56
Harris, Sharon, 194, 239n, 240–1n
Harvey, Elizabeth D., 11, 16, 19
Hawkes, Terence, 9, 31–2
Hays, Janice, 154
Healy, Margaret, 20
hedgehog, 117–19

Heidegger, Martin
  Sein und Zeit, 96
  What is Called Thinking? 35n
Helms, Lorraine, 202, 206, 209, 211, 216
Henderson, Diana E., 182n, 183n, 241n
Henry VI, Part 3, Richard (character), 94–5
Heywood, Thomas, 49
hierarchy of senses, 16–18
historical distance, 31–2
Historical Phenomenology, 16–17, 31–2, 36n
Hobgood, Allison P., 2, 7, 36n, 224
'hollow or void', 178–81, 185n
homosocial relationships, 211–12
honour, 137, 179–81, 206–11, 232
Hornback, Robert, 227
Howard, Jean E., 104, 121, 123–4, 139, 143n, 143–4n, 149, 158, 183n, 184n
humanist tradition, 95, 184n, 208, 229
humours, 3, 46–7, 57, 59, 64, 68
Hunt, Maurice, 149–50, 152, 183n

imitation, 94, 110–11, 113, 226–7, 236–7
immersive theatres, 34n
indirect touch, 229
individual self, 7, 61, 96–8, 107, 179, 184–5n, 191, 201, 239–40n
individuation, 22, 195, 200, 210, 219, 231

infection, 2, 46, 60, 174, 235–7; *see also* contagion; contamination
infidelity of time, 240n
insubstantial, 246–7
interaction, 13–15, 18–19, 66, 79n, 92, 200, 232–3, 238, 241n
interior hatred, 93–5
Irigaray, Luce, 27–8, 33, 183–4n
  An Ethics of Sexual Difference, 145n
  Speculum of the Other Woman, 129, 146n
  'This Sex Which is Not One', 28, 146n, 184–5n
isotopies, 81–2

Jackson, Ken, 31, 37n, 143n
'Jew', 228
Jones, Robert C., 93
Jorgensen, Paul A., *Redeeming Shakespeare's Words*, 183–4n

Kant, Immanuel, 35n
  Critique of Pure Reason, 6–7
  Kritik der reinen Vernunft, 35n
Karim-Cooper, Farah, 11, 14, 16, 17–18, 25, 35n, 37n, 41, 58, 66–7, 78n, 147n, 190, 240n
Kearney, James, 16, 78n
Kehler, Dorothea, 123, 133
King Lear
  crossing of senses, 78n
  deep, 101
  speech as tactile, 77n
kiss and handshake, 92, 177, 195–7
kisses, 25, 89, 151–2, 193, 200, 206, 240n

kissing touch, 201–5, 216
Knapp, James, 77n
knifeman, 115–17
'knot, five-finger-tied', 186–91, 189, 199, 213–14, 221, 230
Kott, Jan, 138
Kristeva, Julia, 'Women's Time', 143–4n
Kyd, Thomas, *The First Part of Ieronimo*, 125

Lacan, Jacques, 95–6, 124, 142n, 146n
Langis, Unhae, 202, 205–6, 209, 216, 218, 240n
lechery, 205–6, 215–16, 222, 237
leering chorus, 204, 220–1
legally binding ceremony, 196–7
Liebler, Naomi C., 127
'Liberty of the Clink', 12
lighting, artificial, 13–14, 36n
linguistics of touch, 158
loneliness, 95–7
Loraux, Nicole, *Mothers in Mourning*, 143n
loss of control, 7, 23
loving touch, 159–60, 169, 217–18
Loxley, James, *Shakespeare, Jonson, and the Claims of the Performative*, 29–30, 160
Luhmann, Niklas,
    Love as Passion: The Codification of Intimacy, 37n, 89–90, 233
    Social Systems, 97, 222, 232

Macbeth, crossing of senses, 78n
McEachern, Claire, 149, 177, 182–3n, 183n

Machiavelli, Niccolò, 95, 98
    The Arte of Warre, 209
Machon, Josephine, 34n
Mack, Maynard, 76n
McNeir, Waldo F., 88, 95–6, 114
madness, 48–50, 55, 73–4, 230, 245
making visible, 45
Marchitello, Howard, 41, 46, 56
Marion, Jean-Luc, 143n
masculinity, 121, 124, 135, 142n, 145n, 150, 154, 158–9, 200–4
Massumi, Brian, 31
    Parables for the Virtual, 27, 37n
Mazzio, Carla, 16
    'Acting with Tact', 11–12, 19–20, 35n, 76n, 79n, 184n
Mead, Stephen X, 200, 239n, 241n
meat, 173
mediality, 39, 42, 52–3, 66, 104–5, 238–9
Mentz, Steve, *At the Bottom of Shakespeare's Ocean*, 144n
The Merchant of Venice
    'Jew', 228–9
    pricking and tickling, 242n
    Shylock (character), 228–9, 242n
metaphorology, 65
metatheatricality, 10, 14–15, 20–2, 29–31, 39–40, 43–9, 52–7, 70, 73–5, 77n, 97, 112, 116–17, 223–5, 231
Michalos, Constantina, 178

A Midsummer Night's Dream
   Hippolyta (character), 77n
   phenomenal world, 77n
   tactility, 78n
   Theseus (character), 77n
mimesis, 113, 227
minoritarian mode of touch, 245, 248, 250n
mirror, 128–30
More, Thomas, *History of King Richard III*, 107–10, 116–17
Mountjoy, Mary, 197
moving in the dark, 76n
moving spectators, 3–4, 42–3, 181, 225–6, 234, 237, 246–8
Much Ado About Nothing, 148–84
   Antonio (character), 170, 174
   audience as voyeuristic, 241n
   Beatrice (character) imperative, 166–78
   Beatrice (character) speaks for Hero, 151–2
   Beatrice-Benedick caresses, 154–65
   Beatrice-Benedick plot as parallel to main plot, 148–85
   Benedick (character), 148
   Don Pedro (character), 148, 154–6, 164, 169, 174
   Friar's double touch, 178–82
   Hero veiled, 153–4
   Hero-Claudio declarations, 151–4
   Hero-Claudio plot, 148–85
   Hero's silence, 152, 159–60, 179, 183n
   Leonato (character), 151–4, 173–4, 176, 178–80
   Margaret (character), 170–2

mutuality, 13, 15, 20, 26, 27, 34n, 66, 165, 216, 244–6, 250
   radical, 5–6
   vulnerability, 30, 245

Nancy, Jean-Luc, 27–8, 37n, 52, 241n
   Being Singular Plural, 5, 69–70
   Corpus, 28
   'The Image: Mimesis and Methexis', 113–14, 144–5n
   'Rühren, Berühren, Aufruhr', 4, 28
narcissism, 95–6, 129–30
nearness, 2–4, 6–7, 29–31, 51–2, 73, 116, 143n, 244, 247–9
neutralisation, 96–7, 105–7, 144n, 157–61, 167–8, 177
New Historicism, 16, 31–2, 37n
Nietzsche, Friedrich, 27–8, 113–16, 118, 123, 146n, 240n
   Beyond Good and Evil, 145n
   The Gay Science, 115–16, 125, 231
   Genealogy of Morals, 98, 100
   Human All-Too-Human, 186, 220
   'Twilight of the Idols', 136
nothing, 183–4n
Now, 86–8

offence, 50–9, 63–4, 66–9, 71–6
Okerlund, Arlene, 200, 202, 217, 238
Olk, Claudia, 122, 143n
openness, 77n, 179, 201–5
Othello, symmetry of male and female, 242n
otherness, 7, 37n

Ott, Michaela, 239–40n
out of touch, 139, 219
outsiders, 22–4, 84, 127, 137, 228, 241, 245
  women as, 139–40, 147n
Outterson-Murphy, Sarah, 46–7, 74, 77n, 79n

Papp, Joseph, 240n
paradox, 2–10, 89–90, 110–11, 155, 162–8, 175, 180, 195, 214, 223, 225–30
passions, 57–8, 68–9, 74–6, 79n, 228
Paster, Gail Kern, 79n
patience, 179, 224–5, 228, 229–31, 237, 247–8
patriarchal order, 23, 124, 139, 147n, 150–3, 158–9, 165, 174, 179, 183n, 184n, 202–4, 213
peace and war, 80–8
perception, 14, 41, 51, 62, 65–7
  to vulnerability, 78n
perfomativity, 29–30
personifications of air, 48–50, 52–5
personifications of war, 80–8
phallic agency, 117–38, 215
phallic speech, 150, 158–9, 175
phallic weapon, 116, 122–8, 146n, 70–1
phenomenology, 65–6, 95
philology and theatre, 178–85
philology of touch, 243–50
physiology, 25, 59–60
pity, 7, 62–3, 69–70, 94, 121, 130, 226
'plain man', 91–3, 115–41
plainness, 130–5

Plato, 141
  The Republic, 45
  Symposium, 232
play-acting, 2, 7, 55, 89–91, 96, 99–100, 109–12, 122, 125, 131, 136, 143n
playhouses, 11–18, 69–70
plays-within-plays, 9–10, 56–7, 61, 169–170
pledges, 167–8
plurality, 228
  of interacting senses, 17
Pollard, Tanya, 11, 17, 25, 139, 143n, 242n
postmodernism, 184n
power, 61, 83, 98, 103–4, 108, 121–4, 137–9, 142n, 157, 159–61, 171, 202, 217, 221, 231, 244
  theatrical, 77n, 110, 114–18, 131–2, 140, 145n, 228, 236, 238, 242n, 246, 248
  of words, 126–8, 135, 141n, 149–150, 169, 182, 192–5, 245
precariousness, 114, 182, 241n
pricking, 11, 117, 147n, 173, 175, 229, 242n
prostitution, 12, 228, 235
protest, 152, 160–2, 166–8
proximity, 13–14, 26, 28, 30–2, 37n, 160, 246
Prynne, William, 236
psychophisiology, 25
public theatre, 12, 69, 224, 235
Puritanism, 227–8

Rackin, Phyllis, 104, 121, 123–5, 135, 139, 143n, 143–4n

radical mutuality, 5–6
Rainolds, John, 236
Raman, Shankar, 3, 16–17, 32, 41, 68, 76n, 78n
Rancière, Jacques, *The Emancipated Spectator*, 241n
reconciliation, 89–91, 100, 142n
repartee, 157, 161
resentment, 98
Residenztheater Munich, 95–8
revenge, 54, 88, 122, 125, 130, 166–78, 180–1, 188, 209–10, 218–19
Richard III, 80–147
   Buckingham (character), 89, 102–3, 106, 109–12, 128, 131–2, 147n
   Clarence (character), 100–7, 134, 136
   Duchess of York (character), 102, 104
   Hastings (character), 89, 103–4, 108, 137, 143n
   King Edward (character), 88–9, 100, 108
   Lady Anne (character), 101, 104, 117–133, 141, 146n, 147n, 245
   Messenger (character), 106
   Queen Elizabeth (character), 93, 100, 104, 127, 132–7
   Queen Margaret (character), 117, 126–7
   Richard (character), 80–140
   Richard (character) as death, 103–5
   Richard (character) 'deep dissembler', 100–15
   Rivers (character), 89, 108
   solo entry, 80–8
   'spectacle of Gloucester's seduction of Lady Anne', 117, 119–30
   spurning touches, 115–41
Richard III 2017, 95–8
Richardson, Catherine, 76n
Rist, Thomas, 55, 78n
Robson, Mark, *Shakespeare, Jonson, and the Claims of the Performative*, 29–30, 160
Rokem, Freddie, 54, 223
Rose, Steven, 155
Ross, Emily, 196–7
Röttger-Rössler, Birgitt, *Affect in Relation*, 26
Ryan, Kiernan, 8
Rzepka, Adam, 31, 37n

Sanders, Eve Rachele, 12, 235, 242n
scattering, 105–6, 144n
schizophrenic soliloquy, 95
Schmitt, Carl, 90, 142n, 204–5, 208–17, 241n
self-conscious theatricality, 143n
sexual orientation, 171–7, 211
sexuality in language, 184–5n
Shakespeare and us, 7–9
Shakespeare Studies, 16, 19, 31–2, 249
shallowness, 83, 89, 112, 115–41, 246
shaped, 84, 93–5, 129, 142n
Shea, Lisa Scancella, 127
Showalter, Elaine, 184n
Sidney, Philip, *Defence of Poetry*, 141–2n
Siemon, James R., 90, 93, 95

sight, 13, 17, 36n, 39–41, 43–5,
    51–2, 73, 75, 78n, 143n, 236;
    see also visual perception
signification, 27, 149–51, 250
Slaby, Jan, *Affect in Relation*, 26
Slotkin, Joel Elliot, 90, 93, 95,
    120, 122, 141n, 142n, 143n
Smith, Bruce R., 15–16, 31–2
    *The Acoustic World of Early
    Modern England: Attending
    to the O-Factor*, 17
    Phenomenal Shakespeare, 16,
    53, 77n, 78n, 79n, 146n, 158,
    183n
Smith, Kristin M., 122–3, 127,
    142n
smoothing, 55, 80–8, 92–5, 107,
    121–2, 128–30, 245
social
    bonds, 187–92, 207, 211, 231
    coherence in severe crisis,
    186–92
    distinctions, blurring of, 12–13
    regime of touch, 193, 205–8,
    213–21, 231–9
    touches, 89–90, 222–3
Southwark, 12, 235
spectators
    involvement, 10, 15, 20, 66,
    237, 247
    moving, 3–4, 42–3, 59, 70,
    114, 234, 246–7
    see also audience
spurning, 118
    touches, 115–41
spurring, 117–19, 123, 137–41
stage and audience, 3, 13–15, 31,
    42, 66, 76, 231–4, 238, 243,
    246

Stern, Tiffany, 16, 18, 25
Straznicky, Marta, 158–9, 183n
style, 118, 128, 134–5
suffering, 2, 5, 7, 46, 51–2, 59,
    61–2, 67–9, 73, 212, 222,
    225, 231, 234–5, 243
    together, 237–8, 241n, 246–7
surface-processes, 82–7
    manipulations, 88, 91, 115–16
    quality, 92–3
suspension, 144n, 165, 169,
    178–81, 210, 244–6, 249
sword, 118–28, 147n, 166–79,
    245
    as phallic, 122–4, 170–1
synaesthesia, 37n

tactile assault, 41
tactility, 14, 17, 19–20, 78n
    and femininity, 147n, 240n
tempest, 60–5
The Tempest, 38–79
    Ariel (character), 49, 59–60, 64,
    67–8, 229
    Caliban (character), 60–1, 64
    conjuration, 230
    court masque, 45, 63–4, 79n
    Ferdinand (character), 61, 63
    Gonzalo (character), 47–8, 61
    insubstantial, 20–1, 246
    intemperance, 78–9n
    Miranda (character), 61–4, 68–9
    Prospero (character), 10, 20–1,
    45, 47–50, 59–64, 67–9, 72–3,
    229
temporality, 5, 20, 22, 24, 26, 87,
    143–4n
textual surface, 249–50
Thalheimer, Michael, 95–8

theatrical
  contact, 9–10, 15
  contagions, 1–37
  contract, 224, 247
  emotions, 2–3
  events, 66
  power and agency, 123, 132, 135
theatricality, 10, 22–3, 25, 29–31, 57, 61, 74–5, 77n, 95–8, 111, 116–17, 131, 143n, 229, 235–6, 247
theatrum mundi, 231–2
'Theory of Participation', 239–40n
tickling, 34, 181, 203–5, 215–16, 222–3, 227, 231–2, 236–8, 242n
Tiffany, Grace, 227–8
time and male and female, 143–4n
tongues, 75, 121–2, 126–8, 139–40, 146n, 155–6, 170, 175, 194, 202–3, 205–6, 233–4
tongue-in-cheek, 162
touch
  audience, 243
  contact-free, 238
  contingent, 201–5
  erotic and, 184n, 206, 216
  indirect, 229
  kissing, 201–5
  linguistics of, 158
  loving, 159–60, 169, 217–18
  minoritarian mode of, 245, 248, 250n
  out of, 139, 219
  of peace and war, 88–100
  prohibition of, 223–4
  social, 89–90, 222,
  social regime of, 193, 205–8, 213–21, 231–9

  spectacle of, 221–7
  spurning, 115–41
  tension of, 72–3
  vision and, 43–4
  with love, 153–4
  without touching, 162–3
  and words, 192–201
touchability, 64–8, 71
  human, 35n
  and theatre, 57–76
touching
  the depth of the surface, 80–147
  fractions, 186–242
  this dreaded sight, 42–50
  the untouchable, 52
  without being touched, 44–5
  without distance, 9
touchophobic, 226
trading, 11–12
tragedians, 109–15, 122, 245
tragic wonder, 47
transcendentalism, 6–7, 29
transgression, 61–2, 243–4
Tribble, Evelyn, 19, 36n, 43, 67, 190
Troilus and Cressida, 185–241
  Achilles (character), 187–8, 211–12, 218, 226–7, 236–7
  Agamemnon (character), 201, 210, 212, 214
  Ajax (character), 187, 210–12, 237, 245
  Cassandra (character), 188, 225–6, 230
  contagion, 1–2, 212, 236–7, 239
  Cressida (character) as commodity, 202–2
  Cressida (character) problem with language, 192–201

Diomedes (character), 186–7, 189, 199–200, 212–14, 216, 221–3, 227, 229, 230, 242n, 243–4
Hector (character), 188, 191, 206–12, 214, 216–19, 220, 226, 237, 245
Menelaus (character), 202–3, 212
Pandarus (character), 1–2, 192–3, 195–9, 215–16, 219, 233–5, 238–9
Thersites (character), 199, 205, 222–3, 237–8, 241n
Troilus (character) man of words, 192–201
Ulysses (character), 187–8, 201–4, 209, 212–14, 219–32, 236, 240n, 247
truth, 5–6, 33, 41, 45–6, 51, 70, 77n, 91–3, 100–1, 110, 121, 124, 132, 149–54, 159–65, 179–82, 184n, 194–6, 199–200, 204, 213, 229–32, 239, 245
turmoil, 69–70, 74, 76

unfolding, 26, 33, 38–42, 44–5, 51, 75, 88, 143–4n, 245, 247, 249
untimeliness, 8–9

Van Laan, Thomas F., 143n
Vaughan, Virginia Mason, 202, 206
venereal disease, 1–2, 12, 234–6
Vernant, Jean-Pierre, 206, 218
Vickers, Brian, 148, 157, 182–3n, 183n

vision and touch, 43–4
visual perception, 14, 16, 39, 41–5, 51–2, 65–6, 78n, 246; *see also* sight
vows, 187, 192–7, 207, 239n
vulnerability, 7, 24, 26, 40–1, 45, 47, 49, 66, 77n, 128, 137, 147n, 217–18, 241n, 245
   and gender, 77n, 159, 219
   mutuality, 30, 32–3
   perception to, 78n

Waldron, Jennifer, 10, 37n, 78n
war, 80–8
   eroticization of combat, 206–15
   'Grim-visaged', 80–8
   and love, 205–20
   machine, 147n
   peace and, 88–100
Wehrs, Donald R., 184n
'welcome ritual', 201–3, 212, 214, 240n
'wild and whirling words', 50, 54–6, 73–5
Wilson, Richard, 8, 31
The Winter's Tale, vision and touch, 43
Wither, George, *A Collection of Emblemes, Ancient and Moderne*, 189
Witmore, Michael, 18, 36n, 79n, 242n
women as outsiders, 139–40, 147n
words and touches, 192–201
Worthen, William B., 20, 36n
Wright, Thomas, *The Passions of the Minde*, 68